COASTAL MISSOURI

Driving on the Edge of Wild

John Drake Robinson

Trade Paperback ISBN 978-1-936688-72-2

eBook ISBN 978-1-936688-73-9

Compass Flower Press
an imprint of AKA-Publishing

COASTAL MISSOURI

Driving on the Edge of Wild

John Drake Robinson

To Cheryl

Acknowledgments

Tony Hawks won a bar bet. His drinking buddies said he'd never be able to hitchhike around the perimeter of Ireland with a refrigerator. In *Round Ireland with a Fridge*, Tony inspired me to think outside the ice box.

Here's a toast to Pete McCarthy, who died too soon, with a hundred great stories still sequestered inside his brain. That's natural. We'll all die with unused food in our refrigerators.

Pete wrote a lively tale about an Englishman touring Ireland. It's the most engaging travel odyssey since Homer. In *McCarthy's Bar*, the Catholic brothers at Pete's grade school described him as "an unpleasant and frivolous boy who talks too much and will never make anything of himself, but he does take a punch well." I found a role model.

Working with most editors, trading punches is part of the process. My rambling style and damaged attention span offer plenty of opportunities for button-down editors to smack me around. For this story, my thanks to Sarah Alban, who drew the short straw to wrestle with a meandering manuscript and a wandering mind.

The State Historical Society of Missouri allowed me to see the impressive E.B. Trail Collection of Steamboating. And thanks to the Missouri Press Association, whose members keep history alive. I continually consulted Tom Beveridge's *Geologic Curiosities and Wonders of Missouri*.

It was an exhaustive process to develop a cover that captures the spirit of this book. When I saw *On the Beach* by Rolla artist Ellen Pearce, I knew I'd found the art to accompany the title. See more of Ellen's delightful work at http://ellenpearce.com.

Thanks to the Missourians, good and bad, who gave character to these stories.

For the 374 people who drowned in Missouri waters during the time I drove these roads and floated these rivers and wrote this book, may your families be at peace. And in the name of the canoeist who died from a bullet to his face, may we all seek a deeper level of tolerance.

Table of Contents

Not All Aboard

"Just throw me off the train."

Even as I spoke, I knew I'd just pushed my own self-destruct button. But the conductor left me no choice.

I was an innocent man. I had just boarded the train, and found an empty window seat. Seconds later, I watched out my big window as we inched away from the train station.

Amtrak was taking me home. I settled back into my seat and listened to the rhythm of the steel wheels on the rails as the train gained momentum. Behind me I could hear the conductor moving up the aisle.

"Tickets." He had his own rhythm. "Tickets," he said with authority as the click of his ticket puncher punched its way closer to my seat. But when he reached me, his rhythm stopped. He looked at my ticket, then he let out a sigh that could only be followed by bad news.

"You shoulda boarded one stop earlier, at Union Station, downtown," he told me. "Now you'll have to buy another ticket."

"What?" I thought he was joking.

"You didn't get on board where you were supposed to."

"What does it matter?" I protested. "I paid for the whole ride. I just joined you one stop later."

"It throws off our accounting. I'll have to charge you for another ticket."

"You gotta be kidding me. I don't have the money to buy another ticket. Tell you what: If I've messed up your accounting, just throw me off the train. I'll get off right here."

"You don't have a credit card?"

"Not for this." I said, looking him squarely in his name badge. "Throw me off the train, Brian."

I knew I'd lost my cool. Brian the Conductor had unleashed my deep resentment of the railroad's attitude. When the railroad barons first blazed their trails through here, they hired ruffians called tie hackers to chop whole forests into railroad ties. The railroads laid the tracks on the backs of dime-a-day labor. Then they murdered all the buffalo. Along the way they managed to piss off Jesse James. And now, me.

"I don't normally do this," Brian the Conductor said. "But I'll call Union Station, and get you added on."

"You don't normally do this? How often does this happen?"

"A lot. People are always trying to get on in Kirkwood, instead of where they bought the ticket for: downtown."

"Then why don't you figure out a way to fix it?"

The conductor sighed and walked up the aisle to the next passenger. "Tickets."

* * *

I was secretly thankful that Brian the Conductor didn't throw me off the train. Even as we hurtled through the middle of America, I knew there was wilderness on the other side of this big window. It's the kind of wilderness that offers good places to hide.

The train rolled across a trestle. I looked down at the Gasconade River, and saw the telltale signs of a manhunt. Posted on each bank beside the trestle were men carrying 12-gauge shotguns. Their green uniforms told me they were prison guards, looking for an escapee from one of the four prisons that hug this area's riverbanks. Around here, when inmates go over the wall and make a run for it, they sneak along the easiest paths to freedom: riverbanks and railroad tracks. It's the fastest way to make it through the thick underbrush in these wooded hills. So the cops post sentries on the bridges, and wait for escapees to show up, tired, cold, hungry. Ready to give up, usually.

The train crossed another river. More green-clad guards with shotguns.

I settled back in my seat and watched the scenery pass by the big window, farms and fields framed by second-growth forests and speckled with wild hemp that grows as high as an elephant's eye. But mostly, I saw wilderness.

I snagged a newspaper from a vacant seat and scanned the first few pages. Within minutes the newspaper crumpled into my lap, and I fell asleep.

It wasn't long before a recurrent nightmare hijacked my dream sequence, as it always does. The nightmare is vivid and real, because the events truly happened to me. Now look, I'm not superstitious, and I'm not prone to interacting with ghosts, holy or unholy. But I do know this: I shook hands with the Devil.

The handshake happened three decades ago. I'd joined a band to play a wedding reception in old Rosati Hall, a sweet relic in the vineyards that drape the rolling Ozark hills on the outskirts of St. James. The wedding reception was like a thousand others, at least from the view of a band. Joyous occasion. Happy crowd.

As we set up our instruments in this beautiful old wooden dance hall, a scuzzy man approached the bandstand and watched silently. He looked rough, the kind of rough that makes you wonder how he'd survived forty years, rough years that made him look sixty. His fingernails were tattooed an oil slick brown. His face was streaked where he'd wiped his brow. Among the other guests, he stuck out like a finger poking through toilet paper. But that's OK, because this is the wild west, the wilderness. And people around here tolerate their neighbors who don't clean up well, even when they come to funerals or weddings.

"What's that hole for?" he asked, pointing to a foot-wide hole cut in the front skin of a big bass drum.

"So we can stick a microphone inside the drum," I answered.

My friendly response prompted him to stick out his hand. "Bill's my name," he said as I gripped his handshake. "Bill Zebub," I think I recall his name, at least in my dream. I could feel the dirty oil on his hand. "I work for Russell Bliss."

Russell Bliss! The name smacked me. That's the same guy who spread waste oil on the dirt roads and horse farms around here, to dampen and seal the thick summer dust. The waste oil was laced with deadly dioxin. I'd just been Tased by a handshake.

As I tell this story, Russell Bliss has been dead for many years. But on that warm summer night in a country dance hall wedding reception, if you shouted his name, everybody would know about Russell Bliss. He claimed he didn't know the waste oil contained dioxin, and he was never convicted of knowingly spreading poison. But the waste oil he spread contaminated roads and fields and horse tracks, even shut down an entire town.

Meanwhile, Bill Zebub kept a strong grip on my hand, one of those grips that lasts while you exchange a few greetings back and forth. I tried not to show panic, looking at my hand when he released it, assuming I'd just accepted my death sentence.

"Excuse me," I said to Bill the Infector, and dashed to the tiny bathroom in the corner of the hall. I scrubbed my hands vigorously for as long as my skin could stand the hot water, chanting my new death mantra, "parts per billion . . . parts per billion."

We played the gig without further incident, I steered clear of Bill Zebub, and I'm still alive today, with only one minor side effect from that handshake. I tell a lot of lies.

But the nightmare recurs. It's vivid because it really happened.

After the dance, the nightmare wasn't over.

Oh, I made a clean getaway from the reception at Rosati Hall. But I knew I carried the time-bomb poison from Beelzebub's handshake. So the next morning, death banged on my brain. I needed something to steady my nerves.

Johnnie's Bar has been serving whiskey in downtown St. James since the Irish laborers built the railroad through here. Even from the outside, Johnnie's looks foreboding, with its big neon Stag Beer sign over a doorway into cold, smoky darkness. It's the kind of place that makes you hear your mother's voice: "I better *never* catch you going in *there*."

"Don't worry, Mom, I'll *never* go in *there*."

But in life, a young boy's perspective evolves. Moms just don't understand that places like Johnnie's have the elixir that can subdue frightful images of devils and demons, dioxin and death.

Or bring them out.

Soon I was immersed in the culture of the locals in the low light of this tavern, a delightful throwback to the days when the barroom was filled with rail passengers and conductors and brakemen and engineers laying over.

Hours later, having dipped liberally into John Barleycorn's reserves, I paid my bill and threw down a liberal tip, and walked out the door.

I was walking to the edge of town, preparing to hitchhike home, when I saw a single car, a sleek silver hearse approaching. It was going my way, but in reverence to its passenger, I showed no thumb, instead placing my hand over my heart and bowing my head. As the hearse passed, it slowed to a stop. Its backup lights told me that the hearse was coming back for me. Even significant whiskey impairment couldn't dull my panic. As the hearse drew nigh to my startled face, the passenger window rolled down and the voice from the driver's seat called out.

"John Robinson!"

I swallowed hard and leaned into the hearse's open window, expecting to meet the Grim Reaper. Instead, I saw the familiar face of an old friend from high school.

"What are you doing way down here?" he asked.

"Son of a bitch!" I think I shouted, as a feeling of relief washed through my veins.

For reasons of good taste and legal advice, I'll protect the anonymity of the driver and his pallid passenger. I have no idea who his passenger was, since the casket was closed. Suffice it to say the three of us had a pleasant ride to my destination, and two of us had a great conversation.

"So long, buddy, and thanks for the ride." I hopped out and he drove away in the general direction of his passenger's final stop.

That's when I always wake out of my nightmare, always with the same nagging questions. Did Bill Zebub know he was spreading seeds of death? Does my dear departed mother know I stopped at Johnnie's Bar? Did that stiff in the hearse ever pick up hitchhikers?

She did on her last ride.

Those events happened years ago. But my nightmare serves as a reminder that the next time a hearse stops to give me a ride, it'll probably be my last.

So this recurring nightmare is a catalyst, of sorts, prodding me to *get busy*.

I awoke in my seat on the train with my face pressed against the giant window. The passing farms and forests and hemp had given over to the rail bed's most constant companion, the Missouri River. Rails and rivers and prison escapees seem to end up together a lot, since they all seek the path of least resistance.

For a short century, this same river hosted the golden age of steamboat travel. Now the river is mostly empty on its surface. But hundreds of shipwrecks hide beneath the riverbed, hundreds of paddlewheel steamers that sank before the railroads had a chance to kill them off.

* * *

Brian the Conductor strode back through our rail car. He didn't stop to chat with me, or even glance at me. I was relieved, but in a way it was sad that we couldn't resolve a problem that was gonna piss off more unsuspecting passengers down the line.

That's just the nature of things, I guess.

* * *

All those things—the recurrent nightmares, the dispute with Brian the Conductor—those things happened before she rolled into my life. She's been with me for fifteen years now, a steady ride for almost 300,000 miles.

Together, we drove every mile of every road on my state highway map.

Maybe she would have preferred a normal life. Smooth highways. Familiar landmarks. But she accepted her fate without complaint.

Along our backroad odyssey, we've dodged rabbits and turtles, texters and drunks. We've slid sideways in sleet, jumped curbs and low-water crossings, even did the limbo under a downed power line. We've hung on the back of the *Toad Suck Ferry*, and every other ferry crossing every river on our map. We've passed every pun on every church marquee, every time and temperature sign, every clip joint and carny barker and corn dog vendor, every barbecue shack and Tex-Mex taco stand. And we've stopped at most of 'em.

We've driven by every brick shit house and half the meth labs in North America, into deep woods that hide chip mills, where forests get chewed up and spit out, and lead mines where brain cells go to die, and lonely backroads where the only sound is hate radio. During the time it took to complete our travels, the golden arches slung another ten billion burgers, I'd guess, and Congress got goatroped by fifty million angry, shouting factions.

We drove on roads that Tom Wolfe assigns to the great flyover. Yet in these backwoods, Joseph Smith found the Garden of Eden. I found the footprints of the world's most notorious outlaw, the world's preeminent adventure novelist, and the world's greatest clown. That's Jesse James, Mark Twain and Emmett Kelly, for the record.

It's dangerous out there. And nowhere is it more dangerous than the wilderness in the middle of America. At the end of every black top road, where the sign warns that "State Maintenance Ends," I knew I was crossing a threshold, a no man's land scattered with rattlesnakes and rednecks, deep woods caverns and cracks named after devils, whirlpools and whiskey stills and puppy mills, meth cookers and cock fights and creeping vines that can smother whole forests and fish that jump up and smack you in the head.

It's dangerous out there. And if you're gonna ride into the wilderness, you need a trusty steed. My ride is a 1999 Pontiac Sunfire named Erifnus Caitnop, and she's sleek and red and hides 120 horses under her hood, and I've rode 'em all, just to get her back to safe haven. Every time I went to the edge of civilization and jumped into the wilderness, she delivered me there.

Her top shows the scars from my canoe, and she's hauled it 10,000 miles or more, dropping us beside dozens of remote riverbanks. I guess there were times that she wondered if she'd ever bring me back home, as she waited for my canoe and me to cover a lot of water.

There's a surprising amount of water in America's middle.

Some folks are silly enough to believe that we've tamed it.

Belching Steam

It was one of my first memories of Hannibal. Mark Twain had been dead for forty-five years. I had been alive for four. From behind the front seat of our '49 Chevrolet, my heart jumped, feeling my father edge our old sedan closer to the Mississippi, that giant river whose black waters blended into the dark night sky. Inching down the cobblestone bank that has been Hannibal's welcome mat for two centuries, we parked among a hundred other cars. Together, we sat bathed in the popcorn glow of a thousand yellow lights outlining the decks of the *Delta Queen*. The Queen filled our windshield picture, wider than the eyes of a four-year-old. In an instant, steam the color of Sam Clemens' hair began belching from a topside calliope, its maestro tapping out the familiar syncopation of "Down Yonder." As the calliope's last throaty steam whistles echoed back across the black water, applause burst forth in a most unique manner. Horns honking and lights flashing, the cars came alive in their enthusiastic approval of a sound, a style, and a mode of travel that the internal combustion engine had driven to the edge of extinction.

But not quite.

The *Delta Queen* was still the grande dame of the rivers.

A few years back, our family rode the *Delta Queen* from St. Paul to St. Louis, a voyage of seven days, with stops in a half dozen river towns along the way. When Cheryl and I first stepped aboard, we lowered the average age of passengers to eighty-five. It's too bad that young travelers have no patience for Victorian pace, no taste for Gilded Age grandeur. With a passenger-to-crew ratio of two to one, we were never more than an arm's length from superb service.

On the day we steamed into Hannibal, passengers went ashore to scour the town, whitewash a fence, get lost in a cave, and generally relive childhood adventures. As the time to depart Hannibal grew near, Cheryl and I sat on our stateroom balcony, reading. For half an hour, the *Delta Queen's* whistle had blasted steam signals, calling passengers to get back aboard the boat. The last long whistle echoed between the bluffs as I looked up to see a lady running, nearly out of control, down the hill toward the steamer, arms loaded with packages. The lady's family and friends shrieked and waved frantically from the Texas deck, hoping the pilot would wait for her to board.

"Cast off all lines," came the call. Surely the captain wouldn't penalize her for having too much fun retracing the trails of Tom Sawyer.

With cinematic flair, and no time to spare, she leapt onto the stage—lubbers call it a gangplank—and the *Delta Queen* shoved off, setting a course downriver to St. Louis.

From the cozy comfort of our stateroom veranda, we heard the calliope hiss and spit a chorus of "Down Yonder," and watched townspeople trade farewell salutes with riverboat passengers. We raised our wine glasses to the town as it grew tiny in the wake of the churning sternwheel.

Our pilot navigated downriver, between forested bluffs that for the most part remain surprisingly unspoiled by civilization.

* * *

Nothing beats the sunset on the Mississippi. Unless it's dinner on the *Delta Queen*. Dinner aboard a riverboat eclipses any feast on a giant modern cruise ship. Every bite is better, as you're seduced by the elegant intimacy of America's inland waterways.

On the second night, Cheryl and I donned our best attire to dine with the captain. After the appropriate ice-breaker chit chat, I asked him directly, "Why don't you take this boat up the Missouri?"

He looked as if I had summoned the Devil to dine with us.

"Dangerous river," he drew out his words for emphasis. "Swift current, treacherous bends. My steamer will not travel up the Missouri." Captain John Davitt was true to his word. With a rare exception in the past three decades, when a steamboat visited St. Charles, the royal sisters—*Mississippi Queen, American Queen, Delta Queen*—avoided the waters of the Missouri River.

As we ate, we watched the scenery through big picture windows. Ol' Man River unfolded to the steady beat of those eighty-year-old pistons that turned the paddle wheel, pounding out a gentle, hypnotic rhythm.

We prepared for another great night's sleep. Next day, we'd fly kites off the stern, then retreat back to a favorite read while sitting on our personal veranda, mimosas in hand, watching Mark Twain's Mississippi from the inside out, the way he intended. Well, it's one of the ways he wanted us to see it. At the time I wasn't aware that the river and I would meet again many times, and I would experience her from whole new perspectives.

* * *

The rules of the river, as reported by Sam Clemens, remain intact. We awoke the next morning to thick fog rising from the water. The ship was noiseless, engines silent. Fog is nature's great eraser, and it had forced each boat to stop and tie up to a tree or two along the river bank. We choked a stump, in riverboat parlance.

The biggest change from Clemens' time is not the shore line, but the river itself, transformed into a chain of lakes thanks to some of our ancestors who thought they could improve on the beaver. During the 1920s, Congress ordered the U.S. Army Corps of Engineers to build a series of locks and dams on this river. The Corps balked, knowing that it couldn't control flooding on this mighty waterway, the continent's main drain. But nowadays, the river is the Corps' domain, and now Congress balks at the cost of taming a river with aging dams.

These broad lakes have spawned hundreds of pleasure boaters and water skiers who dart around the *Delta Queen* and cut across her bow. Looking like a cover on a Mark Twain novel, the *Delta Queen* casts a magical spell over boaters, who routinely sidle alongside the ship, and moon the passengers. Twain would heartily approve, I suspect. So do most of the octogenarians on board.

Moons notwithstanding, the views along the river serve deep inspiration. But the best inspiration often comes from within. It was a revelation at dinner that propelled me to continue my journey inland, to further explore the backroads, to drive every mile of every road in Missouri. It may have been the third dinner course, maybe the seventh, I don't remember. At some point, I tossed my napkin into my plate and leaned back, staring up at the ceiling. The ornate designs of the tin ceiling stared back at me. And I wondered out loud, "Who came up with that gaudy shit?"

Cheryl looked surprised at my blurt, but before she could speak, the server, always at hand, said, "Right in your backyard."

"Do tell," I said.

"There in Nevada, Missouri. There's a place been makin' tin ceilings for more'n a hunnert years. . . . "

I made a mental note to find that tin stamping company. But even as the server pulled the last plate away from the table, a clarinet wailed like a Gershwin, and the dance band lurched into a tango, luring out the most elegantly dressed elderly ladies I'd ever seen, each on the arm of a handsome young dance partner. The ladies wore evening gowns, mostly black, in memory of their dead husbands, I'd like to think. And their jewelry, purloined from Cleopatra's gem box, sparkled in the eyes of their dance partners, these young men, perfectly manicured and tailored in tails.

No doubt about it, this boat specialized in pleasure.

It was tough saying goodbye to this old steamer with its link to the past, its commitment to style, and its doting crew. We docked beneath the Gateway Arch in St. Louis, and I stepped away from Mark Twain's Mississippi, unsure when I'd ever touch it again.

* * *

Less than a shotgun blast from the Arch, Eads Bridge stands against time. The old bridge, made of iron and stone, was the first span across the Mississippi, and it's nine years older than the Brooklyn Bridge. In the shadow of this historic old bridge, the riverfront is called Laclede's Landing, named for one of the city's most prominent fathers. Today, Laclede's Landing offers a carnival atmosphere of food and drink and music and gambling. There's even a place where you can rent wax figures. Kinda like a Midwest Madame Tussaud's, for hire. No shit, the Laclede's Landing Wax Museum, Chamber of Horrors, and Ice Cream Parlor rents wax figures for parties and events and such. You can rent an old Missouri legend, maybe a Steve McQueen, or Satan.

I almost bit. After all, it's lonely on these backroads of Missouri, and I could use some company, a reliable companion who wouldn't talk much, and might scare away hijackers or Sasquatch. So I thought about checking the cost to rent Jesse James or Jesus to ride with me into the bush. You know, the ultimate protection. But at a minimum of $300 per day, these wax bodyguards were expensive, plus they would have to bend to fit into Erifnus' shotgun seat. My biggest concern was for Erifnus: What if things got hot, and Jesse James melted in the car?

* * *

Erifnus took me west a few miles down old Route 66—now called Chippewa Street—to the Hill, the home of great Italian culture in St. Louis. This is the neighborhood that nurtured Yogi Berra's words to live by and Joe Garagiola's gab. It's a tidy community with modest homes surrounding great old storefronts painted green and red, framing big plate glass windows, and cast-iron doorways leading into Italian produce grocers and old-fashioned meat markets.

And restaurants. For lunch, you can't beat the cafeteria fare of Rigazzi's, a favorite of locals, where you drink Budweiser from a giant frosty fishbowl the size of your head. There's nothing fancy about

Rigazzi's, and that's what makes it authentic. There's no need for pretenses. You come for the food.

I had fried catfish and mashed potatoes and gravy with stewed tomatoes and a side of *mostaccioli.*

With a full belly and a satisfied soul, I set our compass east a few blocks to the edge of Tower Grove Park, where St. Louis Botanical Garden unveils its floral treasures. Its nickname is Shaw's Garden, in honor of founder Henry Shaw, one of the preeminent movers and shakers in St. Louis during the mid-nineteenth century.

Shaw was a major landowner, an investor and philanthropist. His botanical garden is his crowning achievement. The highlight of my walk through this cultivated jungle was the garden tribute to my idol, George Washington Carver, patron saint of recycling and crop rotation. Yet the monument to Carver left me feeling a bit conflicted, knowing where I was headed later that day, to confront a flaw in Henry Shaw's character.

* * *

A couple of miles up St. Louis Avenue sits the Griot Museum of Black History and Culture. At the museum entrance, setting the tone was a 170-year-old raffle poster. It announced that a "Dark Bay Horse named Star and a Mulatto Girl named Sarah" will be raffled for chances at one dollar each.

Museum curator Erica Neal met me and showed me around. I saw inspirational exhibits featuring some of St. Louis' greats: Miles Davis, whose horn couldn't hide his emotion. Josephine Baker, who left racism for Paris. Clark Terry, the trumpeter who taught me a bit of his mumbles routine. The museum commemorated the life of George Washington Carver and the trials of Dred Scott.

Throughout the museum, reality smacked me, showing a nasty underbelly of our culture. I folded like an embryo to fit in a life-sized recreation of the hold of a slave trade ship. Even without the threat of seasickness and dysentery and starvation—and the shackles and chains of enslavement—sitting in the cramped underdeck of this display made me physically ill. The saddest part of my museum experience was the realization that not enough children will see what I just saw. And we're doomed to a culture of ignorance. The end is near.

Wide-eyed, I thanked Erica. Erifnus took me back to the river.

Driving to the Mississippi, we followed the Riverfront Trail north to see Mary. But we were 150 years too late. On this river bank, at the site of an old Coast Guard station, there stands a modest monument to Mary.

Back in 1855 on this spot, a vigilante coast guard busted a boatload of folks trying to make it to freedom. Mary was their leader. Like her husband, legendary teacher John Berry Meachum, Mary Meachum was a free black. John established a school on a riverboat in the middle of the Mississippi so young black Missourians could be educated, while Mary risked her life to help local slaves escape through the St. Louis underground railroad.

From this spot, Mary arranged for a group of runaway slaves to launch a boat by the moonlight to cross the Mississippi to the free soil of Illinois.

But Henry Shaw had other ideas. As great as Henry Shaw was with his plants and gardens and science and money and benevolence, some of the people in this boat were his slaves, and he wanted them back. He got them back, too.

Mary's crossing was in vain. Only recently has the city publicly acknowledged this conflict in its history. The Mary Meachum monument is small, compared to the Gateway Arch and Shaw's Garden, and it's accessible only by taking a back road and crossing to the other side of the tracks.

We drove to the Chain of Rocks Bridge, a span that attaches itself to rocky shoals in the Mississippi. The bridge makes an abrupt thirty-degree turn in the middle of the river. For a time, the Chain of Rocks Bridge was part of Route 66. And throughout its history, there have been many bloody wrecks and even murders on its decks. Erifnus couldn't cross it, since the bridge has been closed to vehicles for decades. Pedestrians and cyclists cross the bridge freely, connecting hiking/biking trails on either side of the river.

I walked to the middle of the bridge, where it makes its deadly turn, and looked out over the deadly shoals that can shred boats careless enough to try to navigate this section of the river. That's why the U.S. Army Corps of Engineers built a canal to circumvent this part of the Mighty Mississip.

As I stood in the middle of that bridge, I had no way of knowing that one day soon I'd be paddling into this river in the dead of winter.

Winter Water

The air was cold, a few degrees above freezing. Three of us pushed one long canoe away from shore and paddled out of a swirling eddy into the main stream, thus surviving the most dangerous phase of the trip: the launch into a swift current.

It was early February, and we'd dressed in layers over wetsuits. But the bone-chilling cold reminded us that our canoe was balanced atop a giant swift-moving stream of hypothermia. We paddled away from the Columbia Bottoms access point into the middle of the river. Here, the Missouri is easily half a mile wide, pouring its entire collection of western waters toward the end of its 2,315-mile journey, and the end was almost in sight, a few miles downriver where it greets the Mighty Mississippi.

All three of us were experienced canoeists, and we were confident we wouldn't fall into the icy river. But I guess no explorer plans to spill or crash or drown.

"The Missouri River moves fast when the channel comes close to the bank," Mike Clark said. Mike was our guide. If he were boastful, he could boast about his 20,000 miles of river experience on some of the world's most revered waterways. But even though he's a world traveler, he makes his home just a few miles from this spot. And why not? He knows what the earliest inhabitants of this area have always known: This meeting of the continent's two great rivers is a sacred spot, a giver of life for the billions of birds that follow the flyways and for the fish that don't know the names of these rivers but know the rivers' distinctly different personalities.

I felt comfortable on this big fast water, except for the cold.

We paddled down the middle of this magnificent waterway. In the distance, above the treeline, the only pollution we could see was smoke and steam from the factories of Wood River, on the Illinois bank, the spot where Lewis and Clark wintered before they paddled and poled three boats 2,315 miles upriver. At that thought, I felt more comfortable, paddling downstream.

Mike Clark steered the canoe from his seat at the stern. He shared his paddler's philosophy. "Some people judge others by what they say. I judge them by how much they're willing to paddle."

No problem for me. I pulled my own weight. And the cold subsided as we got into a rhythm and worked up a sweat. A north wind tried to aggravate us, but Cora blocked its best gusts. Cora, the island on our port side, shielded us from the wind until we were almost to the confluence of these two mighty rivers.

"Heron," I pointed off the bow at a remarkable bird in flight, with its wide wingspan and long legs and long neck and long beak. Herons are good luck.

In the distance, south of the confluence, we watched a thousand pelicans take low flight and move like a shimmering school of fish to another feeding spot. Above us, an immature bald eagle flew across the water to the treetops along the bank. Our eyes followed the bird to its aerie, a wooden fortress, a monstrosity in the world of birds nests, bigger than your childhood tree house.

"This is in the middle of a metropolitan area," Mike said. "But out here, we're away from all that."

Most of it, anyway. I glanced at the big white columns of smoke and steam from the Wood River refineries, making jet fuel for a thirsty nation. The north wind pushed the steam down the Mississippi flyway.

We stopped on the peninsula to check on the tree saplings that Greg, our bow paddler, had planted last fall. "I figure one in ten will survive," Greg said, as he bent to examine a protective sleeve around one sapling's trunk. "But with good conditions, half of them might make it." A sapling's life could be cut short by flood or drought. But the biggest predators are deer, who agree with each other that saplings are tasty.

With his left arm, Mike made a sweeping wave toward the north. "Up there is the new Audubon Center, right in the middle of the Riverlands Migratory Bird Sanctuary."

"Audubon picked a great spot," I said.

"The birds picked a great spot," Mike said as he pivoted to face west. "Portage des Sioux is up there," Mike pointed upriver to the spot where Native Americans used to carry their canoes across the narrowest strip of this peninsula, from one great river to the other. By portaging their gear overland, they saved a twenty-five-mile paddle around the point. It was also the site of the Treaties of Portage des Sioux, which hastened the displacement of the Mississippi tribal cultures as a hungry Manifest Destiny moved west.

But the spirits that guided the native inhabitants, they're still here. The plants. The wildlife. The moon. And the point where two sacred rivers join together.

You can feel it, the life-giving power of these waters. Indeed, there's only one reason St. Louis grew so populous. The confluence.

We paddled to the point, where I stood with one foot in the Missouri, the other in the Mississippi. Facing that narrow backbone of land that finally allows these rivers to mingle around my ankles, I saw two bronze nameplates, one embedded in each bank. The north plate spells Mississippi River. Just a few feet away, the south plate is covered in mud. As I scraped the mud off the letters that spell Missouri River, it was living proof that Big Muddy delivers on its reputation. You could grow cotton on top of that nameplate.

Mike Clark and I stood for a photo at this point where two sacred rivers join to mix their juices. In the picture, Mike held his sacred paddle, a paddle that has traveled the entire length of the Missouri and the Mississippi, the Colorado and the Amazon, too. Painted on its broad blade is the Rolling Stones logo, the tongue that first appeared on the *Sticky Fingers* album. You know the one.

The sun set as we paddled down the Mississippi. We stopped on a sand bar and built a fire, boiled some water and drank hot tea. Then we drowned the fire and in the February darkness, climbed in our canoe. We were fearless as we paddled down the Mississippi, black water against black forest, silhouetted in the dim backlight of a major urban center, just over the hills out of sight. The moon rose to guide us to our landing.

Sacred.

Rafting the Mississippi

The days were getting warmer when I got a call from a good friend alerting me that an adventurous soul was about to experience the dream of every American river rat. He'd built a raft, and was looking for crew members to help him drift from St. Paul to the Gulf of Mexico.

Holy Huck! I'm in!

But would I trust my life to somebody I'd never met? After some background checking, I committed to the journey of a lifetime.

I was one of maybe a dozen conscripts who volunteered for the three-month journey. Every one of those volunteers quickly realized that none of us could spend an entire summer floating down that big river. I tempered my dream with a realistic plan. I'd sign on to crew from St. Louis to the confluence of the Mississippi and Ohio Rivers. That would cover a part of the Mississippi I hadn't traveled.

It wasn't a big boat. In terms of cubits, it was a two-by-four. But it had a big backyard, a mile wide and 1,800 miles long. And it became the summer palace for a big thinker who has no problem translating big thoughts into action. Even his name was bold, fit for a John Wayne movie.

Justus McLarty has dipped his paddle in rivers throughout the world. Amazon. Yukon. Patagonia. Colorado. He's plunged kayaks down forty-foot waterfalls and shared the unfamiliar food of a dozen different tribes. But the Mighty Mississippi had eluded him.

No longer.

Most big thinkers don't progress past the idea stage. Justus not only planned the adventure, he built the boat. He spent the better part of a year in the driest of dry docks, in his garage in a tiny West Texas town where the surrounding seas are subterranean black gold. That might seem like a problem, transporting a dream from tumbleweed country to the headwaters of America's seminal waterway. But remember, Justus McLarty thinks big.

He had the luxury of summertime to complete the journey. His job goes dormant during the summer when his employer, NBC's *Saturday Night Live*, takes a production break.

Unlike an *SNL* rerun, you never step in the same raft twice. A raft always has a changing view, and a different danger lurking around the bend.

So what kind of vessel would deliver a passenger from Sorenson Landing, Minnesota, to Head of Passes, Louisiana, in relative comfort and safety?

The design bounced around McLarty's brain for years. Unlike too many of us whose dreams die unfulfilled, Justus was swift and sure. From his own mental design, he began a trial-and-error process that produced a creature as unique to this universe as Mary Shelley's monster or the zilla of God.

At first glance, the boat looked nearly as freakish. The cabin was framed by welded aluminum joists and fit with bright yellow plywood decking. Walls of waterproof nylon, canvas, and clear plastic protected the passenger from the elements and rolled up during a breezeless swelter. The whole house sat atop two bulbous pontoons, blue as a *Simpsons* sky. The pontoons were tough rubber carcasses that sported a patchwork quilt of repairs incurred in a previous life, when the pontoons took a thousand trips down the Colorado River. The boat even had a tiny outboard motor.

So the raft was a bit more sophisticated than a *Huck Finn* production. But Justus McLarty was determined to guide his craft like a raft.

The interior offered the rudimentary comforts of home: a stove, a sink, an ice box. Running water flowed from refillable plastic tankards. Ample shelving supported all the things a body would need for ninety days: kitchenware, food, flashlights, books, even a boom box loaded with a billion river tunes. Since interior space was devoted to cooking, sleeping and storage, the living room sat atop the flat roof, furnished with folding lawn chairs. Not a lot of shade.

Mark Twain endowed us with more than literary masterpieces. He gave us a lasting river lexicon. America's exclusive fraternity of riverboat pilots adopted a term for disciples of Twain who act on their fantasies of wild river adventure: Tom'n'Hucks. Because the boat McLarty built made a cartoonish first impression, it attracted skeptical curiosity from river veterans and barge pilots. That's understandable. The barge pilots are professionals, guiding billions of tons of commerce between the red and green buoys that mark the river's navigable channel. They view primitive rafts the way you view a skateboard on a highway.

They soon learned that our boat was not primitive. They saw it was solid and seaworthy. And its captain earned their tolerance, maybe even begrudging respect. More important, McLarty showed respect to the big rigs and stayed out of their way. In one radio conversation, he patiently answered a tow captain's queries. "Yes, I have a motor." And charts. And navigation experience. And lifesaving gear. And respect for the Mississippi and its rules.

It was after this radio grilling that McLarty overheard his inquisitor talking to another tow pilot. "He's OK," one pilot reassured the other. "He's not a Tom'n'Huck."

There's another telling difference. Best I can recall, Big Jim and Huck Finn never named their raft. Justus has a name for his craft.

From the earliest idea stage, observers pestered him with the same question: "What's the name of your boat?"

"No name yet," he replied. For months he heard suggestions. "*Huck Too*" . . . "*Mighty Miss*" . . . Good God Almighty.

No, really, *Good God Almighty*, there must be 2.4 billion of those corny names on the posteriors of otherwise respectable boats.

McLarty even had an offer to sell the naming rights. But he resisted the temptation to call his floating home the *Acme Bag of Chips* or the *Tip Top Toilet Bowl Cleaner*. He'd poured years into this project, and his goal had nothing to do with marketing or making money. As launch time approached, he patiently awaited the name to come to him. And he was comfortable with the thought that the boat might not have a name until well downstream.

As with all good ideas and most newborns, the name arrived on its own schedule. In a conversation about the project, McLarty recalls his grandfather saying, "Well, my Grandma Alexander always said the worst thing of all is to go through life with a great big wanter and a little bitty getter. So keep your getter bigger than your wanter."

The *Big Getter* was born.

All summer long, river folks gravitated to this hydro-nomad perched on bulbous blue balloons. From a hundred docks, through the locks, along the river bluffs, from the decks of paddlewheel steamers, onlookers tempered their first impressions with one of two thoughts.

"I'd never do that," said the people who rarely step out of their comfort zone. But a larger group felt a sense of envy. The spirit of adventure. Justus routinely invited them to join him. "Drop what you're doing and climb aboard."

Along the entire length of the river, Justus McLarty welcomed a revolving door of passengers and crew, friends and strangers from all over the nation. Each arrived with notions of rafting on Mark Twain's Mississippi. Each departed with a dozen stories to tell and practical knowledge in oarsmanship.

The oars were called sweeps, which looked like long hockey sticks on steroids used to guide a free-floating raft through swift currents. They resembled the flatboat oars in a George Caleb Bingham painting. And although McLarty's boat had a small outboard motor for use in emergency situations, he didn't plan to rely on it much.

But he also didn't plan the weather.

Early in his trip, weather sprung an unrelenting test of the boat's integrity and of the skipper's resolve. Justus launched his boat on June 1, and for three weeks he endured rain and tornadoes and rain and cold and rain and wind and rain—enough water to cause the biggest flood since '93. The flood waters crashed through levees, swamped downtowns, and attracted politicians eager to smile for the news cameras while they sandbagged swollen levees. The flood covered campsites and marinas and reached into the forests to loose a dozen years of dead timber, turning the Mississippi into a flume of driftwood. In a river where snags sink boats, McLarty was sitting on two vulnerable rubber pontoons among a thousand wooden torpedoes.

I hadn't joined the boat yet, waiting for it to get to St. Louis. As I tracked the *Big Getter's* progress on McLarty's website, he fell farther and farther behind his published schedule. I emailed him at one point, passing along a news story I'd watched about shrinking clearance between the rising river and railroad trestles. Sure enough, in an early close encounter, the top of McLarty's raft came within inches of crashing into the bottom of a bridge deck. The next day, for a few days, several of the river's twenty-seven locks were closed to pleasure boats, so Justus laid over to sightsee the Quad Cities.

I wasn't worried about his ability to cope with adversity. But I did get nervous about finding the boat. Timing my jump aboard the *Big Getter* was a bit like anticipating when the message in a bottle will drift by.

Meanwhile, my window of opportunity was narrowing, too. We talked by phone and email a few times, to recalculate my leg of the journey and where I would hop aboard. When the U.S. Army Corps of Engineers reopened the locks, the *Big Getter* rode the flood crest, making up for lost time, reaching Hannibal, then Clarksville, then Alton, Illinois, and nearing my point of embarkation, among the barges near the base of the St. Louis Arch.

I didn't meet Justus until minutes before I boarded the raft.

It was late at night when my daughter dropped me and a duffel bag off at Cunetto's, an Italian restaurant on the Hill in St. Louis where Justus and two other new crew members were loading up on carbs.

I walked into the restaurant knowing only that I was looking for three people with whom I would spend the next four days in close proximity. I spotted them as easily as they spotted me, since all of us had adopted the keen senses of river rats.

Justus greeted me like an old friend, and introduced Margot from Washington, D.C., and her beau Kenny from San Francisco. They had just flown into St. Louis from opposite directions and were as new to the raft as I. Kenny immediately hit the "small world" button when he asked me if I knew a Rocheport luthier who had made Kenny's mandolin. Rocheport is a tiny town that neighbors Columbia, my home.

"Indeed!" I lied to him in the spirit of good conversation. "Well, sorta. Friend of a friend."

We talked and planned and picked up some supplies from a local grocery, then headed for the boat.

My first glimpse of the *Big Getter* came under the light of a full moon. It sat like an aquatic incarnation of *The Little Engine that Could*, dwarfed on three sides by the rusty hulls of empty barges, towering a dozen feet above the raft. The open side looked downriver toward the city's main train trestle across the Mississippi, backlit by the full moon like an x-ray negative. All night long, freight trains and Amtraks and more freight trains repeated a chugging rhythm that seemed to match the churning of the swift river current. Good sleeping.

Despite the close quarters, there were sleeping stations all over the boat. Each bunk or cot featured the single most important tool on the entire craft: mosquito netting. Seriously, it saved our lives. Of all the dangers we encountered on the Mighty Mississip—from barge tows the size of small towns, from felled trees floating like Mother Nature's Minuteman missiles to the phobia of being swallowed by a river turned backward by an earthquake, or consumed by a giant catfish worthy of a Peter Benchley read—the most immediate calamity happens every day at sundown, when a billion tiny Draculas emerge from the shadows to suck your blood.

Other dangers may pose more risk, but they don't cause you to slap yourself so much.

That night, a dozen barge tows passed as I slept, their vibrations relaxing like magic fingers, their wakes rocking me to sleep.

"Where's the shower?" I joked at sunrise, assuming that bathing would come courtesy of muddy Mississippi water.

"On the roof," Justus responded, dead serious. I climbed onto the roof, to find two black water bags. The bags absorb heat from the sun and wait patiently for the opportunity to hang from the side of the boat and spill their guts all over a grateful showeree. I can testify that these solar water heaters work like a charm, and there's no utility bill.

Toilets? There are two. One is a tiny portable throne aboard the craft. The other, well, it's as big as the great outdoors. Take a shovel.

On this morning, I took advantage of my last connection to modern convenience, borrowing the National Park Service bathroom at the base of the Gateway Arch to rinse and repeat. Then we cast off all lines and floated free, out into the main channel.

Barge tows look more menacing when observed at river level, dead on. McLarty's new team learned quickly how to maneuver the craft and stayed a safe distance from those commercial giants.

Stabbing the sky from one corner of the roof, the boat's golden flag adopted the message broadcast by the original thirteen colonies: Don't Tread on Me. No, this flag wasn't a Tea Party sentiment. Our trip predated all that noise. Instead, the flag sent a heartfelt request, since this collapsible craft would be no match in a tangle with a tow pushing forty-two barges. Just in case, an aluminum canoe hung suspended below the starboard deck. Not to worry. This is a big river, and Justus McLarty had no plans for close encounters with barges, so the canoe functioned as a ship-to-shore taxi.

Years ago, when I had a job in tourism, I got some disturbing news that St. Louis tourism officials had discouraged a *New York Times* reporter from rafting down Twain's Mississippi. "Too dangerous," the St. Louisans pleaded. I guffawed at the time. "You can't get a better story," I told St. Louis. "Anyway, a drowned *New York Times* reporter would add depth to the sense of adventure on this river."

Now, I was testing that very concept, skating on thin ice, figuratively. I felt safe. Of course, that was because Justus McLarty is no Tom'n'Huck.

In my lifetime so far, I've traveled three quarters of the Mississippi. I'm always amazed at how small the city riverfronts are in relation to the endless miles of forested shores. Minutes from the bustle of the downtown St. Louis riverfront, the river assumes a peaceful demeanor, absolutely beautiful, as we passed the big Belgian brewery, and just downriver, visible among the trees atop the bluffs, stood the old Jefferson Barracks, the historic army installation where Grant and Lee and a thousand other military leaders put in time.

We drifted past the mouth of the Meramec River at Arnold, and stopped at Hoppy's, an oasis for fuel-hungry pleasure craft motoring between St. Louis and Cape Girardeau. We didn't need fuel, of course. We'd just heard about the legendary Hoppy's, the waterfront welcome mat that leads to the tiny tourist community of Kimmswick. We sat with Fern and Hoppy on the sprawling dock in a mismatched set of Elvis-era overstuffed chairs, and for hours we watched the river roll by while feasting on river tales. Hoppy is among the last of the lamplighters, the guys who made sure the channel-marker buoys had enough kerosene to burn through the night as beacons for anybody silly enough to be on this river after dark. The lamplighters were replaced in 1954 by a system of electric lights.

A couple of neighbors boated in. Roger and Scott brought fresh stories about their recent circumnavigation of the eastern third of the United States. They started from Hoppy's, headed down the Mississippi, hugged the gulf shore around Florida, up the inland waterway along the Eastern Seaboard to the St. Lawrence River, through the Great Lakes, and down the Illinois River back to their Mississippi home base. Justus listened intently, asking about their boat, sailing conditions, rough spots.

For dessert, we hiked a half mile to the world famous Blue Owl, where Mary Hostetter bakes big pies. How big? Some pies have their own zip codes. I delved into a Levee High Apple Pie. Mary's love for baking evolved into the classic business success story. After winning just about every baking competition around, she started selling her sweets in a Kimmswick tea room in 1985. The business took off, though it almost got washed away. The tiny arts community survived the Great Flood of '93 thanks to townspeople who pitched in on a heroic sandbagging effort to keep floodwaters at bay. Today, Mary employs six dozen people in this town of ninety-four residents.

Joining us at our table was a youthful adventurer we'd encountered a few miles upriver. He introduced himself as Adam Book, and his current chapter focused on piloting a kayak down the entire Mississippi. From Adam's perspective, as his faster craft overtook us, the *Big Getter* seemed luxurious, more accommodating. Adam wasn't yet twenty-one, but he had guts and stamina to challenge the Mother of All Rivers by himself in a seven-foot boat.

Next day we bid adieu to Kimmswick, and to Adam, who rose with the sun and swiftly slid downriver out of sight. Unlike McLarty's experience on the turbulent upper Mississippi, our weather featured the traditional August forecast: sunny and hot, perfect for a river sojourn.

Around a sweeping bend we noticed thick black smoke that signaled one of the rarest sights on the river, at least nowadays. Sure enough, a paddlewheel steamer appeared, churning toward us. As the distance closed between our two craft, the steamer stopped dead in the water, the pilot thrusting his paddlewheel into forward and reverse to hold the *Mississippi Queen's* position in the strong current. We drifted within spitting distance of the big steamer. The captain appeared on the bridge and shouted down to us. "Better move out of the channel. Big barge coming down around the bend behind you." We knew that. Still, we thanked him for his courtesy. And we endured every one of the 200 passengers who appeared on the big steamer's Texas Deck to observe our curious craft and to yell at us, "Get out of the way! Big barge coming!" We debated thanking them in the traditional sign language from small craft to these big floating wedding cakes. But mooning those octogenarian passengers after their well-intended advice seemed beneath crass.

As we drifted past the big boat, her pilot signaled the engineer to step on it, and the *Mississippi Queen* chugged up around the bend and out of sight. Minutes later, the big barge tow overtook us and passed without incident.

Taking a brief respite from a Mississippi River journey, our crew navigated our raft through a narrow inlet to port Ste. Genevieve. Appropriate, I thought, since this was the first highway into town, used by explorers and settlers and Lewis and Clark, and maybe even the Duke of Bilgewater and the lost Dauphin, the royal poseurs who tried to sucker Huck Finn. We drifted way back into the protected bayou, greeted by a ghostly dock that had been abandoned after the last big flood. We lashed to the dock and overnighted, never seeing another soul in this overgrown inlet, save a few fishermen in johnboats and 2.6 billion mosquitoes.

Some people in Ste. Genevieve would like to reclaim the dock and the port and open for business to river visitors. But alas, they realize the quest is quixotic, up against a lack of money and a recession and a lack of money and time and materials and a bunch of loudmouth doubters and a lack of money. State and federal agencies appear reluctant to help dredge the inlet to keep it from silting up. And let's face it, tourist traffic from the river probably wouldn't pay for the upkeep.

I walked toward Ste. Genevieve, a distance of about a mile, mostly atop levees. I began to see the town, older than Thomas Jefferson. Built by folks named Balduc, Bequette, and Beauvais, the town leaves no doubt about its heritage. These settlers were from the same French stock that settled southern Louisiana, where their appellation shortened to Cajun.

Thirsty, I stopped into the historic Ste. Genevieve Hotel and ended up dining on the restaurant's signature dish, liver dumplings. The accent was on the dumplings, with the liver cooked to an almost puree, soupy base. An acquired taste for sure, but delightful. Thus fortified with enough iron to attract magnets, or sink mosquitoes, I set out to explore this, the oldest community in Missouri, founded in 1732. The oldest record at the historic Catholic church is a 1759 baptism of one of founder Felix Valle's slaves.

The houses were unique in two ways. First, three homes featured a rare French creole vernacular vertical log construction. And second, they were still standing, despite threats from fire, flood, time and man. These structures even survived the 1811-1812 New Madrid earthquakes, the most violent shakedown in the recorded history of the North American continent.

The town was a quiet walk back in time, thanks to four miles of insulation that separate Ste. Genevieve from the plastic modernity that proliferates along the interstate up the hill.

Next morning we left the abandoned dock, an eerily silent refuge, and worked our way back out to the river, passing a pair of unfriendly bubbas standing on shore beside their old towboat, concealed from the river, illegally burning contaminated fuel on the bank. Suddenly the characters we were encountering on this trip had taken a tilt toward the adventures of Huck Finn. I felt powerless to admonish the polluters. But through the morning mist, as we made our way into the main channel, hope bobbed to the surface, because we were headed to Chester, Illinois, the home of America's legendary enforcer, Popeye.

The mist evaporated, and we sliced up a lunch of mangoes and cheese and crackers. A few hours later, Chester's first icon appeared. Hugging the river on the north edge of town is Menard Correctional Center, one of Illinois' oldest prisons. Poised on the bank beside the prison walls was a camera with a familiar face behind it, snapping photos of our crew as we managed the sweeps and oars. Downriver just past the highway bridge, we disembarked at the Port of Chester.

The Port of Chester is nothing more than a concrete slab to launch fishing boats. It has no Popeye Marina or Olive Oyl Cafe, not even a sign denoting this home of Poopdeck Pappy's favorite son. The photographer, magazine publisher Gary Figgins, chauffeured our dirty, hungry crew to a local buffet to gorge ourselves in Popeyian fashion. Stuffed to the forearms, we launched Justus McLarty and the *Big Getter* back into the Mississippi's main channel, and he sailed solo downriver out of sight.

The raft story doesn't end there, of course. Justus hadn't even reached the Ohio River yet. Little did he know that downriver a ship was sinking, an oil slick was spreading, and a hurricane was brewing, poised to pound New Orleans. And although I warned him that below the Ohio River, the levees were so high that the scenery would be limited, Justus reported that the Lower Mississippi turned out to provide the most beautiful landscape of all.

So what happens to a houseboat when the owner reaches the end of an odyssey? As a bona fide big thinker, Justus had a plan. He pulled the boat onto the bank and deflated the pontoons. He got out his wrench, unbolted the decks and took the frame apart. Like a one-man carnival, he folded the whole thing into the back of a rental truck and drove toward the West Texas sunset. He beat Hurricane Katrina by a few days.

True to his great-great-grandmother's advice, his ideas for the *Big Getter* keep getting bigger. He wants to travel a giant circle around the eastern third of the United States, as foreshadowed by the two boaters on Hoppy's deck.

Such a journey will test his limits. He'll need a stronger structure to withstand waves. He'll get a bigger motor to battle ocean currents and open seas. He'll need to carve out a year away from work, and the comforts of a landlocked home. He might have to kiss *SNL* goodbye.

No problem for a big getter whose getter is bigger than his wanter.

Since his journey to the gulf, a disaster hit Louisiana, one bigger than 10,000 sinking ships and more lasting than the effects of Katrina. Stretches of beach east of Gulfport, Mississippi, were coated in a reflux of tar balls from the world's worst oil spill, the *Deepwater Horizon* oil spill of 2010. If Justus ever makes his trip along America's gulf shore and eastern seaboard, he'll probably find plenty of oil. The end is near.

Burma Shavings

I hitched a ride back to St. Louis, and hopped a train home. Same train. Would it be the same conductor?

"Tickets," I heard the conductor's voice behind me as he worked his way up the aisle.

"Tickets." He drew closer.

I fought the urge to peer around the edge of my seat. Instead I sat staring straight ahead, waiting in ambush. As he turned to punch my ticket, he saw my face. "John Robinson!"

"Jim Lagnaf! Man, am I glad to see you."

The conductor was an old friend. We'd grown up in the same Jeff City neighborhood, so this trip was starting out a lot smoother than the nightmare with Brian the Conductor.

"Whatter you doin' on my train?" Jim asked.

"Headed home. Been on tourism business."

"Tourism. Hmm," he grunted. "I'll be back in a minute." He continued up the aisle. "Tickets!"

* * *

I settled back in my seat and watched the scenery roll past my window. The train followed the river around a sweeping turn called Alert Bend, named after a boat, an early river pioneer that didn't make it.

I knew the story. The *Alert* was steaming a few miles upriver from Hermann when it happened. A lookout at the bow of the boat spotted a sawyer at the edge of the channel. A sawyer is a limb that sticks out of the swift current. It's attached to a submerged tree, so it's a trigger, waiting to spring the sunken tree trunk like a mousetrap and punch a hole in a wooden boat hull. The lookout pointed to the sawyer so the captain would see. The captain already had seen it. Any captain would have seen it, because that's how captains become captains. They see all the obstacles atop the water. But the good ones, the captains who endure, they know what's under the water.

The *Alert* was a side wheeler, "like all early-day boats on the Missouri River," wrote E.B. Trail, one of the Missouri River's foremost steamboat historians. And she ran "an irregular trade on the Missouri." That may have been the *Alert's* undoing. "An irregular trade" means the captain probably didn't know the river very well.

She had beat the odds so far, five years old, still going strong, built in Pittsburgh the same year Sam Clemens was born, 1835. But she had entered a river where most steamboats wouldn't reach their second birthday. On the Ohio River or the Mississippi River, she could chug in relative safety at five or six knots and provide useful service for a dozen years, maybe more.

But this was the Missouri River—swift and turbulent, braiding, deadly.

The captain steered the boat safely past the sawyer and was

rounding the tight bend into a narrow channel when he felt the jolt. His heart sank. The *Alert* had struck a snag. He had evaded the snap of the sawyer, but the sunken tree punched a hole in the wooden hull below the waterline. In minutes the river rushed into the gash and claimed another victim.

To the small fraternity of riverboat pilots whose two dozen boats braved the Missouri River in 1840, that spot became known as Alert Bend. Within the year, two more spots on the Missouri River would take their names from shipwrecks.

There would be more.

* * *

Like Jim the conductor, I grew up beside this river. So I'd heard the stories. This was the first highway of westward expansion. Steamboats shipped a million pioneer families on their first leg of a long journey west. Some families didn't make it, buried in shipwrecks beneath the flood plain, tombs filled with enough provisions to satisfy a pharaoh in the first millennium of afterlife.

Living near the edge of Jefferson City as a kid, I could sneak out of the house on warm summer nights, and hike to the bluffs above the river as it moved silently through the darkness. Back then it was easier to find total darkness, away from star-erasing pollution caused by streetlights and security lamps. The river bluffs offered a clear view of the universe. The night sky entertained me with infinite vastness, rewarding my patience with a shooting star across the Milky Way. But I never waited long before a light saber would stab the black night, waving low across the river, focused laser sharp from the bridge of a towboat, a narrow beam of white light swinging from one fix to the next, marker to marker, buoy to bridge to bank and back again, bright enough to make a new moon full. Back then, riverboat spotlights were common as fireflies. On a dark treacherous river, these powerful beams helped show the way for gigantic rafts formed when daredevils lashed supermarket-sized barges together, two across, four barges long, and filled them with the harvest from America's breadbasket. These daredevils rode the barges from Omaha and Sioux City and Bismarck, pushing their cargo day and night down to their destinations along the Mississippi.

Barge traffic finally died out when engineers dammed the river in the Dakotas. The dams do their best to control flooding in the spring, and they do a better job of offering recreation in the summer. But they also withhold the autumn waters that once ferried the grain harvest to St. Louis and New Orleans and St. Paul. So nowadays grain shipments do what human travelers do: crowd the highways or take a rail route.

* * *

Jim the conductor returned and sat down in the empty seat next to me. In a firm low conductor voice, he warned me:

"Keep Montauk a secret."

And since he was the conductor, I listened.

"Promote the trout fishing at Bennett Springs if you want," he said, "and at Maramec Springs and at Roaring River. But keep Montauk a secret."

Fishermen are that way. Secretive. Possessive. Sometimes down-right paranoid. I think it has something to do with spending so much time alone with beer and worms. Since I was on his train, I lied and told him I'd keep his secret. At least until now. Truth is, there are thousands of secret water spots in the heartland. But Montauk isn't one of them. The conductor knows that. Every fly fisherman within a thousand miles knows about Montauk.

I grew up nearby, near enough to frequent that not-so-secret Ozarks spring near the headwaters of the Current River. And roots being roots, I'm proud of Montauk. I recall my first trip to that remote little trout park.

It was about as far back as my memory goes, back when I was practicing my phonics on Burma-Shave signs. My family unit rolled out of Rolla in a '58 Biscayne, leaving Route 66 in our rearview mirror, headed for the springs. Our car bobbed and weaved on a roller-coaster road that unfurled through the thick woods, deep in free-range country where we had to keep an eye out for deer, but also had to dodge pigs and cows and horses.

When our family arrived at Montauk, not one of us wet a line. We ran around the old mill, and fed the tiny fish in the hatchery and stood in the cold rushing water for as long as we could stand it, and marveled at the natural beauty of spring water busting out from under a mountain.

And I slept all the way home.

* * *

The historic old Montauk lodge is almost unchanged from the picture in my memory. Nowadays a few more cabins dot the hillsides. And the lodge has a new name, but it still serves up the same great Sunday dinner. Real mashed potatoes. Chicken like your grandmother made it.

And the trout have no clue that my friend the conductor might show up soon.

From Montauk, if you didn't have to stay on the curvy swervy roads, it's only about 17,000 frog hops back to Salem. From there a county road snakes south, down to Akers Ferry, where a barge transports cars across the spring-fed Current River into the deep Ozark Mountains. These are the backroads, and one of them goes past the Dillards' old homestead.

You know the Dillards, whether you remember the name or not. They were the backwoods boys who showed up to play bluegrass music with jug-blowin' Briscoe Darlin and his daughter, Charlene, on *The Andy Griffith Show*. And never far from Charlene Darlin was a ne'er do well named Ernest T. Bass, who would demonstrate his devotion to Charlene by strapping love notes to rocks and launching them through plate-glass windows to land at her feet. Briscoe and the boys weren't too keen on Ernest, on account of his terrorist ways. The boys just wanted to play bluegrass music.

In real life, they're still some of the best pickers on the planet. I don't know if they ever ran into Yogi Berra who, like me, married a lady from Salem. It would be fun someday to sit in the dance hall at Salem's Tower Inn with Yogi and tap our toes to the Dillards.

That'll never happen, mainly because they tore down the Tower Inn. And I don't know if the Dillards ever get together to pick anymore. They wouldn't be complete, since their bass player and world-class storyteller Mitch Jayne died a few years ago. Mitch's local radio show was famous for its Snake and Tick Market Report, more meaningful than Dow Jones to folks who trade in rattlesnake hides or who discover a Hoo-Boy White Dot Crushproof Dry Valley Wonder Tick on their scrotum.

Anyway, Mitch is gone, the Tower Inn is gone, and I don't have Yogi's phone number.

* * *

The onslaught of Wi-Fi and cell towers and cable TV and other links to the outside world take their toll on Salem. Call it progress if you want. But Ozark people are slowly losing their insulation from the world—and their unique dialect, and a precious part of their charm. Three decades ago, I called for a friend who was dining at the Davis Cafe on the town square. A well-seasoned lady's voice answered. "May I tell him who's a-callin'?" she asked.

"Mick Jagger."

"Hey Calvin," through a muffled telephone I could hear her yell, "there's a Mitch Jaggard on the phone fer ya."

But nowadays, even Mick has penetrated these hills. And his portrayal of the Devil mixes freely with dozens of local Ozark spots named for the Prince of Darkness.

* * *

So folks in the Ozarks are losing their innocence. As the Wi-Fi generation matures, plugged into social media and tweeting and texting their way through these hills, they're much more sophisticated than my generation. Not necessarily smarter, but more sophisticated. And they accept diversity more readily than their Ozark parents.

A buddy asked me if I ever worried for my safety when I drove deep into the Ozarks backwoods. His exact question was, "Did you ever hear banjo music?"

"All the time." My response startled him. "And when I hear banjo music, I just pick up a doghouse bass fiddle and join in."

When in Rome . . .

The Bullfrogs Sound Like Banjo Strings

I drove down to *Akers Ferry*, which connects the wilderness north of the Current River to the wilderness on the south. It's an area where the bullfrogs sound like banjo strings. That's not a crude reference to the movie *Deliverance* or a slam at Ozark hill people. The bullfrogs really do sound like banjo strings.

The ferry is operated by Gene and Eleanor Maggard. Gene's family has been in the canoe rental business since shortly after the birth of Julius Caesar. As Gene and Eleanor prepare for retirement, their son Marcus will take over operations. It's no small business. Two million people float Missouri's Ozark streams every year. The Current and its major tributary, the Jacks Fork River, are part of the oldest national scenic riverway in America.

Ever since the National Park Service secured these rivers, the feds have licensed the canoe outfitters. Hard feelings persist among folks who, forty years ago, lost their livelihoods when they found themselves without one of the coveted canoe rental concessions.

Such a protected scenic riverway could never happen today. Not with the anti-government conspiracy theorists, who believe it's their God-given right to employ nature to fit personal purposes, environment be damned. Most people respect these waters. But it's stunning how fast a few idiots armed with trash and tractors can destroy the land and foul the streams.

The Maggards know the importance of keeping these rivers clean. They're good at what they do. Gene just got a new pair of knees to support his gentle-giant frame, so he's regained the ability to singlehandedly hoist canoes atop the big five-high canoe trailers. That's something I've never been able to do, even with good knees.

His son Marcus could hoist two canoes at the same time to the highest rung. He's that big. I have a special respect for good-natured giants, and it's comforting to know they're on your side in a land where the bullfrogs sound like banjo strings. Marcus and his dad can keep drunken yahoos in line, if necessary.

Hey, since history began, folks have gathered to get polluted. And on any warm weather weekend along the Current, a natural progression plays out in a bumper-to-bumper regatta, as revelers drink and bake and drink and become victims of their own excess.

Lucky for me I had timed my visit on Wednesday, the best day to float the Current River because it's the furthest day from the weekend, furthest from the rowdy drunken bumper boaters who show up to bong beers and snort Jell-O shots and fall out of their shorts.

Despite all that shiny aluminum traffic and all that beer piss and vomit, the river runs clear, thanks to the hundreds of springs that pour their liquid benefit into the mix. The springs are cold, and when the air temperature pushes 100 degrees, nothing's better than planting your ass in sixty-degree water.

We floated from Cedar Grove back down to the ferry, a distance of eight miles, a four-hour trip. Halfway down the river, we stopped at Maggard's cabin, a favorite hideout for the James Gang as they were terrorizing the railroads and banks in Missouri. This was the spot where the gang holed up after the Gads Hill train robbery fifty miles from here. The hideout has been restored, and the legend preserved.

We hit Welch Spring, home to the concrete shell of a spooky old abandoned country hospital, a sanitarium established by a doctor who built the monstrosity into a bluff over a cave, hoping to lure sick lungs to gasp for clean, cool, cave air. Long since abandoned by humans, the cave is now home to bats.

Drunken canoeists whine and bitch that the bats shouldn't be the only mammals allowed in the cave. But ecologists prevail, the delicate bat nurseries thrive, and the bats show their gratitude by eating their weight in bugs every night. Go bats!

Welch Spring explodes onto the river with the force of a hundred hydrants, and the water is bag-shriveling frigid. So when the air temperature and humidity are right, the cold water emerging from underground hits the warming water in the river, and causes a pea soup fog as thick as anything off Nantucket. The phenomenon lasts a good half mile downstream, during which surprised canoeists can't see beyond their own canoes, and they can only drift, listen to those banjo bullfrogs, and shit their swimsuits.

The cold water of Welch Spring and its wall of fog energized my useful senses as I felt and listened my way downriver to Akers and its real live ferry that keeps Route K continuous. We emerged from the fog and arrived at the ferry crossing in late afternoon, where we emptied our canoes and our trunks and our bladders.

The end of the float brought the same satisfaction that millions of visitors feel each year. The float is not whitewater; novices can complete the journey relatively unscathed. Still, it's an exhilarating escape from the normal daily grind, escape from TV and texters and tweets.

The ferry is nothing much to look at, a flat barge that can hold three cars, maybe four, although there rarely are more than one or two vehicles waiting on the riverbank at one time, even during rush hour. The barge propels itself using an overhead motor that clutches two cables, one from either side of the river, and reels one cable in as it lets the other out. Erifnus has floated the barge a half dozen times, but she wouldn't today. She was waiting patiently for me under the shade of a sycamore tree on the fringe of the Akers Ferry campground. And she was ready for the next leg of our wilderness plunge.

Even as I stepped out of my canoe, Branson was calling, for a bright-eyed, bushy-tailed business breakfast early next morning. But the late afternoon sun still allowed enough time to check out another geologic wonder named after Satan.

Devil's Well is a big stomach, says one of the area's preeminent geologist-explorers. It's Mother Nature's idea of an indoor pool, except that it's cold and dark and underground and scary as hell, hence the name. It is the world's most dramatic peek into an underground river, a hundred feet straight down through a hole no wider than a backyard trampoline.

Before the Devil relinquished this well to the National Park Service, visitors could descend into the stomach, er, sinkhole in a bosun's chair. It was a ride much like the worm experiences when dangled from a fish hook, although the conclusion is less digestive.

On that hot afternoon, I saved a couple of friends. Three of us— Cheryl, Dean and I—walked the steep winding trail down into the sinkhole that drains into Devil's Well. The sinkhole's dimensions are such that it would make a perfect sheath for a small tornado, if Satan wanted to store one here. The hole narrows to the size of an inverted forest tower, descending to a platform where we peered over a ledge through a hole that could easily become plugged by an elephant if it fell from the sky into this tiny vortex. A few dozen feet below the hole is the water. The cavern is damn near the size and circumference of the Astrodome, best I can tell. So this hole is the world's first domed sports facility.

Thanks to well-hung electric lights, we saw the cavern and its pool, which would be the eighth wonder of the world except that it already has a higher ranking as the seventh wonder of Shannon County.

We ascended the staircase out of the hole with the realization that the surrounding terra was not that firma. That was our first unsettling revelation.

Our second unsettling revelation came when Cheryl tried to start her car. Dead battery. Middle of nowhere. No cell phone service, and a gravel road that switchbacked up a steep hill for two miles to the nearest country blacktop. So I started running up the gravel road to find help.

Up the hill, closer to the fringes of the outer beginnings of the path to the edge of civilization, I met a van carrying a vacationing family from Wisconsin, descending into the valley that contains the hole that leads to the Seventh Wonder of Shannon County. Friendly and willing, they provided the jumper cables and the juice to start Cheryl's car and get us out of the vortex of the Devil.

That evening over homestyle fried chicken at a country cafe called Jason's Place, among friends whose jobs it is to set tourism lures, we relayed the story of surprise and despair and the kindness of strangers, all within the clutches of the Devil and his well.

Missouri's Wild Belly

Far back as I can remember, float trips on Ozark streams ended with me riding back home, asleep in the back seat.

Not this time.

After dinner at Jason's pavilion, I set my sights on driving a hundred miles west, as the crow flies, to Branson. Only one problem: From these razorback ridges and deep ravines, there's no direct path to Branson, or anywhere. On my highway map I found my current location, halfway between Salem and Eminence and a half inch to the west, at the confluence of several routes that begin and end with K. The map confirmed there was no straight line to Branson. If I wanted to stay on paved roads, the route would require backtracking on an alphabet soup of blacktops and highways, first going in the opposite direction, then south in a sweeping circle that finally turns west toward Branson. Hours of extra driving.

"What Would Magellan Do?" I mumbled to myself.

Magellan and I are kindred spirits. We both let Columbus go first, and do the dirty work, testing the edge of the world and battling sea serpents and scary stuff like that. Magellan and I both like to travel, except that I have better maps, and don't have a penguin named after me, or the most treacherous strait on the face of the Earth, for that matter, and I wasn't murdered on my journey, either. Not yet, anyway. Other than that, well, we both put a lot of miles behind us. Oh, and we both had a penchant for finding a new way from point A to point B. Seeing no direct route from here to Branson, I channeled the ghost of Magellan.

And I asked directions.

"Got a shortcut from here to Branson?" I asked Gene Maggard.

"Yep," he said. His directions were sure as sundown, and not all that complicated, really. But the shortcut used every kind of back road I'd ever imagined. Blacktop. Gravel. Dirt. Low water ford over the river, and a right turn at a one-room schoolhouse.

That much would get me across the river and point me to Raymondville, and save at least an hour.

"But watch for deer," Gene cautioned. "They're thick, especially at dusk."

The deer own this part of the Ozarks, with its dense forests draped over steep valleys. I thanked Gene and started my journey along the narrowest ridge used for a Missouri highway. The ridge's name? Devil's Backbone, of course.

It was nine p.m. With a quick check of the gas gauge and a kick of my tire with the slow leak, I took off toward the sun, which was burning the treetops along the horizon. First mile of blacktop, three deer darted across the road. A dozen deer later, deep into the woods, I adopted a tactic most similar to the Indiana bat. Every fifteen seconds, a beep from my car horn bounced off anything with ears. Hopefully, the deer would realize that a car was barreling through at speeds upwards of thirty mph.

Don't know if my sonar worked. Didn't see any more deer though. And none of the sparsely scattered neighbors called the sheriff about excess noise pollution. It was a beautiful drive to Branson, I know it was, even in the dark. Not so much because of the time I'd saved, but because I took a shortcut across Missouri's wild belly.

* * *

Branson offered me a surprise this time.

Over my lifetime, I've stayed in some of the world's legendary hotels. Monaco and the Riviera. The Ritz and the Carlton, the Waldorf and the Conrad Hilton. The Fairmont and the Deauville. The Adolphus. The Willard. The Peabody and the Palmer House. The Grand.

But on this night, Branson's Chateau on the Lake offered the world's greatest suite.

Maybe it was because I was really tired. I didn't reach the Chateau until well after midnight. My first meeting on the Branson strip was at seven a.m. I had barely enough time to examine the exquisite furnishings, the leather chairs, iron and wood trim, the rich tile floors with thick throw rugs. A wet bar stayed dry for my too-brief overnight, as did the Jacuzzi. Too bad I was in my room for only four hours. By myself.

Early morning pushed me out of a barely warmed bed. I waved at the Jacuzzi and left for work. Some day Cheryl and I plan to return, and stay for more than a cup of coffee.

* * *

After a battery of meetings, Erifnus took me deep into the Ozarks.

When you slip away from Branson's glitter and strip away the greasepaint, the land and the people shout their own rich culture, punctuated by city-limit signs showing names like Mincy and Pine Top, Gobbler's Knob and Walnut Shade.

We drove south, exiting the state through Blue Eye, population 129, where if you study real hard you can get a sheepskin from Blue Eye High . . . not that I would trade my bloodshot eye education.

Jane & Jesse, Noel & Nakedness

The road reveals unalterable truths. One such truth is this: You can take Jane out of the Walmart, but you can't take the Walmart out of Jane. Jane, Missouri, is the tiny suburb of almost-as-tiny Pineville. Well technically it sits halfway between Pineville and Bella Vista, Arkansas. It's just south of Big Sugar Creek State Park and Huckleberry Ridge Conservation Area. Campers and hikers flock to Jane, since this small town has a mighty economy, boosted by the county's only Walmart.

Local history suggests the James Gang hid in the caves around here. There's no solid proof. But if Jesse was looking for a place to hide, he couldn't find a more remote location. Driving around these rugged backwoods, I can see how outlaws could still hide in its nooks and crannies, and get their supplies from the Jane Walmart.

Back in 1938, filmmakers chose this remote location of Greater Jane for the setting of the movie *Jesse James*, starring Tyrone Power, Henry Fonda, and Randolph Scott. The movie was a hit, finishing fourth at the box office behind *Gone with the Wind*, the *Wizard of Oz*, the *Hunchback of Notre Dame*, and ahead of *Mr. Smith Goes to Washington*. Not a bad lineup.

As word spread about the film location, thousands of fans flocked to get a glimpse of movie stars Power, Fonda, and Scott as they relaxed at Shadow Lake Resort in Noel.

Yep, Noel.

Even though the local motels and the post office get a spike in visitation every December 24th, the town isn't named for Christmas. It was named for a man whose last name was Noel. Willis Bridges Noel. Went by the name of Bridge. Must've been an interesting character.

The town of Noel sits at a sweeping bend in the Elk River, with a reputation as a resort getaway on the cutting edge of wild and wooly.

The Elk River is seductive, coursing along a deep crack in the Ozarks, offering a scenic float through the very southwest corner of Missouri. And on steamy weekends, it can get wild. Drunkenness. Nakedness. Debauchery.

I used a delightful day to kayak Indian Creek into the Elk River from Anderson to Noel. Floaters were having a great time. I had a great time myself, but saw no orgiastic activity. Maybe things were calm because it was a Wednesday. But on any given sunbaked weekend, thousands of sun worshipers gravitate to this charming watershed. And somewhere along the float, a percentage of them lose all their inhibitions, and clothing, and they start freely distributing bodily fluids. Alcohol may be involved.

Not long ago, one Kansas couple brought their two young children for a weekend float. Before they committed to the trip, they pointedly asked the canoe outfitter if the river would be family friendly. "Oh, yes," the outfitter reassured them. "We're a Christian outfitter." I don't doubt that the outfitter shows up in church most Sundays, but to knowingly invite a family with small children to float on a weekend among depraved raving party animals is kinda like encouraging small children to play with a meth lab in the street.

* * *

But the Great Equalizer has a way of evening things out. Drunken idiocy has its paybacks.

It was a hot summer day. A lady took her children to play on their backyard beach beside the Elk River. Along came some chemically impaired canoeists, who floated within earshot. Loud and lascivious, they spewed particularly vile passages from their favorite classic literature, *Bodily Functions of Angles and Saxons*.

Their unclothed cavorting alarmed the mother. She shouted out to them. "Please watch your language! There are children on the beach."

Her request met a chorus of carnal cuss, a semaphore circus of anatomical demonstrations. She pulled her cell phone out of her beach bag. Seeing this, one besotted actor sprung from his canoe, bolted ashore and grabbed the phone from her hand. He heaved it into the river.

Justice bore down swift and sure. In a coincidence that may prove that there is order in the universe, a party of off-duty St. Louis police officers happened to be floating behind the attacker, and they witnessed the crime. Moving with all deliberate shock and awe, the cops nailed the poop-faced perp, pushing his face down in watery gravel. Local authorities arrived within minutes, and the lady's husband, the sheriff, assessed a sobering charge of robbery.

As a result of this and other crime reports, McDonald County enacted stricter rules governing social behavior along the Elk River. The officials are doing their best to modify eye pollution and ear pollution and bloodstream pollution.

The jury's still out regarding the efforts to reduce water pollution. But as of now, according to government tests, some streams in the region, and elsewhere in the state, are impaired. Some folks warn that pollution may be coming from tons of chicken shit, totally unrelated to the impaired chickenshit who landed in jail. The end is near.

Speaking of water pollution, just southwest of Southwest City, along Highway 43, a marker indicates the junction of three states, and I found myself standing in Arkansas, Oklahoma and Missouri simultaneously. I stood with each foot planted in a different state, and whizzed in the third.

Well, I thought about it, anyway.

* * *

Dipping into Arkansas, I took a detour to Eureka Springs to see the giant statue of Christ of the Ozarks.

Besides his regular gig keeping watch over the flock of Pentecostal churches in the general vicinity, Christ makes quite a presence here, towering seven stories atop a formidable mountain. When the statue was first erected, he towered even higher. The Federal Aviation Administration cracked down on the builders of this glorious monument to our savior, saying that Jesus' head was sticking into airspace, and as such, the Lord posed a hazard to airplanes in the area. Obviously, this was an awkward situation.

What would Jesus do?

The FAA's solution was simple: Put a flashing red light on top of the blessed savior's head.

"Blasphemy!" said the faithful, who instead cut Jesus off at the knees to get his head below radar and back to safety. For Christ's sake, the faithful saved the statue from the indignity of a red light. For the statue's knees, the end came with a terrible swift sword.

We turned toward Bull Shoals Lake and rode the old *Toad Suck Ferry* back into Missouri. This isn't the original route of the old *Toad Suck Ferry*, which was on a stream way down near Little Rock. I guess somebody bought this old barge, with the *Toad Suck* name still emblazoned on its hull, and brought it up here. Riding the *Toad Suck Ferry* on the *Peel Ferry* route isn't as romantic as climbing on the back of the ferry in the actual town of Toad Suck. But that's no concern of mine.

And Erifnus enjoyed the float. Deep in the lake, beneath her wheels, giant trophies eyed the bottom of the *Toad Suck* barge as we crossed the water. Well, they're not trophies yet. They're the great-great-granddaughters of the trophies, the Missouri state record walleye, brown trout, yellow perch, striped bass, and largemouth bass. The latter record has stood since JFK's first hundred days.

The ferry dumped Erifnus onto Route 125, and we began probably the most beautiful drive in the Ozarks. I don't know. It was dark. So we headed up to Springfield, and I checked in to the Clarion Hotel.

At sunrise, we'd tackle the heart of hillbilly holler.

* * *

Next day, I stuffed Erifnus with her favorite brand of corn liquor and plunged south from Route 66, where the road less traveled becomes Route 125, winding past Sparta and Chadwick. Like the perfect anthem, the scenery reached a crescendo along the twisting trail through the Mark Twain National Forest in Taney County, south of Camp Ridge, and Cobb Ridge.

Route DD watches Brushy Creek sweep past, on its way to fortify Beaver Creek, and for miles the vista south overlooks the ridges and ravines around Hercules Glade, some of the best ridge-running mountain scenery in Missouri's Ozarks. Wonderful motorcycle roads. Great backpacking too. So I left Erifnus as the lone vehicle in a parking lot at a trail head, and marched downhill into the unknown. The path quickly became man's only footprint in this vast wilderness, at once an intrusion into nature, and a lifeline back to civilization. The trail unfolded over miles, and the absence of manmade sounds refreshed my ear's ability to pick out the warbler and the chickadee, to discern the crow from the red-tailed hawk, and listen for the rustle and the rattle. Good shape and good shoes helped this foot soldier. Without water, I limited my march to a few ridges and ravines, enough to remind me that rugged terrain is harder on the knees going downhill than up.

The moments just before arriving back to the parking lot are always tense. Will Erifnus still be there, undisturbed? She was. And like lunch meat, she was ready. We drove on together, as God intended, man and car, pioneer and petrol.

* * *

Adventure takes on new intensity when you and your car are both granddaddies, and the end of the world is nigh. Along the side of the road, we spied a beautiful little sports car for sale, a Fiat Spyder, vintage 1976, *Car and Driver* car of the year. My Pontiac scoffed, and why not? Her odometer showed six digits and no breakdowns. This little Fiat by the roadside—like its twin sister sitting broke down in my garage at home—might've been in the shop dozens of times over that timespan.

We kept driving, and wound up dead-ended in a holler fat with water, where Beaver Creek feeds Lake Taneycomo. Retreating north, following the whitewater froth of Beaver Creek beside us, we veered off Highway 76 onto Route AA. The road unfolded through thick woods and nothing else, until the blacktop ended. At this point, as with so many other crossroads on my journey, the proverbial fork in the road was gravel . . . and uncharted, at least for me.

According to my map, the next blacktop sat only a few miles from this spot. But which gravel road would lead me there? My state highway map offered no clue, other than the tantalizing image of two blacktops just millimeters from connecting. In a nod to ancient mariners who relied on a fallible technique called dead reckoning, I took the fork to the right, which forked again, and again. Erifnus descended deeper into the forest, along rocky roads, through ruts and ravines and low-water fords and mud and panthers and black bears and homesteads that might be friendly or might not, if I broke down and had to walk up a path to knock on a door.

Deeper into the woods we drove. Erifnus' motor groaned, and her tires ached, as signs of civilization dwindled to a single power line fastened to poles older than Dick Clark, more crooked than Bernie Madoff. Using the sun for direction, I angled eastward, looking for pavement. But ahead, gravel, gravel everywhere, surrounded by heavy forest. Finally my blood pressure and my car's radiator relaxed as the gravel path crested a hill and T-boned onto asphalt pavement.

Seeing no roadsign to tell me our position, we turned south, assuming we might make it back to Highway 125. Four miles down the road, a sign told me we were traveling on Route H, far west of our intended destination. It didn't matter. On a hard surface, Erifnus and I breathed a sigh of relief, after spending too much petrol and daylight spreading gravel around the Ozarks backwoods.

The Real Ozarks

We muscled our way east along the slalom course called Route 76. At Brownbranch, Beaver Creek narrows its wild muscle into a great riffle, where an optimistic backwoods entrepreneur put a canoe rental.

Another great canoe spot down the road at Bradleyville bit the dust, a victim of the economy, no doubt, since the stream still rushes by its back door. The stream doesn't miss the canoes; less traffic is good traffic. But for the locals who depend on the trickle down of tourism, it's bad tidings.

I took another blacktop road, a dead end called Route W, away from Beaver Creek into the unknown. A rabbit ran in front of Erifnus, and barely made it to the other side. On our return from the end of the blacktop, the same rabbit, I'm certain, played chicken with us again, narrowly cheating death a second time. Brave rabbit.

It was then that I remembered to stop and get a little extra insurance: my Ozark air bag. Erifnus doesn't think I need it, because she has implants that will inflate and protect me in a crash. But she's getting older, and I just feel better with an eighteen-roll of toilet paper in my lap, tucked snugly under my chin. My Ozark air bag.

Erifnus, my trusty time capsule, delivered me deeper into the hills, into what locals call the "real Ozarks." There are reasons they call it that: Water. Woods. Hills.

And mills.

We stumbled onto the tiny town of Rockbridge, and I learned why it was the original Ozark County seat. There, on the west bank of Spring Creek, the Rockbridge Mill stands resplendent in its red coat of paint. To avoid the agony of pounding their own grain with mortars and pestles, generations of Ozark families gladly traveled miles over crooked roads to pay millers to grind their grain. This mill became the exchange for social contacts, a hillbilly Facebook-on-foot. While customers waited, they checked their mail, and exchanged gossip, and complained about weather and taxes. And they shopped for necessities and niceties and anything else that struck their fancy at these outposts of civilization. Rockbridge was considered the finest general store in the region, the first supercenter of the Ozarks.

Even today, this place is on the edge of civilization. There is no easy access to the area, by superhighway standards. That's the charm. Visitors follow the ridges and ravines, much the same as early settlers.

Nowadays Rockbridge is a resort. Next to the old gristmill is a general store that rose from the ashes of the original store on the site. Known for fine dining, the general store's restaurant receives locals and visitors seven days a week. For the last fifty years, a private trout hatchery has spawned menu items. While I was there, I helped preserve an endangered icon of American culture: I bought a roll of stamps at the Rockbridge Post Office . . . they're good throughout the USA.

It made me feel good about our United States Postal Service. Even from this remote spot, I can mail a letter to anywhere in the world. Oh sure, FedEx or UPS would be glad to pick up my letter, for the better part of a Hamilton. The postal service does it for less than four bits. Yet people still bitch at its inefficiency. What inefficiency? The postal service is a government agency that balances its budget. Sure, the cost of a stamp has increased over time. Name another product that hasn't gone up in price. You may still want to privatize the mail, but don't expect to send a letter from Rockbridge—or anywhere—for half a buck.

We headed east along a roller coaster called Highway 14, dipping, ducking and diving toward the valley of the Twin Bridges. Along the way, the Devil arose again. From what I gather, popular sentiment crowns a spot along the North Fork of the White River as the preeminent Devil's Backbone in Missouri.

Sprawling along the border of Douglas and Howell counties in the Mark Twain National Forest, this bony ridge crowns one of the smallest of Missouri's eight designated wilderness areas. In wilderness terms, small is relative: My legs yearned to make a deal with the Devil in the middle of this 7,000-acre wilderness. My hike along the backbone itself must have looked like an ant on an ax handle. The nearby Ozark Trail is well marked, but take a map because there are sixty miles of connecting trails. Take water, too. Otherwise, you'll drink from Amber Spring or the wildlife ponds for the rest of your short life, lost in this wild back country.

I made it back to Erifnus.

Just south of the Devil's Backbone, we dropped into a deep valley, bottoming out at Twin Bridges Canoe Rental. I jumped in a canoe and floated down the North Fork of the White River toward the falls at Dawt Mill, another one of the five Ozark County mills that still stand against Mother Nature's relentless surprises.

Halfway downstream to Dawt, the river nearly doubles in size, and drops in temperature at Rainbow Springs. That's where wild trout enter the picture. I didn't see any, since you must sneak up on wild trout. Back in 1882, humans introduced rainbow trout to the North Fork. Then an unusual thing happened. The trout began to reproduce naturally, a rarity in Ozarks streams. Wild trout. Wild country.

And a wild ride down the White River Valley.

Slicing through this rough terrain, the crooked streams never worry for an instant who's in control. They tolerate the bridges and the gristmills that anchor into their banks. They know that when the time is right, they'll wash away any trace of manmade objects. In terms of geologic time, the end is always near for the handiwork of man.

Floating more than paddling, I reached the low dam that spans the river at Dawt Mill. The dam welcomes two types of canoeists who attempt to paddle over it: fools and survivors.

Dawt Mill's weather-beaten countenance reflects a century of tempest. The unpainted look adds to her charm and offers an authentic, unretouched glimpse into the past. Well, it *was* unretouched. A local couple has refurbished the mill and added a restaurant.

It's a tradeoff. They may have erased some history with a facelift, but the structural tuck guarantees the historic building will not slide into the creek for at least a few generations. An artificial millwheel adorns one side of the mill, added to pacify visitors who insist on seeing a water wheel, even though this mill's power comes from a turbine beneath the mill race.

The mill still grinds flour using burr stones. But the property's primary function is nostalgia, a place to peek into the past, and to get food and lodging, of course.

These Ozark County mills survive because they're so remote, and civilization hasn't figured a way to pave over them and make subdivisions with names like Millstream Acres. The mills are close together, no more than a two-song drive from one to the next. As the crow flies, Hodgson Mill sits about four miles from Dawt Mill.

I'd already seen Hodgson Mill, on a grocery store's flour shelf, on packaging that bears the Hodgson name. The old mill doesn't produce flour anymore. In 1976, that duty migrated to a modern plant ten miles down the road in the county seat of Gainesville. But don't fret. Modern doesn't mean the flour has changed. It's still stone ground, and they take away nothing, add nothing. The company proclaims that "Alva Hodgson would be proud."

Alva Hodgson left his powerprints all over the region, as Missouri's preeminent millwright of the nineteenth century. For its 119th birthday, Hodgson's namesake mill received a facelift—really a foundation lift—completed with the help of Amish carpenters from nearby Seymour. The carpenters bolstered the sagging structure with giant timbers cut from the hearts of Douglas firs. Now, Lord willin' and Bryant Creek don't rise, the mill will stand another 120 years.

Before you make plans to visit these mills, there's one item you must bring with you. Search your father's closet for that old pair of Big Smith overalls. While Big Smith overalls may not be the official uniform of Ozark County, your dad's duds might get a kick in returning to the likely source of their stitching, Hodgson or its neighbor, Zanoni Mill.

Zanoni, about four miles downhill from Hodgson, sits on Pine Creek and features a rare overshot waterwheel mill. It was built in 1940 on the site of a mill that operated as far back as the Civil War. Back when the mill was in service, a wooden flume captured water from the Zanoni Spring and channeled it down the hill, pouring it on top of the waterwheel, hence the term overshot. Nowadays, the mill's services are mostly limited to weddings and special occasions. On this day, there was no activity around the mill, so we drove on.

Best I can tell from a review of the Ozark County map, local residents have named sixteen springs, a dozen ridges, twelve knobs, eight hollows, eight caves, five balds, five mountains, two bends, and one sink. There are more than that, of course. After all, a road map can hold only so much information.

But who's counting?

* * *

Only a few miles east of here, the question becomes, "Who's listening?"

On my map an inch north of Arkansas, the home of the Zizzers beckons. Aside from having the world's second-most unique high school team name, West Plains gets credit for nurturing Dick Van Dyke and Porter Wagoner. Baseball great Bill Virdon grew up here, as did big-league pitcher Preacher Roe, who threw a pretty lively spit ball and ran a pretty good grocery store.

For a few years, a faceless group infiltrated the area. To visualize this group, shut your eyes, and listen to the theater in your mind as the opening credits roll: Big national radio voices converge upon an unlikely destination . . . they come to this spot, so remote you can't get there from here . . . and liberally share their creativity in the heart of conservative America. . . .

The National Audio Theatre Festivals ended a long run in Columbia a few years back, and dropped into West Plains. They fell in love with the surroundings. They don't hate Columbia, with its echoes of festivals past. Lord knows Columbia is easier for a coastal resident to find. But that's the charm of West Plains. West is a relative term. So is plains. And this little town with its Zizzers and spitters and Porters and Petrys is flanked by veritable Venus flytraps of Ozark allure. From the middle of town, you can find rugged remotes in the elapsed time of an average commercial station break. The participants in this audio theatre festival loved to get as remote as, well, audio theatre. Within minutes, actors could trade microphones for appendages to help them hike and paddle, and push smoldering sticks under a campfire grill. It's reassuring, in a cosmic kind of way, that folks who create the theatre of the mind came to this remote area to get the inspiration to create the theatre of the mind. They reveled in the revelation that truly, Chicago coyotes just don't howl the way they do down here.

* * *

Erifnus pulled off the highway and waited for me to tap into a conference call. With my headset on and my hands free to drive, we headed back down the highway as I listened to a dozen voices talk about tourism. Nearly in a trance, and in no hurry, I gripped the steering wheel as Erifnus followed a big truck. As the voices droned in my headset, one of the truck's rear tires kicked up a rock the size of your big toe. In one slow-motion second, I watched the rock arc like a diver and smack my windshield.

"Son of a bitch!" My reaction was involuntary.

The conference callers stopped talking. A deafening silence waited for an explanation. Finally a voice said, "Is everybody okay?"

I confessed. "Rock cracked my windshield. Sorry."

We drove on. What else could we do?

Lovely, Dark & Deep

Just outside Koshkonong, a tiny town near the Arkansas border, we rolled into a setting that waited patiently for 10,000 years for the Great Wallendas to cross. The Great Wallendas were a balanced family who formed human pyramids and walked tightropes over familiar places. Niagara Falls. Big-city skyscrapers. And now a brave descendant has crossed the Grand Canyon.

Best I can tell, no circus tightrope ever crossed Grand Gulf. The Wallendas never came.

That's not Grand Gulf's fault, nor the fault of circus people, nor anybody's fault, really. Unlike those familiar places, most people never heard of Grand Gulf. Besides, for most people, Grand Gulf is just too far out of the way. Too bad. It features one of the Cave State's most dramatic members of the sinkhole family. Water flows into this sinkhole and does a Houdini, escaping into thin ground. Ancestors used to pour a bushel of oats into the hole, and watch them reappear in Mammoth Spring, just across the Arkansas border.

Eons ago, the roof of Grand Gulf cave collapsed and plunged thirteen stories into the ground, making a sheer drop that is deeper than it is wide. It would be a tough hike over the surviving 250-foot-long natural bridge and down into the sinkhole, if not for the state park's quarter-mile boardwalk, snaking and undulating and dropping a 118-step stairway into the bottom of the sinkhole, where you can wade in the Shiloh Church Creek. This crack in the world would be a great place for a baptism, right there in the depths of the earth where the saved can thumb their noses at Hell.

Grand Gulf goes by a grandiose nickname: Missouri's Little Grand

Canyon. And until you see it, you'd be skeptical of such a name. I was. But once you see it, you'll fall to your knees, like I did, and throw your arms skyward, and proclaim disbelief that Grand Gulf still seems to be buried in the Witness Protection Program.

Well, some folks think obscurity is a good thing. They don't mind that you don't know about their favorite geologic formations. They know that less traffic makes it easier to preserve such natural wonders and easier to enjoy, all to themselves.

* * *

It's a short hop from there to Thayer, an old railroad town that reigns as the biggest town within a mile of Missouri's southern border. And in their soft southern drawl, the 2,200 residents turn the word Thayer into a distinctive dialectic destination, stretched to the edge of three syllables.

Up the road is Alton, which, as we all know, spelled backward is "Not L.A." Alton residents seem comfortable with that. After all, Los Angeles has a lot of stuff, but it doesn't have Booches' old screen door. At the Eleven Point River Canoe Rental, I put my hands on that familiar old door knob. It's the same screen door that had slammed a billion times as the guardian of Booches, an ancient pool hall in Columbia, 200 miles away.

Most residents of Alton don't care that generations of Mizzou students learned as much on the nights they walked through this old wooden green screen door as they did from sleeping through economics class. It's a relic that means nothing to the uninitiated. But if you've ever walked through that door, or stumbled back out, you know the significance. Sure, Booches serves Stag Beer, and you can shoot a game of snooker or billiards. But gourmands worldwide know something else: the Booche Burger is the world's best.

For most of its life, the old screen door opened only for men. Women weren't welcome in the pool hall. But as a succession of owners softened their stance against infiltration by xx chromosomes, the door's knob began to feel a feminine grip.

When the old door retired, Ryan and Brian brought it to Alton to work as a flystopper for the Eleven Point River Canoe Rental. Ryan urged me to let go of the door handle so they could drop my canoe and me in the river.

My canoe has a name, too. I bought her brand new, before she'd ever been dipped or tipped or swamped, before the tough polymer of her deep green skin took on scars from the gravel along shallow Ozark streams. She started her life as a Guide, a sturdy boat made by Old Town. But to make her unique, I removed the decal letters along her bow, the ones that spelled "G-u-i-d-e," and rearranged them to spell "G-n-e-i-d." Thus, she became one of a kind and, as such, impervious to thievery.

Or so I hoped.

Ryan gave me some parting advice: "You'll float fast, since the water's a foot higher than normal."

As it turned out, the swifter current saved me, since the cows along this remote river were ready to call my bluff. Shortly after shoving off downstream, I came upon a herd of cows in the pasture along the river. Rather than exhibiting the customary bovine shyness, these heifers and steers charged my canoe. I'm convinced that in the grand master plan of settling old scores, these cows practice canoe tipping. Or maybe they didn't like my canoe's name. Whatever their reason for being aggressive, the beef balked at the swift current, and they let me pass. I escaped downriver and congratulated myself on choosing such a delightful day.

An eagle launched from a tree and flew close overhead. A blue heron led us downstream, flitting just a few yards ahead, always just safely out of reach.

The Eleven Point River enveloped me in layers of isolation as we bisected the Irish Wilderness in a ragged, rugged slash. Resident mammals along the river showed a behavior largely uncontaminated by human contact. Yeah, there are floaters. But the floaters who reach this remote spot are respectful of the river.

* * *

Back when my job involved promoting my state, I found myself in a Manhattan office, face-to-face with an editor of a major publication that shall remain nameless, except to say that it's national in scope and geographic in nature. The editor was cordial, but all business. "Why would I want to visit Missouri?" he spat. "My readers want wilderness. And adventure."

"Precisely," I answered. He looked surprised. "The Irish Wilderness covers as much area as Manhattan," I offered, "but only one-millionth the population.

"There may be a lonelier place than the Irish Wilderness, but I don't know where." Roads are few, making it a perfect host for the Ozark Trail to penetrate through it.

It's one of wild America's best-kept secrets, the Ozark Trail. And cross-country drivers and magazine editors would be startled to see the beauty that unfolds along this rugged footpath through the wilderness, away from interstate highways and the world's most concentrated crop of billboards.

I told him that the Ozark Trail is the Appalachian Trail's newer sister, lesser known and one third as long but no less a challenge, as it crosses the continent's oldest exposed rocks, named for pachyderms and johnsons.

I told him about rivers with foreboding trolls named Smash Rock and Devil's Rake, and holes in the earth like Slaughter Sink.

In an instant the magazine editor unfolded a map across his table, and we plotted his course through Missouri's wild abdomen.

But that editor never made the trip. A few weeks after my visit, he was transferred to another magazine. *C'est la vie.* And more than a few Ozarks natives are happy to remain undiscovered.

* * *

As I paddled Gneid down the Eleven Point River, I knew that within the better part of a county in every direction, I was a population of one.

Along the river there used to be a town named Surprise. It's long gone. Gone too is its centerpiece, Turner Mill, although the mill's old rusty iron water wheel survives, overgrown with climbing vegetation, looking like it rolled downhill out of a Spiderman movie. As if on cue, inside a cave a few yards away, I met the biggest spider this side of a Goliath Bird-Eater Tarantula.

The arachnid that lurks on the walls of Turner Mill cave sees few people, and she likes it that way. Isolation has its soothing benefits. And she doesn't have to endure wave after wave of drunken idiocy, as exhibited on more accessible Ozark rivers. The spider drilled me with a fangy stare—a deathly silent fearsome fix that suggested I leave her alone. Fine with me.

Downriver, I found a suitable gravel bar where I beached Gneid, to climb the riverbank and set up camp deep in the Irish Wilderness. Because the wilderness deserves a "leave no trace" campsite, I packed light: a tent, sleeping bag, water, and a small amount of food. Oh, and whiskey. This is, after all, the Irish Wilderness.

I sat alone by the campfire and thought about the strange evolution of this area: wilderness, then settled and clear cut and stripped, then abandoned and back to wilderness. A few tiny hamlets remain. One is a two-building town named Wilderness. It's a half-day hike from there to Handy, Missouri, where the nation's smallest post office (6'x 9') kept in touch with civilization until it disappeared.

The wilderness itself is named for the Irish families who busted their backs building railroads westward. Tough work. After they finished the job, Father John Hogan led the spent workers to decompress in the wilderness. But the people vanished sometime during the chaos of the Civil War, unable to fend off raids by confederates, Union troops, and bushwhackers. Now, the land is wilderness again, with hardly a human trace.

During the past century a new growth forest has reestablished. It's a bit weaker genetically than the old forest, but more trees cover the same territory. The heavy forest cover is especially noticeable when you fly over the rugged remoteness of the Ozarks. You see miles of dense forestland, pocked only occasionally by a town, or a clearing that might indicate a chip mill lurking around the fringes of these woods, grinding and pulverizing acres of trees to be used in plywood and particle board. Chip mills are the human equivalent of termites. They hide out of sight and exercise their appetites for wood until, before you realize it, whole forests can disappear. Maybe it's the pressure from the environmental movement, or maybe it's just the lay of this very rugged, remote terrain, but chip millers seem to conceal their clear cuts from public view, away from busy highways.

As darkness fell and a full moon rose, I remembered the last time I camped in this forest, deep in this wilderness. It was a December night, and my campfire bolstered me against the cold, but also against the coyotes that circled at a distance, in a pack whose chorus sounded like a hundred dogs. In reality, the pack probably numbered a half dozen. Their night howls came first from the south, an hour later from the east. As the full moon reached its midnight zenith, they howled from the north. I couldn't help feeling like a can of Alpo, opened and heated.

But I was prepared, with my most important defensive weapon: a good campfire.

Lack of preparedness is always a danger. . . .

* * *

They didn't think they'd get in trouble.

It was a balmy day for January. A father and his two boys went for a hike, as they'd done a dozen times on camping trips into the heart of the Ozarks. They had good shoes. But they were dressed for seventy degrees and sun. Two hours into their hike, when a cold front hit them, a miserable rain soaked them to the bone.

Even deep in this wilderness, a pickup truck passed them as they walked along a remote road. The driver asked them if they needed a ride. They declined. Who knows why? A mistrust of strangers, maybe, or determination to find their own way out.

It gets dark fast in January, and the trio became disoriented. Lost. Shivering wet.

Back at camp, Mom became worried as darkness settled in, and the temperature dropped. She called for help. Search parties combed the rugged wilderness all night. They found three bodies the next morning. Hypothermia.

You wouldn't think that in this modern age, people could still fall off the edge of the earth. Not here in the middle of America. But it happens a lot. Sometimes it's bad luck. Sometimes it's carelessness or not being prepared. Sometimes it's lack of training, or a lapse in judgment. But there's one other ingredient:

This is still the wild west.

* * *

Next morning, alive and unmolested by coyotes, I rose early, broke camp, and restored it to wilderness. I packed Gneid so she'd balance through the rapids and riffles along this wild river. She performed beautifully, agile as a dancer through the chutes, around the bends, dodging root wads and water moccasins. She delivered me unscathed, once again, to where Erifnus waited.

Gneid hugged tight to Erifnus' top as we climbed the swervy gravel roads out of the river valley.

Back on the swervy curves of Highway 19, we reached the tiny hamlet of Greer, with its all-purpose precursor to the supercenter. I didn't stop, even though the store had a big Busch Bavarian Beer sign. It was only mid-morning, and Richard's Canoe Rental probably hadn't tapped the beer yet. I'll keep driving and make up for lost time, I promised myself, mustering a remnant of puritan shame.

But I made it only a few miles when Erifnus felt that familiar gravitational pull off the road. This time the pull came from Greer Spring, a gushing wonder that could fill 220 million milk jugs a day with real spring water. The spring pays big dividends for hikers willing to descend a mile to see it. I made Erifnus stay in the parking lot, and I took the plunge down the trail.

The National Forest Service lets the poison ivy form its three-leaf fence on both sides of the footpath, thus encouraging me to stay on the trail. Ingenious.

But poison ivy isn't the only danger. Friends worry that on one of these solitary walks into the wilderness, I might be killed by a bear, or a feral hillbilly. I worry more about a fall from a cliff and a broken back. I'm wary of the surprise bite from a copperhead or a cottonmouth. Neither offers the fair warning of a rattlesnake before she strikes. I wonder if I could climb a mile uphill with a tourniquet around my leg, and make it to Erifnus before I lost consciousness.

Most dangerous of all, I knew that when I returned to Erifnus and we hit the road, we were much more likely to be maimed by a texter, lol behind the wheel.

Still, hostile human confrontation happens, as I would find out down the road.

I walked deeper down the ravine. The first glimpse of the rushing water came from a stone observation deck built by a descendant of the land's first European owner.

As it busts out from under a bluff, the spring makes the sound of raw power, rushing over boulders dressed in watercress, water tumbling down the mountainside, pushing toward its wedding with the Eleven Point River. The spring emerges after its underground journey from as far as forty miles away near Willow Springs. It reminds me that this water will remain crystal pure only if the folks upstream are careful what they dump atop these karst catacombs of limestone and dolomite.

A few years back, there was a sewage leak in a nearby town. Anybody who came along shortly after that spill to drink the pure water of Greer Spring might've got a dose of human fecal coliform with it. But the hydrology of the underground river lets new water flush the spring and await the next sewage leak.

Hiking back up the hill to the parking lot, I followed the switchback trail as it crossed wooden bridges that span deep ravines. This is nature nearly unspoiled, and you don't see beer cans or cigarette butts or candy bar wrappers because lazy, thoughtless assholes would never walk this far into the woods.

Reaching the parking lot I was relieved to see Erifnus, with Gneid hugging her top, just like I'd left them. We rejoined the road.

Only minutes north of Greer, we drove off-road again to McCormack Lake, a setting for reflection and rejuvenation, insulated by miles and miles of Irish Wilderness. The morning sun filtered its rays through the thick canopy of pines and hardwoods, forming a real live Gainsborough painting. In these thick woods, it's easy to seduce yourself into a sense of hope that natural ecosystems still have a fighting chance.

Up the road we ran into a test for CSI fans. Just west of the waterfalls and chert shut-ins of Cowards Hollow, Tupelo Gum Pond offers two remarkable distinctions. It's a rare sinkhole because it holds water. And the tupelo trees that surround the sinkhole pond have no relatives this far north. Up here the word tupelo is more closely associated with Elvis Presley and Van Morrison. And like the singers, the tupelo trees are not native to this area, not for eons. This isolated island of tupelo gums tells something about this sinkhole. It's ancient—and protective.

* * *

Winona is a crossroads in the middle of the Mark Twain National Forest and an unofficial forestry capital in these deep woods, thanks to logger heads who envisioned a monument to the surrounding forests and the folk heroes who harvest them. Built by private interests more than a decade ago and called the Missouri Forest Heritage Center, the $4 million museum had big plans.

Today, sustainable forestry has taken root. Even as tourism grows, the timber industry remains the biggest money maker in this dirt-poor region, and responsible logging operations thrive.

But way out here in the middle of nowhere, the museum foundered until the Missouri Department of Conservation came to the rescue and established the 456-acre Twin Pines Conservation Education Center. Now the museum is stable, preserving insights into past dangers that threatened this forest. Inside are priceless histories sketched by a local named Lennis Broadfoot. He told about life here during the Great Depression, before electricity reached the region, when feral hogs nearly rooted out the entire deer and turkey populations.

People all over Missouri bitch about the Department of Conservation, one of the state's biggest landowners—and one of the state's biggest law enforcement agencies. "Conservation has too much money," some say, "and too much power." But without the agency, what would happen?

The forests have rebounded to record density since their low point, when the railroads came through and cut down damn near every tree. Poor forest management and poor hunting practices killed Missouri's last bear, the last cougar, the last elk.

Now, they're all back.

But there's still work to do. Tallgrass prairie once covered nearly one-third of the state—15 million acres. Today, less than one percent remains. If not for conservation efforts, even that one percent might disappear.

We jumped back onto Highway 19 and passed a rural church, whose marquee announced an upcoming Summer Quake. Erifnus' engine shuddered as I shifted.

We pressed onward past Overcup Oak Sink, north and west to my favorite spot on Earth, the prongs of the Jacks Fork River.

From a gravel bar upstream from a culvert bridge, I've launched canoes nearly two dozen times, through the culvert and down the river, in fair weather and foul, in low water and high water, in wind and rain, and on one memorable occasion, during a sleet storm. But the most dangerous conditions had nothing to do with the weather or the water.

A few years ago, I joined a group who came to this spot to begin a four-day float. Sitting around the campfire in the middle of a gravel bar on the night before the launch, we heard a vehicle approaching. We watched headlights turn toward us, leaving the gravel road and descending down a path toward the river. An old rusty van splashed through the shallow water onto the same gravel bar where we sat, a hundred yards downriver from our campfire. Within minutes, the van's occupants poured gasoline onto an old tire and ignited it.

As we debated the dangers of sending a greeting party to offer to build them a natural fire, the van drove away, leaving the flaming tire behind. The whole bizarre event suggested the influence of meth. We extinguished the tire and packed it with other trash we'd picked up around the area.

My Favorite Spot

The painting always captivated me with its small-but-mighty presence. For years, the painting presided over the dining room of the Missouri Governor's Mansion, absorbing whispers and tall tales as mansion guests stood under its influence.

On those occasions when fate summoned me to the governor's table, Thomas Hart Benton's *The Rapids* never failed to lure me through its portal and transport me to that scene of serenity. Outdoor lovers succumb to Benton's mastery of that landscape, a towering river bluff, displayed on a canvas stretched to the size of a Big Chief tablet.

Benton loved the Ozark streams. "Down the river is freedom from consequence. All one has to do is jump in a skiff at night and by the morrow be beyond the reach of trouble. . . ." he wrote in *An Artist in America* (1937).

The painting no longer hangs in the governor's mansion. It moved on to its next stop, at a museum somewhere. But wherever the masterpiece emerges, it remains a powerful paean to rugged Ozark beauty, a raw iron-ore magnet to those who whisper under its spell.

Benton completed the work half a century ago, but the painting's rocky bluff has overlooked the Jacks Fork River for a million years, inspiring thousands who have made the journey deep into wilderness to gaze into its natural wonder.

Through that one work of art, I've kindled a kinship to the artist, because I think I know the spot where he set up his easel to capture the beauty of the river and its majestic bluffs. Maybe I'm right. Maybe not. It doesn't matter. The scene repeats a dozen times downstream, featuring ever-changing gravel bars built and rebuilt by the force of the water. The water and the wind combined to sculpt one of the oldest, most diverse gardens on the continent.

For nearly thirty years, I've joined a gang of Ozark free thinkers who have made a ritual journey down that river, launching from its headwaters in early spring, when the water runs fast and full, and floaters are scarce. These guys are possessive of their river, not really interested in sharing this treasure with the rest of the world.

For the most part, their secret is safe. In conversations with national media, I've discovered that this stream remains a hidden treasure, unknown to most outdoor types, even folks who should know about it. The Jacks Fork River is OK with that, as it tumbles down steep valleys to deliver some challenging surprises.

Like Smash Rock.

* * *

Sure, there are bigger rapids. Niagara Falls comes to mind. And several spots along Benton's favorite, the Buffalo River. But each spring, Smash Rock stands between me and inner peace.

As my rendezvous with Smash Rock approaches, I concentrate on little else. My sole mission hardens into a successful negotiation past this looming Lorelei. Smash Rock could care less, having stood like a giant troll at the gate for a good forty million years, as a swift current barrels under its jaw.

The initial sensation is auditory. Even before you see it, you can hear the force of the water colliding with the giant boulder, easily the size of a Lincoln Navigator.

I tilt my bow toward Smash Rock. The river gulps my canoe toward its face, until at the last moment, I dig furiously to veer left, brushing Gneid's stern against the rock as I pass. It's a signature of sorts left upon the rock's face, a guest book of canoe scrapes, each canoe leaving a layer of its skin: silver, green, red.

Here, the danger begins, as canoes slalom through a boulder field the length of Graceland's driveway. The water level determines the degree of difficulty. High water offers a glide over the rocks. Low water lets canoes carom through them. Middle water, most dangerous, turns the rocks into fists that lurk just beneath the rolling surface, ready to snag a keel and turn the boat sideways into the torrent. A Tilt-A-Whirl is a gentler ride.

I've never succumbed to Smash Rock: safe passage every time I've tried. Credit concentration. On the other hand, I've dumped canoes in easier waters. Those surprise dumps happen during lapses best described as rectal-cranial inversions.

On my most recent pass by Smash Rock, I thumbed my nose at that troll at the gate. Downriver, geologic wonders unfolded like the legs in the front row at a Tom Jones concert. The blue herons guided me downstream, as river turtles waited to the last moment to abandon their rocky sun decks and dive to safety below the water's surface.

When we reached our second night's camp, Mark already had a good fire going. Mark has been on this river many more times than me, and as one of the organizers of this float, he always paddles ahead of the rest of us, gathers wood and builds the campfire.

Around this campfire, cooking is an art. Fellow floaters pack exotic foods and the cast iron hardware to prepare it. I generally underachieve in the gourmet department, relying solely on the two basic food groups: peanut butter sandwiches and beer.

* * *

"Bury your shit!"

Usually, Mark was calm, laid back. But on this morning as he spoke over a breakfast campfire, he held the attention of everybody in the camp, especially the sons and grandsons on their first trip down this river. "I'm tired of walking into the woods and stepping in your shit. Take a shovel, and bury it."

He was right. It's a matter that goes beyond hygiene. It's a matter of respect. After all, even dogs bury their shit. Well, they try, anyway.

We broke camp, and policed the campsite. We drowned the fire and stirred the ashes. We loaded our canoes, packed our trash aboard, and launched silently into this river. Respect.

After several hours of negotiating rapids around hairpin turns and dodging root wads with nasty snags, we paddled to a cave so remote, the only practical way to reach the spot is by river. Or by helicopter.

Jam Up Cave is a barn-sized hole at the base of a sheer rock cliff. The cave entrance stands about three Shaquilles above the water level, a deep cathedral of a cavern that opens into a sinkhole directly behind the cliff's face. I tied Gneid to a tree at the river's edge and climbed a switchback trail to the top of the towering bluff. The sinkhole itself drops from the mountaintop like a funnel, big as a Piggly Wiggly parking lot at the top, small as a teachers lounge at the bottom, where a cold dark pool awaits. Because the sinkhole is so deep, and the cave faces north, only indirect light penetrates to the bottom of the sinkhole. As a result, plant species thrive there that have not existed anywhere else in the Ozarks for 10,000 years. Like a fly in a pitcher plant, I climbed down into the sinkhole and reached the pool. In the murky darkness, it's a leap of faith to plunge into black water and swim to the cave's back entrance, even if it's only a dozen feet. Worse, the water is colder than a well digger's ass.

My first dozen visits to Jam Up took the same approach: Float down the river, tie off, and climb into the cave or climb up the bluff to the sinkhole. But recently, on a trip with friends, I saw the best view of Jam Up Cave, from across the river on a mountaintop in the Greenwood Forest. As I looked down the slope, the cave yawned a mile away, just above the treetops. Perhaps the only thing more inspiring than that view of Jam Up is the vantage point where I stood.

The modest homesteads in Greenwood Forest are made of wood and rock, solid and comfortable, functional, self sufficient. Inhabitants compost their own waste and produce their own electricity by using solar collectors and other natural energy sources. Good thing. The nearest hot wire seems light years away. Yes, there are fossil fuel-eating generators around in case of emergency. But they're a last resort, a sign that even the most ardent environmentalist family must make some concessions while it makes the transition to sustainability.

Peglegs & School Marms & Horse Killers

Shannon County is a synonym for wilderness, with a few small settlements scattered across the deep woods. It's a great place to hide, or get lost.

From border to border, as the Jacks Fork River slices across its face, Shannon County is one of nature's most entertaining theme parks, featuring some of the most remote regions in the Ozarks. That's why I like it, and I think ol' Pegleg Shannon would like it, too. He'd be pleased that somebody named this county after him.

Judge Pegleg Shannon—I don't think anybody called him that to his face—would have a blast in this neck of the woods, assuming he wasn't sick of rivers and caves and general exploring. As a pup, George Shannon, the youngest member of Lewis and Clark's Corps of Discovery, had a knack for getting lost. On one mission to round up the company's stray pack horses, he returned to the wrong part of the Missouri River and stayed lost for almost two weeks. Years later on another mission, he lost a leg. When it comes to getting lost in the woods, the county that bears his name would make him feel right at home.

I left Jam Up Cave and its sinkhole and hopped back into my canoe. Every time down this thirty-mile stretch, the river is different, cutting new channels, serving up a whole new set of rootwads, logjams, and snags. But some things don't change. Around the next bend was a fortress. But instead of steep walls, this fortress was bordered by a split-rail fence. This fortress doesn't need walls, because the inhabitants are so powerful that intruders become mere truants in the face of ultimate authority.

The fortress is a private resort. Viewed from the river, the log buildings in the resort look like a gathering of parochial school girls, all dressed alike in dark patterns with white highlights. Uniformly clad in black, creosote-soaked wood with whitewash trim, two dozen tidy cabins surround a pavilion and a little one-room school house and a chapel, everything a vacationing teacher needs to escape and recharge the batteries. The resort's official name is Bunker Hill, but my buddies call it "Teachers Camp," and they're not wrong. It's the prized possession of a wealthy group of teachers.

Well, of course the teachers are not wealthy, at least they're not wealthy as a result of teaching. But their organization is an immovable object called the Missouri State Teachers Association.

As every surviving school child will attest, old school marms are fearless, beating back bullies and bad actors. Bunker Hill stands as a tribute to the prowess of these stalwart teacher lords.

Sitting within the Ozark National Scenic Riverways boundary, Bunker Hill would be a perfect lunch stop, except that if you go ashore onto the property, a teacher just might kick your ass.

When the feds decided to swallow the Jacks Fork River valley into America's first national scenic riverway, the teachers association resisted. Today their property survives, a monument to the unyielding will of public teachers.

As a child of two teachers, I remember coming to Bunker Hill. Now, like all the other river travelers who encounter this utopia in the wilderness, I marvel as I float past, but I never stop on their gravel beach, lest a stern disciplinarian roar down to my canoe and rap me on the knuckles with a ruler. Sometimes, in some ways other than financial, it pays to be a teacher.

I've been bitched at by a battalion of teachers. Mostly they accused me of grand displays of underachievement. But until this float trip, I'd never been bitched out by a duck. He was a fearless duck, as far as ducks go, a daffy-dressed mallard. Proud. Pushy. He knew we had food. And he knew I was underachieving, in terms of filling his quacking gullet. A fellow canoeist threw him a few chunks of bread, which he gobbled, then he paddled closer to my canoe, quacking impatiently. I kept telling him, "I have no food." He didn't believe me. He jumped in the front of my boat and waddled around between the gunwales, peeking and poking for food. I kept telling him, "No food for you." He kept telling me I was an asshole. He finally jumped out of the canoe and accosted the next floater who sailed into his domain. The floater gave him food. He's gonna be a fat duck.

Several miles downstream, I passed Alley Spring Mill, painted barn red. Some folks claim this mill is the most photographed spot in Missouri. Maybe, but it's probably a bit too remote for the casual paparazzi. The spring itself is a blue goddess.

* * *

I paddled Gneid to the takeout point and strapped her on top of Erifnus Caitnop. I loaded the car with the tired wet remnants of a four-day float. Showing the power of a much younger car, Erifnus climbed up the steep gravel road, out of the river valley.

Cresting a hill, Erifnus missed killing an offroad dirt biker by about six feet. The kid darted across the road like a deer, without looking, and he never saw us until we'd passed. It's a recurrent theme that jumps from the back of my mind every time I have a close call. What if I have a wreck? A breakdown? Kill somebody? I drove safely for at least the next hour.

Holing up in Eminence for the night, I shared the town with a civilian cavalry: 3,000 horses and their riders, who definitely make an impact on this town of 600 people.

Upriver from all those horse barns, the River's Edge Resort is my Ozark outpost. The resort is a work of art, and owners Lynette and Alan Peters made me feel right at home.

The resort is a living lesson in hydrology. After one raging flood a few years back, the stream changed course and carved a new channel a hundred yards away from the River's Edge back door. It'll meander back some day. Meantime, the River's Edge enjoys a more expansive beach, a delightful walk across the gravel beds. Unlike the beach of your dreams, the gravel bars along this river require sturdy soles on your feet—sandals or shoes. But each gravel bar is worth the walk.

These beds don't contain ordinary stones. These rocks are the gods of gravel. Some are fist sized, or shoe shaped, or liver sized or perfectly round or the shape of dinosaur eggs. Most would show off if they joined the rock border in your backyard garden. Orange and black, blue and crimson and maroon, many of these rocks were forged in conflagrations long ago, and pushed up from deeper than the pits of Hell. Because the Ozark Mountains are among America's oldest, the giant Precambrian bluffs have weathered and cracked, shifted and slid, subdividing into ever smaller units, the way seashells turn to sand. For eons, ten trillion stones, one by one, made the pilgrimage from the mountaintops to the streambeds. But gravelation got a big boost from mankind when the real Devils—railroad builders—chopped down every tree to make rail ties. With no trees to hold the karst hillsides in place, the fractured rock rolled and tumbled and slid downhill into the streams.

In the past, the feds thought about dredging the streams. But they realized that it would do no good. The ancient hillsides, steep and rocky, will continue to crumble.

The gravel is unstoppable.

The small stones near the streambed are polished smooth. Some are flat, made for skipping. For anybody who skipped rocks as a child, this gravel bar is an Olympic venue, with a thousand perfect skippers within reach and a beautiful stream ready to host a record skip. It's that way all along this river's forty-six miles of gravel bars. Wear a helmet.

Speaking of helmets, we drove along the river upstream for about a half mile to the Eagle Falls Ranch Zipline and joined a steady stampede of thrill seekers who hook their torsos onto big guywires strung through the treetops. The zipline sent me flying through the trees for the better part of a mile. This experiment in semi-ecotourism has been so successful, ziplines are popping up like zits all over the state's forested face. And now for you night owls, you can zip through Eagle Falls at night, kinda like Space Mountain, I guess.

After dinner, I walked up into the hills. The folds of the Ozark mountains are dramatic. What those hills lack in height, they make up in geologic somersaults. From the highest crest overlooking Eminence at twilight, I looked down into the tiny clearing surrounded by layers of dense forest, a town tucked comfortably into its twilight nest in a way that only Grandmother Earth could provide.

Next morning the smell of coffee and the promise of hash browns caused a traffic jam at Ruby's restaurant. Inside Ruby's, exactly half of the customers looked like a waiting room for the next wagon train. Cowboy boots beneath cowboy jeans buckled by cowboy belts below cowboy shirts under cowboy hats.

The other half looked like a refugee camp of scraggly-clothed river-rat castaways.

The difference in attire demonstrates two differing philosophies. Horse people are serious about their gear, and they proudly wear their boots and spurs and belt buckles. It's more than a statement. It's a way of life.

Stetson hats. Wrangler jeans. These are sacred symbols for the weekend cowboy.

In contrast, float trippers don't give a shit what they look like, dressed for comfort with mismatched outfits in day-glo colors dredged from the bottom of the drawer, keeping in mind the very real possibility that they will lose everything in the river. Flip flops and cutoffs, T-shirts emblazoned with silly puns about beer and "Stupid," and hats that no cowboy would ever wear.

* * *

Many folks around Greater Eminence are aware of the delicate balance between preserving the river and using it for tourism. Sometimes there's friction. Some riverfront landowners resent the trash and disrespect heaped on their property by fog-brained floaters.

And then there's the horse issue.

Behind the nation's biggest trail ride, a new horse trail cuts into the hills, away from the river. Conservationists generally applaud the new trail that encourages horse riders away from the delicate river ecosystem. But many of the riders want contact with the river. After all, that's why they came here. The issue arises when a thousand horses cross the river in one spot. Some folks believe that too many horses can damage the delicate stream, and that the animal waste, in higher concentrations, could affect the stream's chemistry. Horse enthusiasts point to the trash and bodily waste left behind by thousands of canoeists. Both sides have a point: Overcrowding and overuse of a spot can become a problem, whether the crowds are man or beast. But try as they might, canoeists just can't poop like a horse. And horses don't fling cigarette butts.

Downstream a bit, a feud has brewed for decades. At the heart of the fight are wild horses along the Jacks Fork and Current Rivers. Back during the Great Depression, a farmer turned loose his herd of thirty or so horses. He could no longer afford to feed them, so he freed them to fend for themselves. The horses evolved into several distinct herds, which have roamed wild for decades. When the U.S. Department of the Interior established the Ozark National Scenic Riverways, the feds became concerned that the horses' hooves were damaging the fragile karst topography, causing increased erosion. So they began stalking the herds to shoot the horses and eliminate the problem.

That's when the Missouri Wild Horse League formed to stop the federal assault, taking the shooters to court to silence the slaughter. Eventually, with the slogan "Wild and Free, Let Them Be," horse lovers won, and the herds survive today.

A few years back, a hunter spied one of the wild herds and killed several of their number. Locals were outraged, and they tracked down, prosecuted and imprisoned the killer. The surviving horses hope he was rode hard and put away wet.

Today the horses graze at different times of the day in the Shawnee Fields outside of Eminence. I've seen them in the Broadfoot Fields above the spot where the Current and Jacks Fork Rivers meet. Legend is that at the apex of the harvest moon, in honor of their fallen sisters, the two herds head in different directions and stampede the homes of game poachers.

* * *

Downriver from the Broadfoot fields and the wild horses, past Coot Chute, one robust creek flows from springs in the steep hills over an impediment that 10,000 horses couldn't erode. And when I reached it, the specter blew me away.

Rocky Falls is a ship-sized outcropping of rhyolite, and it ranks among America's oldest exposed rock formations, the gatekeeper to a shut-ins that channels water down the rock's broad back. The giant rock gets slippery when wet. But on the day I visited, nobody else was there to fall down. This may be the best-kept secret among Shannon County's geologic wonders.

I left Erifnus in the parking lot and hiked downstream on Rocky Creek, along the Ozark Trail to Klepzig Mill. Built of wood from the first sawmill in the area, the old structure still stands on its stone foundation, and I peered down into the turbine hole, where the millrace water would plunge and force the turbine to spin the shaft that turns the grindstone, grinding the grain between burrstones two stories above the water. The shallow dam that diverts water to the millrace is still visible. I crept carefully beside the remnants of the millrace and strained to imagine a time when this spot was the center of local commerce.

The millwright, Walter Kleipzig, was a trendsetter for the area. He was the first settler in the area to use barbed wire and woven fence wire together. During tough times, he kept poor people from starving by grinding grain for them for free.

Nowadays the neighboring Cedar Bluff camping area offers seclusion rivaled only by a prison super-max cell. Just as a secluded, neighboring Peck Ranch is an inspiration in studying Ozark ecology, and restoring an elk population in Missouri.

I retreated to find Erifnus unmolested, and we headed to the bluest water in the Midwest.

* * *

After squeezing through Coot Chute and rounding Owl's Bend, the Current River joins the Ozark Trail for about five miles. Along that stretch, many floaters miss the stunning blue water of Blue Spring, even though it's only a quarter mile from the Current, an easy hike beside the spring's rushing stream.

The water's vivid color comes from dissolved limestone suspended in this incredibly deep spring. You might see turquoise or aqua or azure, depending on sunlight.

Called "Spring of the Summer Sky" by native inhabitants, the water charges from deep in the ground, at the base of a high bluff that forms the back wall of a box canyon. Halfway up the bluff, a dead cedar trunk, taller and straighter than most, stands on the canyon wall like a spar on a clipper ship. In reality the tree is a diver, frozen in the beginning of her leap into the 300-foot-deep spring. Eventually, in geologic time, she'll finish her dive.

I paused to watch an otter fish in the cold aqua blue spring waters. Local fishermen hate otters the way rival quarterbacks hate each other. It's understandable, since otters have a definite advantage catching fish, unencumbered by limits or seasons or game wardens. Bipedal fishermen are resentful that after they'd painstakingly rendered otters extinct in Missouri and sold all their pelts to hat makers, state conservation folks reintroduced the otters to the rivers a few years back. Now the otters thrive, and the fish must spawn like crazy to supply enough otter fodder.

Still, there is relative harmony in this wondrous ecosystem.

Except for one thing. Walking back to the Current River, I picked up enough beer cans and cigarette butts to fill a mesh trash bag. I know most people respect nature. But a few idiots express their freedom by jettisoning their trash in these pristine areas. They really work at it. They must procure the crap a dozen miles away and transport it into this remote spot to deposit. I'm not a vengeful person, so I only suggest that transgressors should perform hours of community service picking up trash. With their teeth.

Highway 19 crosses the Current River at Round Spring, another wonder to the eyes, but also a wonder down under. That's because geologists believe that ground water crosses under the Current before it empties into the spring.

I emptied back at the River's Edge in Eminence.

Sinkholes & Gar Balls

Climbing north out of Eminence, Highway 19 becomes a switchback trail over the ridges that guide the Jacks Fork and Current Rivers to their eventual matrimony.

If you visit the Current on a summer Saturday, you may think its annual half-million visitors came on the same day. At first glance, considering all the waste and trash and human droppings that half a million people can create, the river seems to remain in good shape. On the surface, the stream appears to clean itself and heal relatively quickly.

But river biologists see a different picture. Look down through the crystal clear water to the river bottom. Hiding among the rocks, you should be able to spot mussels and crayfish and maybe even a hellbender, that most ancient of salamanders. But those animals are showing signs of stress. While crayfish remain abundant, with more species in the Ozark streams than just about any other spot on earth, the hellbenders are disappearing. Hellbenders can live to be fifty or sixty years old. Some of the old timers are still around. But biologists find few young hellbenders. Why?

The waters of the Current at Round Spring aren't talking.

Springs get a lot of credit for providing pure water. It says so on the label of that bottled water at your fingertips. But springs aren't magical. Contrary to popular belief, the percolation of water through the springs does not purify it. Underground springs don't have kidneys. If you dump oil into the ground, it won't magically biodegrade. Of course, everything that campers, canoeists and horse riders dump in the river stays in the river.

That's distressing news for the poor mussels living in the river. They can't go get their food at a drive-thru. They're stuck in the stream, with no choice but to suck their lunch from the same aqueous teat, every day of their lives. The mussels are filters, but they're not oil filters. And they have little tolerance for suntan lotion, no taste for mustard, and no desire to eat horse shit.

* * *

As we drove into the deep Current River valley, a sad story crackled on the radio news. "A hunter who was tracking a deer died today when he stepped into a sinkhole and fell seventy feet to his death."

Long before America got concerned about the ground opening up and swallowing whole houses, sinkholes have been a way of life around here. They're everywhere.

On cue, we took the roads that follow Sinking Creek upstream for a few miles to find the Sinks natural tunnel, Missouri's only natural navigable tunnel, and former home to the world's most sunken bluegrass concert. It's on private land, but the owner let me see the tunnel, a hundred-yard hole through a hill, carved by the vigorous water that still flows through it, with enough headroom to float a canoe through at low tide. Just downstream, I launched my canoe for a ride on Sinking Creek, one of the biggest—and cleanest—tributaries to the Current River.

Good rains made the stream navigable, even though it was the day after Summer solstice, a rare opportunity to float a smaller stream so late in the spring season. Sinking Creek usually runs fairly shallow by summertime. But after a good rain, the stream becomes one of the most delightful rides in the Ozarks.

The whole trip was clean. Unlike the Current, which bulges at the seams with weekend floaters, I joined two buddies and we had the entire Sinking Creek to ourselves. The stream is spring-fed, and in the summertime it produces warm and cold running water. The upper spring waters slowly warm in the hot summer sun as they flow, only to greet another spring, which dumps cold water into the mix. I beached my canoe to sit in the stream where a new tributary offered its cold underground water on my left side, and the warmer stream water on my right. I felt a twitch in one of the tiny holes in my Crocs. Looking down, I saw a crawfish trying to enter my shoe. I wiggled my toes, and the crawfish retreated, but a moment later it returned, determined to wedge into this Croc shelter. You won't find that trust between crayfish and people on the Current River. The crayfish are there, but they're conditioned to stay out of your way.

There's another difference on the smaller streams: Less trash. I picked up one errant aluminum can on six miles of Sinking Creek. In that same space along the Current, I'd fill more than a pair of trash bags. At the end of this ride, I passed Camp Zoe, site of an honest-to-God Earth-people settlement. Assholes call them hippies. The camp is clean and quiet, and the only commotion happens when deputies raid the place, looking for sex, drugs, and rock 'n' roll.

Along this peaceful stretch of river, there is one snag: A series of portable foot bridges usually cross the stream. Fortified with welded iron and anchored by big, cement-filled barrels, these bridges, when spanning the vigorous creek, could rip off the head of an unsuspecting canoeist. On the day I passed through the area, the bridges had been pulled from the river to let high water pass.

* * *

At the end of the ride, Gneid and I hopped onto Erifnus and headed north on Highway 19. Several segments of this highway convinced me that I had gotten on a roller-coaster ride without buying a ticket. We looped through the deep, dark woods, mountainous terrain with tiny clearings, outposts named Bunker and Melton and Reynolds. In the back of my mind were the words of an old country doctor from these parts: "The folks who live around here, a lot of 'em are tie hackers," he told me. "If you're in trouble, they'll give you the shirt off their back. But if you cross 'em, they'll kill you."

I have a tendency to believe old country doctors. And knowing that he was talking about the descendants of the people who cut down the forests to make railroad ties, I knew their general demeanor.

They came here for two reasons: available work and escape from a civilization that was becoming too refined, too confining. They were hardy pioneers who relied on the entire family to survive in a rugged wilderness. They didn't trust outsiders, preferred to be left alone. Those were the hill people of the Ozarks. Popular culture began calling them hillbillies, and though most of their descendants today have cars and indoor plumbing and electricity, they still maintain a fierce independence. Fierce.

How fierce? Diet can be one clue. Beyond delicacies like squirrel and possum, some folks around here eat gar balls. A gar is a particularly ugly fish, long and bony with a toothy snout that looks like needle-nosed pliers. Its tough, scaly hide has been used to cover the wooden blades of primitive plows. Still, the flesh is edible. Use a little flour to roll the meat into fish meatballs and fry them in oil. Mmm. Gar balls.

In this remote bastion of self-sufficiency, where people are perfectly content to eat gar balls, a restaurant better be good if it's going to survive. That's the case with the barbecue joint in Gladden. According to my careful count, Freddie's BBQ appears to be one of about two buildings in the town. Its major traffic is seasonal, for the most part, as it caters to hungry floaters retreating from the rivers with wet money. Yet the place is well kept, the folks are friendly, and the barbecue keeps Freddie's in business.

* * *

It was late Saturday afternoon as Erifnus meandered along Ozarks backroads—past Howe's Mill, through Boss and Bixby, where we stopped at the old Bixby Country Store for a great deli sandwich.

Up past Viburnum, the brown sign to Dillard Mill snagged me off the road. This mill may be America's best demonstration of a turn-of-the-century gristmill. It cranks. The mill ceased commercial operation in 1956, but the building stands solid, a relic fixed firmly against a hairpin turn in the Huzzah Creek, a vigorous Ozark floating stream often overlooked until it meanders nearer the more popular Meramec River. We passed Cherry Branch, a great, gushing spring that contributes to the Huzzah, and Erifnus got a kick out of going through Cherryville, boyhood home of her mechanic.

Taking the backroads, we crossed the Huzzah three times more, including a stop in Hucky Puddle at the Davisville General Store, where "if we don't have it, you don't need it." At the end of Route Z, I occupied a tiny cabin, and spent the day combing the gravel bars of this most overlooked float stream. Sure enough, I saw no floaters. Next morning I reluctantly departed this remote paradise and, as I drove north, slowly began to see the signs of civilization in all its wondrous vestiges. Chief among those vestiges is a decaying sign for the Cutthroat Sewing Company, which sits on the edge of Steelville right before you descend into town. The word "Cutthroat" may refer to a type of trout, I suspect, but it can have a lot of other meanings. Certainly, it offers a memorable description of any business that employs scissors and knives and needles. But I still haven't run across Cutthroat Hospital, or Cutthroat Barber Shop or Cutthroat Bank.

If there's a recipe to make another Steelville, you'd mix equal parts beauty, luck, attitude, and charm. As the self-proclaimed "Floating Capital of Missouri," the town caters to lovers of the great outdoors. But there's something else that's fun about Steelville.

Before there was a Luckytown, Steelville won the lottery. Well, to be precise, the town is the beneficiary of a lottery winner. In 1990, telephone regulators held a lottery to determine which phone companies would provide rural service to the burgeoning cellular phone demand. Among the winners was tiny Steelville Telephone Exchange, a company with the distinct advantage of being owned by the people it serves. The company parlayed its lottery windfall into great service for telephone customers, but also donates to the community and its schools. That's a healthy attitude.

Steelville is enriched by a collection of canoe chic. Scattered around town is Canoehenge, a series of canoes seemingly buried bow-first into the roadside, and each canoe sticks its stern into the sky with painted murals on both cheeks. Around the corner, the entrance sign to Indian Springs Lodge is a canoe standing on twenty-foot stilts.

Down the road is the world's largest private family residence sign. Doesn't sound like much until you see it. The name Neumann's is spelled out in three-foot-tall aluminum letters. In an earlier life, the letters used to perch on the family's restaurant in St. Louis. Now they splay across forty feet of front yard at the family's rural retirement home.

The sign will last only as long as the Neumanns live there, of course, unless they can sell their home to some other Neumanns, Neumanns who like to see their name in big letters.

Wild Woods

The music you bump into in these remote hamlets can be surprising. So are the venues. Of all the hundreds of places I've played, none resonated so sweetly as a spot just a stone's throw off Highway 19. Atop the first hill out of Steelville, Wildwood Springs Lodge has offered up spectacular views of the Meramec River Valley for damn near a century. Lately, the old lodge has turned into a hotspot, an intimate venue where folks mingle up close and personal with bands like the Amazing Rhythm Aces and Asleep at the Wheel, legends like Arlo Guthrie, the Guess Who and Ozark Mountain Daredevils.

Wildwood Springs Lodge has clung to its lofty perch for eight decades. And like many of the icons of '70s music who still come to perform in the cozy lobby—Leon Russell, Dave Mason and Poco—the lodge is a survivor. Like most ninety-somethings, the lodge has endured peaks and valleys, times when visitors flocked to its doorstep, times when its doors were locked.

Today the lodge thrives, thanks to management and staff who lovingly maintain it. It wasn't always healthy. The sprawling lodge, built of stone and stucco and native hardwoods, had slowly slid into decline when Robert Bell brought the old place out of mothballs and saved it from becoming a ruin. Bob Bell knew the history of the old lodge, a Roaring '20s retreat where folks could escape the soot of the city and hunt and fish and float, then dress to dine at tables spread with linen and china and silver. And he's resurrected the lodge's elegant dignity, with a twist.

Of all his renovations and innovations, Bob is proudest of his marketing plan. He should be. He's assembled a mix of talented hotel staff and kitchen magicians who provide wonderful cuisine. But his big draw appears on Wildwood's web page, which lists an entertainment lineup that attracts fans from all over the world to this hidden Ozark nirvana. Every year, he assembles a who's who of classic rock 'n' roll musicians, boomer icons like the Marshall Tucker Band and Hot Tuna and Brewer & Shipley.

The musicians love the relaxed atmosphere and the chance to mingle with the crowd. Everybody—on both sides of the guitar—keeps coming back.

Bob has revived a long history of great music and great times at the lodge. But it takes a lot of fixit to keep things rolling. His secret weapon is a guy named Bill Freeman. A retired state trooper, Bill is affable, polite, knowledgeable. Aside from his knack with tape and string and spit to keep the hotel's systems humming, Bill's also a walking history book, readily telling stories about the river, the region, the lodge.

Ah, the lodge. The lobby's charm overflows, especially when a crowd gathers around Dr. John or Michael Martin Murphy, or America, during what Bob Bell calls the "Living Room Concerts."

Bill Freeman showed me around. The long dining hall could be a movie set. Its hardwood floors, linen tablecloths, and gorgeous floor-to-ceiling French windows serve up a splendid view of the rugged ridges and ravines.

Like a proud grandparent, the lodge displays its photos. Adorning the walls are visuals of pleasures and performances past. It was here that young St. Louis musician Gordon Jenkins honed his chops. Jenkins later became a famous producer for Decca Records. Listen to Frank Sinatra and Nat King Cole, and you'll hear Gordon Jenkins' handiwork.

The handiwork on tap for this evening's show involved some classic Ozark pickin' and grinnin'. Silhouetted by a spectacular sunset over a picture postcard valley, five musicians launched into crisp vocal harmonies punctuated by a fine fiddle. Their stage was a concrete poolside tarmac. The crowd sat in lawn chairs and sprawled on blankets in this natural amphitheater, a pleasant slope softened by thick bluegrass. I settled back in my lawn chair for the show.

Traditional bluegrass fans have little tolerance for a band that strays so easily into Buddy Holly anthems. But this crowd loved the Stringtown String Band. The setting helped. Hours later, full of libations and lively tunes, I retreated to my sleeping quarters.

The guest rooms adopt a European style. Their comfortably Spartan appointments offer a subtle hint that rooms are for sleeping. Daytime calls for action and a vigorous examination of the great outdoors.

Well, then, let the examination begin.

Mussels Are Smarter than Smallmouth Bass

So I went out, got in a canoe, and over sixty miles and six days, I learned about the Meramec River. It was a journey of discovery that turned into a biology class. Organizers had invited a group of reporters to examine the river up close.

Our hosts wanted to publicize the precarious health of a river that does triple duty: it drains a dozen smaller streams to the Mississippi, it carries a million tourists a year, and oh, by the way, it's among the oldest, most complex ecosystems in North America. But on this tour, few media showed up. Only two of us—freelance writers—floated the whole six days. Nobody showed from the big city newspapers or big city television stations, or big city radio. Too bad. The story of the river is compelling, done right. Here's what I mean:

You might call them crayfish. Or crawfish. Maybe crawdads. I call 'em mudbugs. Most people associate them with Louisiana bayous, but they also thrive in the spring-fed rivers of southern Missouri. They're plentiful and fearsome looking, and tasty. Beyond that, my mudbug knowledge resembles the water in my mesh trash bag: a drop or two. That changed one Sunday morning when our team of river explorers met to embark on our six-day expedition down the river.

Our guides, Wild Bill and Jody Miles, operate a lesson factory called Earth's Classroom. From the very beginning, they began spilling an amazing amount of knowledge about our riparian environment.

It was Monday, so the usual assemblage of recreational floaters were all safely home, calling in sick to work. We had the river to ourselves, surrounded by blue herons and swallows and painted turtles called red-eared sliders. We stopped for lunch at Cane Bottom, on a sand bar just above a riffle. Jody's parents met the group and catered lunch, replete with fat slices of homegrown tomatoes. River appetites don't need help, but home cookin' on a great gravel bar takes living to a new level.

On the bank, we watched Bill and Jody cast nets into the shallow water to catch and examine a few critters. Sure enough, they landed a diverse catch that typifies this river, home to hundreds of unique species. We felt the rough scales of a small water snake, less than a foot long. The snake was terrorized by all this human handling and expressed its displeasure by biting my index finger. It didn't hurt. The snake's lightning-fast lunge startled me much more than any sting from its tiny Barbie Doll bite.

We examined a few small bluegill and minnows and a darter, and released them one by one back into their home. Then we studied the mudbugs. Jody explained that more species of crayfish live in the Meramec Basin than just about anywhere. They thrive because the water emanates from springs that filter through limestone formations and infuse high levels of calcium into the water. Crayfish need calcium, since they shed their exoskeleton armor seven or eight times during the warm growing season. Each time a crayfish sheds, it also regurgitates its entire stomach and esophagus. Not to worry, a new stomach already has formed around the old one, with a calcium stone the size of an oblong pearl wedged between. When the old stomach exits, the new stomach dissolves this calcium pill, which hits the bloodstream and emerges as the material for the new exoskeleton. Nifty.

The crawdad we examined had no pinchers. "No problem," Jody said. Any animal that can grow a new exoskeleton seven times in a summer can grow new claws. Besides, the animal won't starve. It catches food with its front legs and eats like you and I: hand to mouth. The crawfish reserves its claws for protection. And, seeing how anything that molts seven times in a summer must be a patient animal, the crawfish is content to hide under a rock until its new defense weapons grow.

After lunch, we met a pair of water craft that looked like they plowed right out of Joseph Conrad's *Heart of Darkness* or Bogart's *African Queen*. These boats glided rather than chugged upriver, having replaced the *African Queen*-ish smoke-belching steam engine with jet engines aft. Seated aboard were two dozen Kate Hepburns, by my count, looking every bit like fish out of water. The boats serve a very unique market: motorists looking for adventure. It's easy to get hooked. People traveling Interstate 44 can't ignore the giant colorful signs painted on barn roofs, luring them to see the Jesse James hideout at Meramec Caverns. When folks take the bait, they drive down toward the river on a road that used to have more billboards per square centimeter than Highway 65 into Branson.

But the old billboards are gone and the drive ends in a handsome payoff. The caverns are a treat, worth the visit not only for the cave's beauty, but also for its history. Eighty years ago a guy named Lester Dill bought the cave and became a walking how-to book on tourism promotion. Not only did he paint dozens of barn roofs across Middle America—visible from the great flyover—but he is credited with pioneering the bumper sticker.

During the 1940s he claimed to have proof that Jesse James hid in the cave, and lo and behold, he revealed 102-year-old Jesse himself, still very much alive, hiding under the pseudonym J. Frank Dalton. That story was one of the legends that eventually got Jesse's old dead bones dug up and tested for DNA. If you believe science, Jesse died on April 3, 1882, from an assassin's bullet. Nevertheless, Dill's story put 102-year-old Jesse back in the spotlight, and created another tasty legend.

During the Cold War, Dill advertised the caverns as the "world's first atomic refuge." And since a goodly number of Soviet nukes were aimed at Missouri's Minuteman II missile silos, the cave's claim got attention from folks who wanted some end-of-the-world insurance.

Anyway, the P.T. Barnum-style promotion continues, and now it incorporates the Meramec River. In the cave parking lot, visitors discover Sand Springs Access and the extra option of the riverboat excursion up the Meramec.

As our floating classroom canoed down the river, we saluted the flatboats with the customary neighborly waves and river greetings. No mooning this time. We could hear only a few words from each pilot as the boats passed us and the loudspeakers reached our ears.

I hope the guides told the passengers about the secret self-bulimic rituals of the native Missouri crayfish. The story offers much more depth than any platter of boiled mudbugs, which after all, is the end of the road for the crawdad.

And I hope the guides warn the passengers that the river is endangered by the careless hand of man, as it was back in November 1981 when a fertilizer pipeline failed and dumped 80,000 liters of liquid ammonium nitrate into the Meramec Basin, which killed 10,000 Salem cave crayfish and 1,000 southern cavefish. Say what you want about saving crayfish, but I bet losing 80,000 liters of liquid ammonium nitrate might put a dent in the meth industry.

Suddenly, just downstream and out of the corner of my eye, I thought I saw Spiderman fly across the river. Turned out it was a zipper, a passenger on the Caveman Zipline, one of the growing number of ziplines in the Ozarks, just like its cousin in Eminence, where thrill seekers hook up to glorified clotheslines and fly at breakneck speed through the treetops. Folks weighing between eighty and 270 pounds with no body piercings or heart problems can hook onto a ride that reaches fifty mph and lasts an hour and a half. So the Caveman Zipline requires a reasonable investment in time and money. Just up the road, for a similar price you can spend all day flopping around on mechanical thrill rides at Six Flags. But this experience is different . . . in terms of a semi-natural setting.

Semi-natural is the best way to describe the Meramec River today, with the constant concentration of humans along this ancient ecosystem. The river is showing stress, and Brian Wilcox joined us to explain. Brian is the naturalist for Meramec State Park, and he's been watching what's happening to nature. He told us the story of mussels, something I'd never really thought about much.

First thing I learned were the names: There are butterfly mussels, and three-ridge mussels and round pigtoe mussels, and pimplebacks and spectacle cases and ladyfingers and pink heelsplitters.

Next thing I learned is that these animals move around using their feet. Feet! Well, foot. They may not be fast, but they're smart. The female pocketbook mussel has been fooling smallmouth bass for longer than there have been fishermen.

She produces thousands of glachidia—tiny mussel babies—in a sac she holds inside her shell, and she waits for the right time to release them to the world. Well, she doesn't really wait; she waves. She sticks her fleshy foot out of the opening in her shell and waves it tantalizingly like a kerchief, except that this foot looks exactly like a minnow. Its outline is in the shape of a minnow; it even has a dark dot for a fake eye. It's enough to fool a smallmouth bass, and the fish tries to eat the fake minnow. When the fish bites, the mussel expels a thousand babies into the fish's mouth, and the babies hook onto the gills of the startled bass.

The bass becomes a host, with baby mussels hanging on and growing for about ten days until they're strong enough to drop to the bottom of the riverbed and fend for themselves. The whole process doesn't hurt the bass, and if he's annoyed that he didn't get the fake minnow, it doesn't stop him from trying again next time.

Brian is concerned about the health of the stream, and the mussels can give us hints. For starters, I'll bet they're high on Prozac and estrogen, dumped into the water by careless floaters.

* * *

The river and the tourism business both endure ebbs and flows. Each inflicts damage on the other. But one event nearly changed the face of the region forever. Three decades ago, the specter of a dam loomed in the Meramec valley. Meramec Dam would have flooded hundreds of square miles of the valley.

The idea of damming the Meramec goes back to 1830, when the Iron Works at present day Maramec (that's the way they spell it) Springs Park near St. James suggested that a dam would help navigation to move their iron-ore product. The most recent plan would have impounded forty-two miles of the Meramec River, nine miles of the Courtois, and twelve miles of the Huzzah.

Sure, dams can provide flood control, power, and a recreation byproduct. But at what cost? A group of concerned Missourians realized that many Meramec treasures would be lost. Among them, Onondaga Cave, a jewel in the underground crown of the cave state—and now a state park—would find itself beneath the waves. Several groups, including the upstart Meramec Basin Association, united to defeat the dam, even as construction had begun. It was a noble effort against the formidable momentum of the federal government. And some folks claim that it was the first time ordinary citizens defeated a federal government hydroelectric dam plan in progress. As a result of the protesters' success, much of the river's geology and history escaped the fate of a watery grave.

At nearby Meramec State Park, I joined some folks who had gathered for a discussion about the success of stopping the Meramec Dam project more than twenty-five years ago. The local discussion became livelier thanks to one guest, the mayor of nearby Sullivan, who expressed his fervent support for the dam and for the economic benefit it would provide for the region. A lake would bring fishermen and vacationers and boats and marinas and resorts and money. It's a heartfelt sentiment, still shared by more than a few locals.

With equal civility and passion, Jerry Sugarman, a leader in the "Stop the Meramec Dam" effort, recounted the political battle that ultimately led to decommissioning the dam.

That evening, I pitched my tent in Meramec State Park and fell asleep, breathing fresh air, glad there would be a river to explore tomorrow.

Next day, full of piss and vinegar, I wrestled with the river—and almost broke my leg.

State herpetologist Jeff Briggler inspired us to put on a snorkel and dive into the Meramec to find an eastern hellbender.

In the process, I found out something else.

Earlier in the day while paddling downstream, I caught myself bitching that the Meramec's current was slower than the rivers to which I was accustomed. Then I put on the mask.

State herpetologists don't mince words. He promised: "You'll eat more and sleep more than you ever have in your life, when you finish a day searching for hellbenders."

Jeff was passionate about finding even one of these primordial salamanders. They're more than endangered, he said. "We can't find small hellbenders. Maybe that means the big ones are not reproducing. Anybody who finds a young hellbender gets a free steak dinner."

We were hooked. This gaggle of swimmers and snorkelers waded into the water as if we were at a revival. We didn't want a steak dinner. We entered the river to find a hellbender. We dived to the bottom of the river—no more than four feet—to overturn big rocks. Big flat rocks. That's where the hellbenders are.

So we hoped.

The current was swift. Just as the herpetologist said, even a small person can overturn BIG rocks—the size of a coffee table—by using the current and an underwater judo move. In the middle of the stream, I tried to maintain my position by digging my feet into the gravel bottom and leaning my skinny frame against a four-foot wall of moving water. I dived, found a rock, overturned it. Before the muddy cloud dispersed, the river swept me a dozen yards downstream.

I dived for an hour. Maybe it was ten minutes. I'd swim ashore, walk upriver, and dive again, the current sending me downriver.

Every time I dived, I knew about the submerged tree, about six body lengths downstream. It was a big tree, sunk in the middle of the stream's channel. If it was in your backyard, it would shade your two-story house. It would take two adult family members to join together to hug the entire circumference of the tree. Now, it lurked in the water like an alligator, waiting to snag a careless fool.

The last time I dived to overturn a rock to find a hellbender, I missed grabbing the rock. My fingers slipped over its mossy pate. The current swept me downstream, and I crashed into the root wad end of the big submerged tree. My shin took the shock, and I instinctively clutched my leg. In that split second the swift current pinned me against the root wad, and I was quickly sucked into a tangle of tree roots and dragged underwater. As I fought against the strong current to free myself, jagged broken root stubs jabbed my sides and held me underwater. I was pinned by the current, tangled underwater in a spaghetti mass of roots, where I would drown. But grabbing one root stub at a time, I pulled myself against the current, and upward toward the water's surface, and stuck my face above the water to gasp for air. Eventually I pulled myself around the edge of the root wad and the current pushed me downriver, tumbling and clutching my leg, until good sense directed me to gather my fortitude and walk ashore.

The tree didn't intend to hurt me. But that sunken sucker taught me a lesson:

The river is bigger and stronger than all of us.

It's more important than any of us, too, because it's the lifeblood of an entire ecosystem.

Yet even though the river is bigger and stronger, any one person can inflict harm.

I can only hope that a hellbender sits under that slippery rock I missed. As the state herpetologist suspected, nobody found a hellbender. And another species that's been around for 60 million years looks as if it's taking its last ride. The end is near.

At the end of my river journey, where Arnold City Park watches the Meramec empty into the Mississippi, I jumped out of my canoe, back on terra firma, and slipped into Erifnus Caitnop to resume my trek across those unnatural asphalt capillaries that feed my addiction.

Oh Hell, Dolly

My wheels veered onto America's blues aorta, Highway 61, the route of every great blues guitarist who ever left the Mississippi Delta for Chicago. Erifnus knows the blues. Countless ballads have pulsed through her speakers.

These legendary blues pioneers would've passed through St. Mary's, too, I thought, as the town came into view. St. Mary's is built around a church on the river, like so many other tiny communities in this wilderness. But the river has its own religion, and it abandoned the little town a few decades back, skipping like a jump rope and cutting a new channel, forming an island that some people believe is cursed.

The curse was leveled at a prominent fur trader from Kaskaskia, across the river in Illinois. To stop his daughter from eloping with a young Native American man, the trader tied the young man to a log and sent him into the river to drown. Indeed, the poor man drowned, but not before leveling a curse that the trader would die in the coming year, and the town would be washed away, and the dead would float to the surface. Sure enough, the curse followed course. The old man was killed in a duel. A succession of floods chased residents away and destroyed most of the structures, including the church altar in the 1973 flood.

Oh, and during the flood the bodies in the cemeteries floated to the surface.

South of this Midwest Atlantis, between blues alley and the river, the road led us through Frohna. The smell of baking bread wafted from a brick oven, and I stopped to learn that just beyond Frohna's border grows the beechwood used to age Budweiser. I didn't gather any beechwood, since my own aging process is damn near complete.

Nearby, Tower Rock Winery is named for a landmark in the Mississippi that every riverboat captain knows. The rock is about the size of the Jefferson Memorial, an irregular cylinder that pushes out of the river like Bart Simpson's noggin, a sheer limestone nonagon with a thick head of forest atop it. Mother Nature insists on forcing the river channel through the narrows between the rock and the riverbank, where enough riverboats have been dashed that river captains toast each successful passing beyond the rock. On this day the rock was preparing to absorb its billionth beating, this time by a weather system spinning counterclockwise out of the tropics.

With an eye toward a darkening sky, we turned away from the river and crossed Cinq Hommes Creek, which was named not for five men (the literal French translation), but for one man: a French priest named Father Saint Cosme. In French, St. Cosme sounds like *cinq hommes*. In this instance, according to Robert L. Ramsay's *Our Storehouse of Missouri Place Names*, the French settlers—not their Saxon neighbors—changed the spelling.

We rolled south on 61 to a beautiful bridge at Old Appletown. The bridge, painted apple red, was built in 1879, so its back has hosted the heels of every one of those blues travelers headed to Chicago. Within spittin' distance downstream from the bridge, an old mill dam forms a deep pool, and the water was thick with swimmers on this hot day, even with an imminent threat of rain from storm clouds billowing out of the Gulf of Mexico. The impending storm was the remnant of Hurricane Dolly, and it still packed a punch, as I would find out.

We took a turn into the wilderness. We circled down through Pocahontas and Oak Ridge and Daisy, the birthplace of the inventor of the world's first coin-operated electric hobby horse. Otto Hahs left Daisy and eventually landed in Sikeston, where he turned his invention loose on Depression-era children. The original mechanical horse was a free-range toy with big wheels, the precursor to the stationary mechanical horses you see today in front of grocery stores.

We found the peaceful homes of Friedheim, then passed through Dissen and Lixville and crossed the Whitewater River, three successive harbingers of the deluge that was about to hit us.

The community of Scopus sits at the confluence of routes B and M, and for some reason, I began to think about my next colonoscopy. Sounds silly, but it's a conditioned response. Roadsigns continually remind me about works of nature given anatomical names, many of them with satanic undertones. I haven't run across the Devil's Asshole yet, but there is a Devil's Elbow and a Devil's Tongue, also known as Lizard Rock or Devil's Dick—pick one. The Devil's body parts poke and peek from crags and crevasses throughout the state, where many of our most vivid geological wonders bear the name of Satan, like the twenty-four Devil's Backbones that jut out from Hell. The Prince of Darkness is well-stocked in Missouri, with the Devil's Ice Box, the Devil's Sugar Bowl, even a Devil's Tea Table. The Devil's Bake Oven got its name "perhaps, because it does not powerfully resemble anybody else's bake oven," according to the leading authority on deviltry in Missouri: Mark Twain. Wait until dark, and drive south of Joplin to witness the spooky Devil's Jack-O-Lantern. Then descend into Table Rock Lake and find Devil's Dive Resort. Or splash into Devil's Pool, and feed at Devil's Pool Restaurant at Big Cedar Lodge.

As you walk to these natural wonders, keep an eye out for Missouri native plants like Devil's Claw, Devil's Darning Needles, Devil's Walking Stick, Devil's Trumpet and Devil's Shoestring. It's the Devil's version of Walmart in the wild.

And if you feel particularly dirty after delving into all these devilish delights, there's a spot to cleanse and refresh: Just off Route 66 west of Halltown, dip into Devil's Wash Pan.

The sky darkened as we continued down the backroads. Next to big fields of green, we passed an irrigator, which became an impromptu car wash, even as the first fat raindrops from Dolly splattered Erifnus' windshield. Erifnus felt clean.

We pulled into Marble Hill, where I met *hypsibema missouriense*, Missouri's only known native dinosaur. Skeletal remains from these giants lie in the Bollinger County Museum of Natural History. It's an impressive effort for this town of 1,500 people to keep an old school building's doors open and fill it with artifacts. Cool artifacts, too. Concretions and pseudo-fossils. Native-American stuff. Civil War stuff. An account of the sinking of the *Montana*, the largest sternwheeler ever on the Missouri River. And the story of Ira Biffle, a hometown boy who grew up to be an aviation pioneer, and taught a budding daredevil-to-be Charles Lindbergh how to fly.

But the museum's biggest star is *hypsibema missouriense,* the Missouri dinosaur. She was a hadrosaur, a plant eater with a cartoonish bovine head at the end of a long neck attached to a massive brontosaurus body with a long tail. Museum curators took me to see the excavation site, on private property west of town near Glenallen, where a guy who called himself Dinosaur Dan first identified the fossils.

A greenhouse structure covers the dig site, so archaeologists can work year round. The Missouri Ozark Dinosaur Project continues to unearth heavy clay containing dinosaur bones. The clay goes to the museum lab, where the bones are carefully retrieved and cleaned. It's quite a project for such a small museum. The Smithsonian and other big museums watch the dig with interest, offering helpful suggestions here and there.

Erifnus didn't care. She needed fossil fuel if we were going to continue our drive through the rainy countryside. I obliged, pouring a dozen gallons of Sinclair into her belly. That's the kind of dinosaur she can get off on.

Pushing east on Highway 91, we passed the Hooe Missionary Baptist Church. For an instant I thought maybe the sign used to say "Hope Missionary," and maybe it lost the stick from the "p." But on this rainy, blustery day I could see no sign of hope, just Hooe. Down the road in Bell City, the Born Again Resellit Shop waited for converts.

Bollinger County rolled back under our wheels, and raindrops distorted my view. I avoided turning on my wipers for as long as I could, because the driver's side wiper blade was broken in half and kept slipping out of its rocker cradle. With each revolution of the broken wiper, the arms were scratching grooves in my windshield, arced high like a ballerina's eyebrow. My better view was out the driver's side window, where I spied a giant round hay bale painted to look like a John Deere tractor, the words "Happy Birthday" appeared beneath.

At the Castor River, I turned north on Route H, the third curviest road in the northwest corner of Western Southeast North America. I reached the end of the blacktop just as the rain intensified. A gravel road lay before me, offering two directions. Which way was a shortcut to the end of another blacktop? My car rolled right. With the sunset obscured by heavy black hurricane leftovers, Erifnus bit into the gravel road that pointed through sheets of rain, down a hill into the woods, around a bend, out of sight of any civilization. We descended, my loyal Erifnus and I, deeper into the woods, down rough gravel roads with washed-out ruts that led to an infestation of low-water crossings. Dolly was still a tempest, and we splashed through flash-flood streamways that were evolving past the trickle stage. I patted my dashboard, and thought about the right rear tire with the slow leak.

We ground through the endless gravel until gravel became dirt, fast becoming mud under the deluge. I glanced out my side window for the appearance of a power line or a telephone pole, any sign that maybe I was emerging from this deep-woods desolation, toward civilization. Nothing but rain and wind and lightning and mud and woods and more low-water crossings. Deeper we went as darkness enveloped our headlights and formed a tiny cocoon of light while the storm raged. I stopped again to reposition the broken wiper blade. The repair lasted for a minute, then the wiper slid off its track at both ends. I stopped to fix it again. Finally my Pontiac's nose pointed uphill, and we snaked up slippery ruts for what seemed like six months, through rains more easily measured in feet, until my tires hit the hard surface of Route EE. It was still a twenty-mile zigzag in the darkness across a trio of backroad blacktops to Perryville. Erifnus' headlights pointed into a billion spooky reflections of raindrops hurtling at our windshield in the howling wind.

At last under the friendly neon of an AutoZone sign, an attendant made his last sale of the night. Then he turned off the neon. I thanked him, and walked outside to replace the defective wiper in a dim, deserted parking lot while Dolly dumped a deluge from her ample bosom. She showed a surprising reserve of stamina, full of sound and fury.

The wiper worked as promised. But the tempest dissolved my short-term memory, and in the thrashing gale, I turned the wrong way out of the AutoZone parking lot. Traveling a dozen miles with no recognizable landmarks, I came to a lonely dead end. Ahead in the blackness, beneath my headlight beams, I could see the shimmering waters of the Mississippi River. Good thing I was driving at a snail's pace, or I might've joined Kaskaskia's resurrected cadavers at the bottom of the Mississippi.

There wasn't much of a way to turn the car around. The mud road was narrow, its ditches filling with water, so using the manual gearshift, I carefully moved Erifnus forward and back, forward and back in the middle of the road, each time turning the wheels slightly, shaving points off the compass, pivoting slowly like a locomotive on a roundhouse turntable. At last, with our backs to the bleak black coldness of the river, we drove into the teeth of Dolly. The windshield wipers rocked while I fumbled around the radio dial for a good blues station.

We rejoined Highway 61 and I regained my bearings, turning north. Cinq Hommes Creek was bank full as we crossed it the second time. Maybe it was a sign, but as we drove north and passed the old Lithium Baptist Church, things got calm.

I found refuge for the night in a Microtel at the Ste. Genevieve exit along I-55. I would have preferred a favorite bed and breakfast down the hill in Ste. Gen, a house with the name "Somewhere Inn Time." Hey, they had to name it something. The stay would have been therapeutic, with a trail that leads through a swimming pool and a Jacuzzi and a wine glass. But since wind and lightning and swimming don't mix, I opted for nine hours of sleep.

Next morning, the storm was gone. In its place, steamy morning sunshine offered to make mushrooms. Like the bad golfer that I am, I put yesterday's round behind me and headed down the automotive fairway in search of birdies.

Good Water Gone Bad

It's the greatest water park in the world.

A summer afternoon at Johnson's Shut-Ins will make you forget about manmade water parks. That's because it pushes humans through some of the most hair-raising chutes a body can stand without drowning. Or so I thought.

The rushing water is entirely natural, no chlorine. And the ride is free.

On a recent visit to this dependable waterworks, I joined family members who turned themselves into torpedoes, sliding through a maze of hydraulics that has yet to meet its manmade match.

The ride never breaks down. Flowing over the oldest exposed rocks in North America, a mountain stream gets forced through a narrow granite canyon strewn with boulders the size of Volkswagens, and the water smashes into this boulder field with the force of your favorite log flume. Visitors come from hundreds of miles away to camp in the campground and spend whole afternoons riding the chutes and spills through this maze, Mother Nature at her playful best.

On a hot summer day, our family participated willingly, alongside a thousand other water worshipers, who were there that day tumbling out of control through fissures that could easily render us dazed or comatose. Surprisingly, all afternoon we didn't see an injury worse than a sunburn. I'm amazed that in this modern age of limits and lawsuits, caveats and crowd control, such a thrill ride still exists.

But one early morning a few years ago, things went horribly wrong. A tragic event revealed that not everything along this slice of fun is natural.

High atop Proffit Mountain, a manmade reservoir regulates the mountain stream. This mountaintop lake is operated by a large utility company, which pumps water up the mountain to the reservoir at night when electricity is cheap, and releases it through turbine generators during the day when electric demand is high. Proffit Mountain, indeed.

Well, a series of mishaps atop the mountain caused the reservoir to overflow the dam, which broke, sending two billion gallons of water scouring down the mountainside. While the rocks of the shut-ins didn't budge, the torrent ripped through the state park, sending a wall of water and boulders and trees that pulverized the campgrounds. The force of the water performed a facelift so complete that it shut the park down for several years.

It was a major catastrophe, an event every bit as turbulent as the Johnstown Flood, but because of timing and luck, nobody died. If the flood had happened in the spring or summer or fall, it would have killed hundreds of campers. Instead, it happened on December 16, and the campground in the state park was empty, except for the park superintendent and his family. The flood unhinged the park superintendent's house, and dashed it against canyon walls downstream.

Searchers found the family the next morning, hugging the tops of two trees that had withstood the raging water. All five family members were plucked to safety. They were suffering from shock and hypothermia, but alive. It's damn near a miracle that the youngest child, a five-year-old, hung on to a tree limb through the night. That five-year-old was fortunate. I had no way of knowing that a few years later, this park would witness the tragic drowning of another five-year-old.

* * *

Driving home from a tour of the flood-damaged park, my mind searched for ideas to save tourism in this washed-out part of the stunningly beautiful Arcadia Valley. Along the way, a small brown sign pointed to Pickle Springs.

I took the bait.

There's a reason. The night before, I had been summoned to a donnybrook downstream from the busted dam. It was a meeting with concerned citizens in the remote little town of Lesterville, a hardscrabble community built on rocky hillsides that offer little support for agriculture. So a lot of folks around here squeeze out a living by renting canoes and campgrounds to vacationers. The townsfolk were angry because they felt like big city television stations were telling people that the flood destroyed the whole valley.

These same television stations were filming this Lesterville meeting, poised to send live reports. So I encouraged the crowd to spin their story positive. "Your eggs are not in one basket. Talk about the valley's other charms. Show your giant boulders at Elephant Rocks State Park. Describe the view from Taum Sauk Mountain. Retell the Civil War's single most bizarre escape at the Battle of Pilot Knob."

They weren't listening. They were angry. These folks had a strong distaste for the word "government" and anybody associated with government. Even though many in the crowd were receiving some kind of government assistance—Medicaid or food stamps or unemployment or disability or aid to families with dependent children—they view government as the problem in their lives.

I told them that state tourism had arranged radio interviews in St. Louis and Chicago to highlight the wonderful Arcadia Valley vacationland, and dozens of stories for Sunday newspaper travel sections. Deaf ears.

From the back of the restless crowd, one man shouted out "Pickle Springs!"

In my mental Rolodex, Pickle Springs was a blank page.

Just then, representatives from Ameren, the electric company—owners of the reservoir and dam—showed up late. The crowd gave them a standing ovation. I was puzzled. Why would these victims applaud the company that douched them with a two billion gallon flood?

The answer is simple: Follow the money. The townspeople wanted the utility company to rebuild the dam. Yes, the company was responsible for setting up the elements that wreaked disaster on Lesterville's livelihood. But locals also realized that Ameren pays more local taxes than just about everybody else in Reynolds and Iron Counties combined. So to keep the public schools open without raising taxes on themselves, the residents needed Ameren to rebuild the mountaintop dam.

Mother Nature, patient and quiet, must be rolling her eyes.

I left the meeting, retreating to my hotel room up the road at the Fort Davidson Motel. The motel is an aging property. But it's solid and friendly, has a nice pool, and a great breakfast next door. And it's protected by the Civil War ghosts of Fort Davidson, who knew how to raise hell. Most important, at this late hour, the motel had the two things I needed.

Flat on my bed, with mankind's most important appendage in hand—the TV remote—I surfed through presentations of the 10 o'clock news. My worst fears were confirmed: All my coaching fell on deaf ears. I watched the locals rant at the television reporters that "All you want to talk about is that we're shut down!" In a classic case of self-fulfilling prophecy, the locals reinforced the boob tube impression that the Johnson's Shut-Ins flood had shut down the whole area.

Damn. Failed.

* * *

Next morning, along the road home, the brown sign sucked me in. Pickle Springs Natural Area. At first, my plan was simple... drive into Pickle Springs parking lot, circle and leave, satisfied to add this spot to my "Yeah, I've been there" list.

But I knew that was dishonest.

I parked next to the only other vehicle in the lot. Stepping out of the warm security of my car into smatterings of old snow, I walked a few yards toward the trail, following fresh footsteps, bending an ear toward the woods, listening for the owners of the pickup parked next to my car. In the February crisp, there was no sound.

At the head of the loop trail, their footprints turned left. I took the trail to the right, stopping after a few yards to peer into the wilderness. Realizing anew that winter affords a better view of the forest, I kept walking. Within seconds, steep walls of a box canyon enveloped me. Sandstone boulders the age of Pluto towered over my head, spring water seeped beneath. One foot followed the other down the path, lured by this unfolding carnival for the eye. With perfect theatrical timing, mother nature arranged her priceless sculptures before me.

Headwall Falls. Rockpile Canyon. Pickle Springs.

I wondered if John Muir or *National Geographic* ever visited this spot, with its collection of weather-beaten sandstone shapes, creations that Bryce Canyon would be proud to display.

Dome Rock. Owl's Den Bluff. Mossy Falls.

A part of me wants to keep these charms secret. They're rewards for observant visitors who've done their research. Another part of me shouts to the contrails that crisscross the heavens, punctuated by gleaming silver dots that carry passengers to Los Angeles and New York.

"You don't know what you're missing!" I yelled.

"And the best is ahead of you!" a voice responded.

The response startled me. Collecting myself, I greeted two backpackers as they approached. These were the guys from the pickup truck parked in the lot. Father and son, by the looks of them. Never did I feel intimidated, despite the warnings of a few radical anti-trail folks who suggest that trails attract serial killers.

Rational people know that most murderers hate to hike. And the only serial this duo had in their sights involved other nearby geologic gems tucked into the St. Francois Mountains. The virgin pines of Hawn State Park. The valley panorama from Buford Mountain. The whitewater thrills of Millstream Gardens.

We marveled at the stunning beauty of this place. The hikers foreshadowed what would unfold on the rest of my two-mile trek along the Pickle Springs trail:

Terrapin Rock. The Keyhole. Cauliflower Rocks.

I was amazed.

The discord of last evening's town hall meeting seemed a billion miles away. In reality, you can cover the distance from that town hall to Pickle Springs in the time it takes to watch the 10 o'clock news. Fresh on my retina is the face of a television reporter telling 250,000 visitors to Johnson's Shut-Ins that the road is closed. Meantime, if they scratch a layer or two deeper into these oldest mountains on the continent, they'll find what I found.

Crappers & Poachers & Busty Encroachers

Bob Franklin looks to be about my age. And like many folks who came of age in the '60s, Bob has a deep respect for land and water and air. Visiting Bob at his river outfitter business, Franklin Floats, was a visit back to 1968. It's not so much the long hair or the relaxed clothing, the kind with tie-dye accents. It's the attitude, an attitude of concern for the river.

Bob's intentions seem as noble as the skycrapper that stands proud on his property. The skycrapper, a solar-powered composting outhouse, was the object of scorn from Senator William Proxmire, who gave the contraption a Golden Fleece Award back in the '70s for wasting taxpayer dollars. Well, in the grand scheme of the cosmos, Proxmire's body lies composting in some saintly sarcophagus, and the skycrapper is still around, composting human waste so it can be used as fertilizer.

Some of Bob's neighbors won't grant him access to the river to launch canoeists. Much of the land along the river is private property, and many landowners would prefer to keep the river private.

Bob Franklin and I reached the public access point to launch my canoe. I started on the West Fork of the Black River. The water was delightful, running rapid and crystal clear over Mother Nature's colorful collection of igneous rocks in the gravel bottom. The landscape is marred only by the several "Private Beach" and "No Trespassing" signs that dot the riverbanks. Well, you can't blame landowners for controlling their property. Some of the property owners say that the reason they deny access is because of the trash left on their banks. That trash makes me sick, too.

Enforcing laws on these remote rivers has always been an issue. Sometimes, the problem goes beyond trash or trespassing.

A few years ago, a sheriff of neighboring Carter County was bust-ed for distributing crystal meth. And I remember stories about a period of time a generation ago, when a few law enforcement officials would hide in the bluffs overlooking these beautiful spring-fed streams and watch canoeists float down the rivers. If a cop spied canoeists smoking pot, the law enforcer would swoop down out of the hills and bust the floaters; It's hard to say how much money law-enforcement agencies made doing this. Granted, smoking pot was illegal. But the area got a reputation for harassing outsiders.

Ask *National Geographic*. A local told me the following story. A few years back, the sheriff in a neighboring county arrested a photographer hired by *National Geographic* who took a photo of some underage kids drinking beer in front of God and everybody.

So the story goes, the sheriff quickly turned the tables on the big-city magazine photographer, accusing the photographer of buying the beer, giving it to the minors, and turning around to photograph these same kids drinking beer. Local folks won't say much about the incident, except that some of them think the sheriff might've been covering somebody's butt for selling beer to minors. What better way to neutralize the *National Geographic* photographer than to blame him for buying the beer?

After tense negotiations, the photographer was allowed to leave the county. His editor was incredulous: "We've never had problems like this, even in third-world countries!" he fumed.

Needless to say, a few rotten apples in the law-enforcement barrel can strain the fragile trust between the public and its watchdogs.

Lumped in that same barrel, Missouri conservation agents seem to get a lot of scorn, especially from people who want to hunt and gig and fish whenever they want.

Without these agents, the poachers would liquidate whole animal populations. It's happened before, right here, a century ago when abundant deer and turkey populations were wiped out.

Conservation agents call themselves the "thin green line," a reference to their green uniforms and sparse ranks compared to the territory they cover. And their duty can be as tricky as it is dangerous: Poachers commit armed robbery, and they wallow in the scent of blood.

The Ozarks' most infamous poaching incident involved a sheriff, according to local legend. Several years ago, as locals tell it, the sheriff was driving along Highway 19 when he spied a deer in the woods near the side of the road. He slowed his truck and pulled a rifle from the rack in the back window of the pickup. A bullet brought the deer down. Well, the deer should have dropped in its tracks. But since the deer was a dummy—a decoy monitored by a conservation agent—it simply absorbed the bullet.

My source—not Bob Franklin—tells me it was the same sheriff that harassed the *National Geographic* photographer.

* * *

I hit the Middle Fork a mile and a half down river, which then joined the East Fork, which clouded the river bed with floculates, tiny electrically-charged bits of clay from the disastrous flood. Looking down, I noticed that the rainbow-bottomed riverbeds beneath the rushing water were coated with a slick slime, turning the rocks a dull gray.

The float was relaxing—and beautiful—as long as I didn't look at the bottom of the river or at the "Keep Out" signs posted everywhere. I didn't see any other floaters. Bob picked me up in his van, and we drove back to Erifnus.

Leaving the Black River, I drove back into Lesterville. In the heart of these hills, laden as they are with lead ore, my radio could pick up only local stations, all preaching Jesus. Their message of hope is impervious to lead.

Wall Art

I like pictures. Other folks do, too. After all, pictures are efficient; few of us have the patience anymore to stop and admire a thousand words.

Like other self-anointed art critics who root for the resurgence of real American downtowns, I'll always appreciate Wall Art. Because Wall Art celebrates local places. Always.

Everywhere Erifnus takes me, main street murals capitalize on this fact, offering local variations of a giant photo album. It's a phenomenon that's gaining momentum. As dozens of downtowns grow older, and vacant buildings decay and fall, neighboring buildings expose blank walls that offer perfect surfaces for local artists.

Sometimes the art is uninvited, spontaneous symbols that appear overnight, declarations of affection or of turf boundaries. Some cities fought the losing battle with graffiti the best way they could, with scouring powder and elbow grease.

A few towns even offered graffiti walls, to channel budding artists. But more and more, towns are getting into the act themselves, hiring artists to tell their stories.

Splayed across the side walls of buildings, these murals tell the Cliff's Notes version of a town's history. Vivid portrayals play out on brick and stucco in Missouri towns from Cuba to Houston, Chillicothe to Mountain View. And so far, in my detours, every mural has been worth a smile.

One mural project stands just a bit taller than the rest, as much for its story as for the paintings themselves.

A few years back, Cape Girardeau transformed an ugly floodwall into a masterpiece. Through those murals, through the project, magic happened, and a downtown coalesced.

Whether you believe it takes a family or a village or both, one thing is for sure: It takes a lot of pluck to pick up the scattered spirits of proud downtowns, punished by neglect and desertion. The people of Cape Girardeau embraced their history, their downtown, and each other, in smacking an artistic grand slam over a twelve-foot gray floodwall. And the murals have helped spawn a renaissance throughout downtown Cape Girardeau.

Cape is lucky. But as the priceless floodwall vignettes illustrate, the people of Cape Girardeau always had a hand in producing their own good luck.

A few years ago, Erifnus and I joined the townsfolk to help dedicate Cape's new wall art. That night, I was at the end of a long list of folks scheduled to speak to a banquet.

The crowd had become restless. It had been a long evening, stuffed with historical data and factoids. The audience sat in the comfortable cool of a big banquet hall, a relief from the hot afternoon dedication of the new murals. The lavish feast had settled into eyelids young and old. The post-banquet speeches, laid end to end, proceeded like one of those long freight trains that pulse through town, blocking the view of the murals.

Don't misunderstand: The evening was a blast . . . just long. It takes some time to laud an artistic feat that stretches along a thousand feet of floodwall. And as the evening began, 400 eyeballs sparkled, reflecting the colorful reproductions of twenty-five panels and five vignettes.

A true celebration it was.

Frank Nickell, the town's *de facto* historian, told a tasty tale about a *New York Times* reporter who visited Cape Girardeau a few years ago. The reporter wasn't kind, complaining that the drab gray floodwall gave the city a medieval appearance. The wall separated the city from its lifeblood, the river, and discouraged visitors. Listeners nodded in agreement that in retrospect, the *Times* was right.

But with one bold artistic feat, Cape Girardeau emerged from the Dark Ages. In fact, look for future historians to categorize Cape's history as Pre-mural and Post-mural. The visuals are that good.

Frank reminded the crowd of a story they'd heard many times and taken to heart. When the city announced a search for the perfect muralist to transform a barren wall, several world-class artists offered their services. Many had impressive credentials. They talked about their muralistic conquests across the globe. They proudly portrayed their portfolios.

Then a visionary young painter named Tom showed up, wearing a cheap suit and a red pork pie hat. Other artists attempted to win Cape's favor by boasting of their prowess and finesse. Tom took a different approach.

"Who are your characters?" Tom asked. "What is your history?" He courted the town and the town courted Tom, and they struck a relationship that sank deeper than a coat of paint.

Immediately Thomas Melvin stood apart from the pack. Locals began to recognize him because he always wore that bright red pork pie hat. They spotted him everywhere. Rather than zipping into town for a quick interview and leaving in a whoosh of self-important urgency, Tom stuck around. Like a fiddler on the roof, he perched and squatted in every possible spot to perceive the town and its rich fabric. He talked to the townsfolk, and asked about things that were important to them and to their city. He dined with them at Port Cape Girardeau, a restaurant where, looking out a giant picture window, patrons and *New York Times* reporters saw an imposing gray floodwall. Tom saw a blank canvas, awaiting.

He got the job.

You can tell when a product has been created by loving hands. And the banquet crowd relished as Tom talked about his inspirations. He told how he watched as the swallows that roosted under the old Mississippi River Bridge left for the winter and returned next year to find the old bridge gone. The swallows promptly christened the new bridge with bird shit, signaling this structure as their new avian condo.

He watched the red-tailed hawks soar above the bluffs, as he learned how the native American mound builders trained the hawks to hunt.

With his paintbrush he translated old tales of DeSoto and Marquette and Joliet, Jean Baptiste Girardot, and Napoleon in a bathtub. He recounted one of the few kindnesses along the Trail of Tears, when Cape residents prepared baskets of food for the Cherokee people as they crossed the Mississippi River.

His paintings showed the fate of three steamboats, all named *Cape Girardeau*, piloted by famous Cape steamboat captain Buck Leyhe. Buck's legendary dog, Toodles, appears on one panel. Toodles often accompanied Buck, and on one trip in St. Louis, Toodles met a tragic end under the wheels of a street car. Toodleoo.

Tom Melvin, a Chicagoan, and his crew of seven talented artists—including his daughter May—depicted life on the Mississippi . . . floods and fires, traders and explorers, hot riverboat jazz and jagged ice floes.

History came alive, in scenes that jumped through the *trompe l'oeil* stone arches painted on the floodwall.

The audience loved him. They didn't become restless until a half-dozen speeches later. I was the last one to speak.

It's an undeniable fact that fidgeting is a high-art form practiced to perfection by all children everywhere. Yet as I gazed out at the audience, the gradeschoolers sat perfectly attentive. The adults looked like they needed a break.

Drawing upon my experience as a child, and summoning all my wisdom as a parent, my speech was forty seven words. Thirty seconds. I spoke to the children directly. "Thank you for your patience tonight. Congratulate your parents for working hard to bring these paintings to life. And a few days from now, when they're rested, remind them that their work is only half done. Now it's time to paint the other side of the wall."

Then I sat down. The crowd looked relieved. I knew then that my mother was right: "Never miss a good chance to shut up."

Later that night, after the banquet, a few night owls from the group joined the revelers at Port Cape Girardeau. The joint was jumpin'. The band played songs I hadn't heard since I was in college. I sat thoroughly entertained by the spectacle, watching the silhouettes dancing in front of the big picture window that framed the town's new floodwall masterpiece. Sure enough, everyone was dancing with the guy in the red pork pie hat. They loved him. And he loved them.

On my next visit, I returned to that table in front of the big picture window at Port Cape. I traded a picture of Andrew Jackson for a dose of the Original Port Cape Ribs, the dinner that keeps this restaurant on the map. The ribs were bathed in smoke for seven hours and glazed three times before they ended up on my platter.

The windows were bathed in murals.

* * *

Next day, I communed with Ol' Man River.

South of town, out of sight of river-hugging Highway 61, and even farther from the interstate, the Port of Cape Girardeau is a busy barge feeder, or eater, I'm not sure which, with lots of trucks and conveyor belts and pipes that can belch or suck hectares of grain, and water-tower sized gulps of gas.

Erifnus and I drove past New York, which isn't there anymore, since it fell into the river. We snaked south along the levees toward the land of azaleas.

The azaleas around Charleston were beautiful, surrounding stately old homes, which reminded me that if the Old South is a Ferris Wheel, I was at the pinnacle.

West of there sits an old town. Old. The fortified walls of Towosahgy were built a thousand years ago by Mississippian Indian Mound Builders. The walls are long gone, but the mounds remain. Archaeologists describe the walls as a stockade with watch towers, which adds to my perspective about the sophistication of mound builders. For some reason, they abandoned the town six centuries ago. I followed suit, and headed south to the site of an inland tsunami.

Calamity

Dorena died so Cairo could live. To keep Mississippi floodwaters from ravaging Cairo, Illinois, the U.S. Army Corps of Engineers blasted a levee at Bird's Point on May 2, 2011, sending a 15-foot-high torrent of floodwater down a spillway on the Missouri side of the river. This inland tsunami smashed into Pinhook before it hit Dorena. Pinhook was a historic black farming community with about fifty residents, whose great-great-great-grandfathers had purchased this land.

For seventy-four years, ever since they built levees along this mighty river, the corps knew that this day might come. But nobody thought they'd ever need to blast the levee. Now, the towns in the spillway have been decimated and covered in sand, the rich fertile farmland scoured and carried away, most of the hundred homes gone.

Tucked into the winding Mississippi, what's left of Dorena is surrounded on three sides by Kentucky. The nearest bridges across the Mississippi are thirty miles north or fifty miles south. So the *Dorena-Hickman Ferry* does a brisk business for those folks willing to shell out fourteen dollars per car, although you can get discounts for multiple trips.

North of the *Dorena-Hickman Ferry*, east of East Prairie, as far as Highway 80 would take me without dumping me into the Mississippi

River, I found Belmont, another spot where the feds did some blasting. But this time, somebody returned fire. Today Belmont—what's left of it—has a grain elevator near the river, along with a historic marker denoting a Civil War battle. History books describe the Battle of Belmont with words including "unremarkable," "inconsequential" and "unnecessary." The town of Belmont doesn't appear strategic. Even during the Civil War, the village had only a few buildings, though it was the site of a river ferry.

But it allowed Brigadier General Ulysses S. Grant and some untested soldiers to gain battle experience. Grant had trouble keeping his own soldiers in line. To keep his troops from wantonly looting the Confederate camp at Belmont, he had to set fire to the camp. Shortly thereafter, his troops retreated hastily in the face of a re-energized Confederate Army at full charge.

During that day, Grant was almost killed three times. First, during the early battle his horse was shot out from under him. Later he narrowly escaped rebel snipers while he rode on a solitary reconnaissance mission along a cornfield. Finally, just after he coaxed his second horse onto a retreating steamboat, he went up to the wheelhouse to survey the scene.

In his memoirs Grant describes his third narrow escape: "Our smoke-stack was riddled with bullets, but there were only three men wounded on the boats, two of whom were soldiers. When I first went on deck I entered the captain's room adjoining the pilot-house, and threw myself on a sofa. I did not keep that position a moment, but rose to go out on the deck to observe what was going on. I had scarcely left when a musket ball entered the room, struck the head of the sofa, passed through it and lodged in the foot."

The Battle of Belmont is a mere footnote in Civil War history books, but from the rosters of soldiers involved, it featured more brigadier generals than the average bank has vice presidents.

This site is every bit as remote as the rest of the riverfront along Mississippi County. It's such an isolated area that the roads would be perfect for a bike race. Sure enough, America's corniest name for a bicycle tour comes from right here, the Tour de Corn.

The Tour de Corn is not a Branson show, and although it involves thousands of bicycles, it's not a race, either. It's a ride of varying distances along Route 80 and connecting roads. The entry fees are donated to charities, including the East Prairie Nutrition Center for senior citizens.

On my drive this day there were no bikes, no cornstalks.

But there was a senior nutrition center. And from experience, I knew that senior nutrition centers offer a good lunch at a good price, and great stories from great people. I missed the chance to dine at the senior center, since they eat lunch early, and I was driving late into the lunch hour.

Driving through East Prairie, the streets were sleepy. But when the corn gets as high as a cyclist's eye, things will be hoppin' all over town, at feedlots, and at watering holes with names like the Hog Pound and the Depot, the Southern Pride and the Prairie Queen, and McDonald's. By the way, that's McDonald's Food Mart, a grocery store, and not the ubiquitous golden arches. That grocery store must have been there a long time to get away with keeping that name.

* * *

Erifnus rolled toward the world's most elastic town. Reaching the Mississippi River's most dramatic bend, where the river traces the imaginary outline of a giant keyhole, we found New Madrid sprawled across the north side of the keyhole. New Madrid looks peaceful, but it sits on one of the most potent fault lines on the continent. Two hundred years ago, the fault unleashed the most powerful earthquake ever recorded in North America, turning the land into ten-foot waves, sending the Mississippi River backward, and changing its course. It even rang church bells in Boston. New Madrid residents actually felt the earth move more than a thousand times over a month and a half.

In the *History of Southeast Missouri*, eyewitness Godfrey LeSieur gives this account:

"The first shock was about 2 o'clock a. m., on the night of December 16, 1811, and was very hard, shaking down log houses, chimneys, etc. It was followed at intervals from half an hour to an hour apart by comparatively slight shocks, until about 7 o'clock in the morning, when a rumbling noise was heard in the west, not unlike distant thunder, and in an instant the earth began to totter and shake so that no persons were able to stand or walk. This lasted a minute, then the earth was observed to be rolling in waves of a few feet in height, with a visible depression between. These swells burst, throwing up large volumes of water, sand and a species of charcoal, some of which was partly covered with a substance which by its peculiar odor was thought to be sulfur. Where these swells burst, large, wide and long fissures were left running north and south parallel with each other for miles. I have seen some four or five miles in length, four and one-half feet deep on an average, and about ten feet wide." LeSieur reports that a second, equally devastating series of shocks occurred three weeks later, whereupon residents "fled in dismay, leaving behind their stock and even many of their household goods, all of which were appropriated by adventurers and carried away in flatboats."

In the 1905 *History of Dunklin County*, eyewitness Michael Braunm described what he saw: "in one particular place on the Mississippi the earth rose like a great loaf of bread to the height of many feet, the uprising being accompanied by a terrible rumbling noise. The swell finally burst with one of the most severe shocks of the period, and great quantities of sand, water and a black sulfurous vapor, was thrown out to nearly the height of an ordinary tree, completely darkening the atmosphere for some distance."

According to Iben Browning, a scientist who studied the fault, there was a fifty-fifty chance that the second cataclysmal New Madrid earthquake would happen on December 3, 1990. He produced enough proof—planetary alignment, gravitational pulls and such—that locals became convinced he was right. They stocked up on food, and schools closed so everybody could prepare for Armageddon. Reporters swarmed the little town, and it sagged under the tonnage of nearly fifty satellite trucks poised to report the earthquake.

Silence.

Iben Browning died a year later. Today, more than two decades hence, the fault still hasn't popped. In that two decades, the fault has saved up enough extra energy to launch a thousand TV trucks like popping corn. Anticipation has waned with time, and most people, even at ground zero, have become complacent, as evidenced by the fact that they still live along the fault line. It's a situation similar to the folks in Southern California and San Francisco; people love the area so much they're willing to take the risk. Or maybe it's a display of faith, that God will protect them. Or maybe they just put it out of their minds, and go on with their lives. Although a strong Midwest quake would damage St. Louis and Memphis, the New Madrid fault would affect exponentially fewer people than California's San Andreas fault, so New Madrid gets little attention.

The town itself is quaint, with nice museums and Civil War-era homes. And before the *Delta Queen* went stagnant and quit plying the Mississippi River, she occasionally would steam into town and dock along the riverfront, and townsfolk would dress in antebellum costumes and greet the passengers, who showed their approval by spending thousands of dollars in the shops.

It was a windfall, as this sleepy town patiently awaits the ghastly end. In the back of everybody's mind is the thought that at any moment, the streets will start undulating like a Tilt-A-Whirl floor.

Even today, New Madrid is only a fraction of the size of Pompeii. In the years before AD 79, Mount Vesuvius sent warnings to the people of Pompeii and Herculaneum. The people stayed. When the end came, they were overwhelmed so quickly that they petrified into a museum of culture at the time of Christ.

* * *

Deeper in the Bootheel, Caruthersville is a fun town. What else would you expect from a place founded by two guys named Johnnie Walker and George W. Bushey? Even the town's name is fun, rhyming with Smothers Brothers. Forget the fact that it's named after a congressman; this is the home of Cedric the Entertainer.

With a casino on the river, the whole county has a history of playing fast and loose. Talk about gambling: At times, the county has led the state in percentage of unwed mothers. But Mother Nature dealt the town its most devastating blows: A 2006 tornado damaged sixty percent of the town, and folks still were rebuilding when a paralyzing ice storm hit.

Living along the Mississippi River, people know how to rebuild from floods and earthquakes. But Caruthersville actually missed the first bout with Armageddon, since it didn't incorporate until decades after the great New Madrid earthquake of 1811.

Much of Caruthersville's fun flows in and out of its riverboat casino. Like all the other modern casinos in Missouri, it was built to conform to modern Missouri law, which said that gambling can be conducted only on riverboats. Further, the law only let you tug the one-armed bandits or rake in your chips when the boats actually were cruising the rivers.

But soon after the new gaming law went into effect, riverboat owners realized their profits were compromised severely by high insurance premiums to cover shipwrecks. So the law was amended, and modern gambling boats don't sail. Most of them don't even have engines. They're fastened securely to the bank, while technically fulfilling the requirement that they are boats.

For a while after the boats were moored permanently dockside, you could board only at two-hour intervals, and if you showed up even one minute after boarding closed for your fake cruise, guards would not let you board for two hours, even though you were only a step away from the ship's gate.

This boarding procedure caused a problem for a Missouri senator who sponsored the law. This senator, an affable guy, was a member of the state tourism board, which had scheduled a meeting at the new casino at ten o'clock. The senator arrived five minutes late, and missed the boarding. Despite his protests to the gatekeeper that he needed to attend a tourism meeting onboard, he was instructed to wait until the next boarding period, two hours hence.

"But the boat is right here. Can I just step on board?"

The guard at the gate stood firm. Rules are rules. Law and order. The senator sat down on a bench, defeated by his own law. A couple visiting from out of state also had just missed the ten o'clock boarding and offered their commiseration: "Whoever made that rule is an idiot." The senator sighed, and agreed.

Leaving the casino and Caruthersville and New Madrid and the Bootheel, I had no idea that the next time I would see this area, it would look like a war zone.

Skating on Thick Ice

The digital sign by the roadside flashed a stark warning to travelers headed south: "Last chance for food and fuel at Exit 99."

At that point, I realized I was driving alongside a convoy on a mission. A line of utility trucks extended from my windshield to the horizon. Behind me the line of bucket trucks stretched beyond the limits of my rearview mirror. The convoy rolled south on Interstate 55, past that last-chance exit at Cape Girardeau, into an area that looked as if it had been flattened by an atomic bomb or a hurricane. The land was laminated in thick ice.

The trucks with their booms and buckets formed a rainbow of colors, a jamboree of logos representing scores of electric utilities from a dozen different states. They traveled single file like an army supply line, amber lights flashing, into a hundred-mile-wide glacier that draped like a deadly sash across America's belly.

Mixed into the convoy, I spied familiar red trucks from my hometown Columbia Water and Light, and the green logos of Boone Electric Cooperative. These guys from my neck of the woods had responded to the SOS, and they were in for a long slog. They knew it. Most of them had done duty like this before.

The convoy entered the war zone. As if on cue, sunshine disappeared, and a gray overcast sealed the icy cold. The invader, the Ice Storm of '09, had rolled through the day before and encased the Bootheel in a layer of ice as thick as a brick. I-55 was the only semi-clear path across this glacier, and with every mile, this armada of bucket trucks rolled into deepening devastation, past whole forests splintered by a billion tons of freezing water. On both sides of the interstate, the few remaining unbroken trees pointed their icy boughs into the ground. Hell frozen over.

A state official crackled on a radio newscast, estimating 4,000 telephone poles were down in Dunklin and Pemiscot counties. That early estimate would turn out to be woefully inaccurate. The two inches of ice that coated power lines weighed sixteen times more than the half inch of ice the lines were designed to withstand, and the power grid in a dozen counties came crashing down.

"It was a mess," recalls Travis Lynn, a journeyman lineman who ended up spending twenty-two days amid the devastation. Lynn has seen devastation before. He helped restore power in Mississippi and Louisiana in the wake of Hurricane Katrina. He says the Bootheel storm repair "was by far the worst one I've ever worked on."

Line foreman Roger Walker agrees. "The crews we worked with that came up from Alabama said they'd much rather work after a hurricane—at least it's not freezing cold!"

Just south of Exit 99, I found a fuel stop still open in Scott City, powered by a gas generator. The young attendant repeated her message through the intercom: "Credit cards won't work at the pump. Transmission lines are down." As she accepted cash from customers, she sighed, "This is terrible. This is a mess."

It got worse. I was just on the edge of devastation.

Route N plunges south of Scott City. The storm transformed the road into a swerving, undulating hockey rink. Two inches of ice separated tires from asphalt.

Amid this treachery, shell-shocked rural residents had begun to break the ice off their car doors and windshields, seeking warmth from a car heater and news from a car radio. Some local radio stations were powerless to help, with no electricity to send a signal. Eventually, the first few brave residents began to drive into towns, looking for supplies or sources of heat.

The first bucket trucks filtered into the area, facing a monumental task. The devastation was so complete, it's hard to imagine how they knew where to start. Just north of Sikeston, a half dozen utility trucks dotted Route Z, their buckets raised to surviving power poles, draped in icy lines that had crashed to earth.

I pushed south, where crews found road signs layered with two inches of ice. The storm pasted these signs like cosmic *papier mâché*, and left CSI-style fingerprints that revealed the storm's fury. Drop by drop, the rain froze on the sign faces and formed icicles off the signs' bottoms, shimmering aqueous stalactites that did not hang straight down, but curved from the force of the wind, the storm pushing and shaping the water as it froze.

A few gas stations and grocery stores struggled to open their doors, even with no power. They offered a gathering place, communal shelter in the light of Coleman lanterns.

One scene reminded me of the '73 oil embargo. In New Madrid County, residents heard that a gas station was open just south of Sikeston. Cars flocked to the pumps, and the lines quickly snaked out of the parking lot, nearly reaching the interstate exit.

Reports began to surface about an insidious predator that crept into homes in the disaster's aftermath. Some people were succumbing to carbon monoxide poisoning from generators not properly ventilated.

News reports warned listeners that some areas would not see electric power for weeks.

And the bucket crews from Columbia and Colorado and Carolina continued their work. For fifteen to sixteen hours each day, they stitched the grid back together, one line at a time, one pole at a time. They knew they might not see their families for weeks. They would miss ball games and birthdays, home-cooked meals and their own warm beds.

As the sun set behind the gray overcast, a half dozen bucket trucks retreated to a truck stop along I-55 at Benton. They joined a scene reminiscent of a science-fiction movie: a parking lot full of bucket trucks—four or five dozen—arranged randomly, as if dropped haphazardly by the same storm that summoned them here. Yellow lights flashed on their crowns and cranes as crews sat, tired occupants taking a brief respite, eating or sleeping or planning their next move.

Further south, my hometown linemen found shelter in a Blytheville, Arkansas, Holiday Inn forty-five minutes from their work site. "This was the closest hotel that had rooms available," said Vicki Kemna, Boone Electric's communications manager. "The first three nights in the hotel, the workers were in the dark. The hotel's electricity hadn't been restored yet, but they had a soft bed to sleep in. In the past, our linemen have had to sleep in their trucks while working on mutual aid efforts because cots or beds were unavailable."

Next day the sun rose to magnify the devastation. In the stillness, falling ice crackled like gunfire as it hit the icy ground. Entire highways remained closed, rendered impassable by a deadly duo of ice and a crumpled power grid. In the remote rural area between the interstate and the Mississippi River, power lines draped the highways, waiting to snag unwary travelers. Power crews and emergency workers attached red flags to the lines, or placed orange cones beside lines hanging inches above the road surface. But not all of them. There were so many. In the two counties that form the Bootheel, the storm felled 12,000 telephone poles. Twelve thousand poles!

I was losing daylight in the late January afternoon and decided to drive back to the safety of my hotel room in Ste. Genevieve. From Route 77 in southern Mississippi County, I was two hours from my bed. I turned on my headlights, and in the near distance I saw it. A power line was hanging from a broken pole on the right shoulder, and the line draped over the road, unmarked. Even at only forty mph, I couldn't stop Erifnus in time, so we hugged the right shoulder, still covered in two inches of ice. The nose of my car is shaped like a catfish, so when we hit the power line, it didn't catch her grill. Instead it skittered up her hood with a crackle, snagging the driver's side rearview mirror, ripping it off and flinging it thirty feet in the air behind me. We slid to a stop, realizing that Erifnus was lucky to have lost only a mirror, and I was lucky I wasn't fried. After a deep sigh, I opened my car door and stepped onto the icy road, walked back and picked up the shattered pieces of the rearview mirror. I was careful to stay away from the dancing power line.

Darkness was closing in. There were no houses in sight, no other cars on the road, and likely there would be none. We continued up the road toward the safety of the interstate, slower this time, eyes straining to see the next electric snag hanging over the road.

That night, I slept the deep sleep of a man who had cheated death.

Firewater & Timber, Clearwater & Beer Bongs

In an area that has been depressed since the shoe factories shut down and moved overseas a generation ago, Missouri holds one potent advantage over neighboring Arkansas: the powerful economic benefit of sin.

Many Arkansas counties still ban the sale of liquor, a virtue Missouri counties abandoned about the same time Pat Nixon's husband abdicated the throne to Betty Ford's husband.

Latching on the rim of this massive Arkansan dearth of spirits, Missouri entrepreneurs sit like vultures, just a bunt from the Arkansas line. An archipelago of liquor stores stretches across Missouri's southern border, along the most unlikely outpost roads, in the middle of cotton fields and nothing else. There, capitalism takes root, with prime commercial frontage along the battle lines of sin.

Fagus is one such outpost, sitting on the map like the head of a cobbler's nail in the instep of the Bootheel. It used to be a timber town, until they cut all the trees down. The whole zip code that surrounds this little town shows only a few dozen people.

Yet the town's solitary business thrives. "It's odd to see a store out here in the middle of nowhere," said the young woman who rang the cash register at Robison & McIver. "But Clay County [Arkansas] is dry." Indeed, in many Arkansas counties, voters still defeat the local sale of liquor. So stores perch on Missouri's borders sitting like eighty-proof ATMs to service the needs of Arkansan back-door Baptists who drive sixty feet into Missouri to buy enough hooch to wet their whistle. They come from neighboring Piggot and Rector and Corning.

"They used to not sell lottery tickets, either," she notes about her good Arkansas neighbors. "But now they do." So that's cut into her business. No matter. John Barleycorn still provides a good living, down here in the land of cotton, and the mindset of Cotton Mather.

* * *

We reached Doniphan, the seat of Ripley County, down in the valley of the Current River, where we ran smack dab into a thousand strokes of genius. Knowing the two best ways to stimulate the economy in this poor region, Doniphan struck gold by combining timber and tourism into the annual Timberfest.

Your favorite rock band doesn't come close to making as much noise as a portable sawmill rig on a vintage flatbed truck. Mick Jagger himself never jumped around as much as a lumberjack in the ironjack decathlon. "The crowd tripled the entire population of Doniphan," gushed Nancy Smith, a local writer. Just as important, she told me that "the move toward certified sustainable wood products has made great strides in the past two years." That's code for "It's OK, environmentalists. A managed forest can be a good thing." In fact, proper harvesting of forests can help areas avoid catastrophes including pestilence and rampant forest fire. Remember what Smokey T. Bear says.

I caromed through displays of old photos of the local timber industry, which was once the site of the largest sawmill in the nation. Folks gravitated to the chainsaw exhibit, including an early model that needed three men to lift it.

That night, I tapped my toes to Miss Crystal and the Codgers, who stayed true to solid bluegrass roots. During the show, it struck me that if Hank Williams were alive today, he'd still be only eighty-eight years old. Getting into the spirit, I decided to request an obscure old Hank tune, and shouted, "My Son Calls Another Man Daddy!" Folks looked at me as if I was on a lost highway.

Lumberjacking wasn't the only game in town. There's racing, too. The River Valley Lawn Mower Racing Association offers proof that in this world, you can find anything.

Next morning, I left the comfort of this clearing on the edge of civilization and drove into the deep woods. The woods are beautiful, but, hey, so are lions and sharks. I guessed my way across a half dozen gravel roads to connect the ends of backwoods blacktops. I also probably risked my life back there in those deep woods, nicknamed Marijuana County, where decades-old rumors say that booby traps await snoops.

In this poor remote region, a significant part of the economy was built on whiskey stills. Nosy revenuers were the enemy. They still are. Modern bootleggers—pot farmers—set booby traps for law enforcers who snoop around.

I have no problem with pot. And I'm not a law enforcer. But out here in the middle of the woods, one wrong move and my obituary labels me a victim. If I make a wrong turn, I might hit a trip wire and get a Steve Martin makeover:

"They'll find me with an arrow through my ears," I patted Erifnus' dashboard. And when folks read the circumstances of my death, half of them will think I accidentally wandered through a pot farm. The other half will think I was there to steal it.

As we drove deeper into the woods along this gravel path, it seemed more and more like a timberous tomb. Through the thick forests, Ripley County's zigzag roads are confusing, even without pot. I crept along dirt roads for what seemed like hours—probably twenty minutes—until I hit a blacktop road that signaled my lifeline back to civilization.

It dawned on me as we drove out of the deep woods that the biggest danger in the Ozark outback is not from pot patches or whiskey stills, but from volatile meth factories and their volatile owners who lurk in the countryside.

Not long after this episode on the fringes of civilization, I asked a highway department employee if they had detailed county maps. Of course they do. Now, wherever I go, laid across my back seat are 115 dog-eared, coffee stained, table-sized county maps that show the way, right down to dirt water crossings. The maps offer security. They've also saved the planet from at least 45,000 extra miles Erifnus would have needed to backtrack and retrace our trail.

Back on blacktop, we reached a high rate of speed when we almost ran up somebody's ass. A ten-point buck jumped in front of Erifnus, running diagonally into our path. We both were startled, the buck and I, and he dug as fast as he could go as I hit the brakes. He dodged my bumper by the length of his bob tail. The encounter gave us both a thrill, and both of us lived to remember the experience. It was then that I tested the value of my Ozark Air Bag. Now I need to work on my Ozark diaper.

* * *

Pushing south, I found a state road that wasn't even on the map, and a four-way stop in the middle of nowhere. If four cars ever meet at this intersection, I'll eat the bugs off Erifnus' bumper. This area is so remote, I passed Many Springs, Missouri, whose city limit signs were back-to-back on the same post. Many Springs, one pole.

A few miles west, I glanced at an aging hand-lettered sign on a building: "NERD PENTECOSTAL CHURCH." I did a double-take and then actually drove up the driveway to inspect it. My apologies to the Nebo Pentecostal Church, but I recommend that the sign maker remake the sign.

Further west I found a dilapidated trailer, barely inhabitable, door sprung so it would never shut tight. But bless 'em, they had a reassuring sign out front: "There is life after death."

I wondered about life in that trailer.

* * *

We beat a retreat north into the hill country, headed to a cabin at one of my personal favorite state parks, Sam A. Baker.

As Erifnus delivered me nearer to the park, the signs jumped out at me: "Transporting firewood prohibited." I knew why. In my backyard at home, my seventy-year-old ash tree looks healthy. But its cousins around Sam A. Baker have been infected with a shiny green bug called the emerald ash borer. This pest must have the jaws of a pit bull, since few hardwoods are harder than ash. That's why baseball bats are made of ash. Nevertheless, the bug kills these hardy hardwoods. So far, the ash borer has been found only in this park, brought in among sticks of ash firewood in the backs of pickup trucks from Illinois or Michigan or Ohio. But I know that for my back yard tree, the end is near.

Sam A Baker State Park snuggles into rugged foothills of the St. Francois Mountains. The park is situated along Big Creek, where it empties into the floatable flow of the St. Francis River as it whitewaters its way to vacation at Lake Wappapello. Most of the cabins were built of native stone and timber by those venerable Depression-era lifelines: the Civilian Conservation Corps and the Works Progress Administration. How venerable? A hundred thousand unemployed workers found jobs building a thousand acres of campgrounds in the state, and erected 111 lookout towers to watch for fire. They planted forty-three million trees, built and stocked two dozen fish hatcheries with a million fish. They built trails and truck roads, stone picnic pavilions and big log lodges. Most of their handiwork survives seventy five years later.

After breakfast at the lodge, we skirted the north edge of Mingo National Wildlife Refuge, and drifted east past Eaglette and Brownwood and Toga. After a pit stop in Advance, pronounced "ADD-vance" by locals, we swung through Leora, which locals used to call either Toadsuck or Crackskull, depending, I guess, on the time of day and the blood alcohol levels.

Route H ends at Webb Creek Boat Dock on Clearwater Lake. Like most major lakes around here, Clearwater is managed by the Corps of Engineers, so there's little development along the shoreline. But driving down toward the water, I passed dozens of little weekend cabins and retirement villas, modest for sure, but functional, each with its big fishing lure sitting in the carport: a bass boat waiting to take the short trip to the end of the road, which drops straight into the water. The concrete boat ramp feels a lot of rubber, where dozens of fishermen in pickup trucks back their boat trailers to the water's edge, and begin their fishing odysseys. Some of them end their perfect day of fishing by stopping at the Lower Bar, a tavern that hides in plain sight, the back of its roof tucked tight against the foot of the roadbed, its front door only a spin-cast from the boat ramp.

The bar was owned by a guy named Matt Dillon, so the fishermen behave. But maybe that's a fish story.

The lake seemed like a fisherman's paradise, but sometimes the fish play second fiddle. Despite the fact that it was dinnertime for the crappie, it was happy hour for the fishermen. There were no boats in the water, the boats were all snug in their trailers, safely attached to the pickup trucks, all parked at this secluded little bar.

Erifnus backtracked to the next blacktop junction and drove east, past idle sawmills surrounded by rotting pallet wood. A truck for sale.

Traveling to starboard on the map, south of Van Buren, we reached Big Spring, largest spring in the state. I went to the office. It's not uncommon for springs to have offices, especially if they're tourist attractions. This particular office is busier than most, because it's the nerve center for managing the Ozark National Scenic Riverways.

I found Noel Poe. He's the park's chief, and an ally in the effort to preserve our natural treasures. Noel has a relaxed style, a folksy affable aura that becomes all business when the subject turns to stewardship. He was concerned. The riverways have been victims of their own beauty, attracting hordes of floaters and campers on summer weekends. Even with federal limits on the number of rental canoes, a summer Saturday sees an endless succession of boats, resembling a life-sized Grab-A-Duck game on the carnival midway. Crowds produce trash, and worse, they bring glass bottles, and beer bongs, and other tools of self-flagellation that tend to end up falling into the stream, breaking into shards, slicing feet, affecting other folks. So Noel's crew banned glass, and beer bongs. The ban makes sense. I even support restrictions on motorboats, and prohibiting all-terrain four-wheelers from driving up and down the fragile riverbeds. But when they talk about limiting the number of beers to one six-pack per floater, I knew I would probably end up breaking the law.

Face the reality: Everybody comes to these rivers to get away from it all. Some folks come to party. Other folks come to reflect. I feel strongly both ways: environmental and impaired mental. Truth is, rivers and frosty libations go well together, both being composed primarily of water.

I just worry that if I carry no more than a six-pack of beer, I'll have to figure out how to keep six 200-ounce beer cans cold.

When I asked Noel about his crew's ability to enforce such bans, he was realistic. He knows they can't stop every transgression, and he really doesn't want to put a damper on anybody's good time. But he can't stand by idly and watch idiots destroy his river. He knows I'm not the problem, even if I take two cases of beer down a river. He knows I'll end up with more than forty-eight cans in my trash bag. It's such a simple concept: Pick up more trash than you bring in, and leave the river a little bit cleaner than you found it. Respect.

I walked to the spring. It's a stone-cold gusher, a beautiful blue blast of water boiling up from the crack at the foot of a mountain, crystal clear and as clean as the water in that plastic bottle at your fingertips. But right there on the path around the gurgling spring, I spied three cigarette butts and a beer can on the ground. The end is near.

The unfolding road awaited to take me past towns with mystic appellations like Rat and Flip and Low Wassie, Not and Gang.

Licking, Balls, & the Road to Success

Licking is in a sweet spot. According to the 2000 census, Licking was seventeen miles south of America's population center. Ten years later the town was seventeen miles east of America's population center. So the middle of America has passed Licking by. The locals don't seem to mind. Like most of us, they're more interested in paychecks than population centers.

I passed Licking's old Rawlings plant, where folks in greater Licking used to gather and sew names like Musial and Maris, Brock and Broglio on the backs of Cardinals jerseys. It was a great day for Licking when, in 1953, Rawlings, the St. Louis sporting goods manufacturer, shifted its production of all major league baseballs to this small town. From that point on, all of Preacher Roe's spitters were Licking balls.

But when the Licking plant unionized, Rawlings moved the baseball-making business offshore to Puerto Rico. When Puerto Ricans established a minimum wage, the business went to Haiti. When Haiti became unstable, they made the balls in Costa Rica. It appeared that for a long time, Major League Baseball had trouble growing balls.

Now the most visible industry in Licking is the new prison, where business is stable, and inmates make well below the minimum wage. When the rumor first surfaced that Licking might get a prison, many residents fought against the idea. They didn't want rapists and murderers and child molesters living in their backyards. Now, decades later with no successful escapes over the facility's electrified razor-wire fences, the locals not only tolerate the prison, they profit from it.

* * *

I aimed Erifnus toward the Big Piney River, soaking in the beautiful scenery on the fringes of the Mark Twain Forest. The drive went through a forest so thick it was like threading my way through a pine sweater, a trip made sweeter because this is the road to Success.

Success (SUCK-sess) joins the billion or so Missouri towns mispronounced by locals. It's a local art form, this stubborn adherence to nonconformist nomenclature.

This tiny town with an unknown population remains relatively unchanged, avoiding the trappings of, well, success. Of course, success depends on your own personal definition. Some people want money; others want a backyard full of deer and wild turkey. And driving through this obscure gateway to the big forest and the Big Piney River, I reminded myself of the two keys to success:

1. Don't tell everything you know.

We drove through neighboring Old Success down to Boiling Springs on the Big Piney River, and along backroads that pointed to the sunset through deep woods that are good for hiding from revenuers and people who want to break your kneecaps. Of course, if they ever catch you in this remote wilderness, nobody else will ever find you.

Miles of tall pine trees border the road close enough to shade its shoulders—if the road had shoulders. The pines form a veneer separating the highway from the rest of the forest, a mix of hardwoods, thick woods, and lost in the woods. The only sign of civilization hangs several miles into the wilderness, a unique display of Ozark art. During my travels, I've seen brassieres hanging from tavern ceilings, and chain saw sculptures of hillbillies. I've seen countless exhibits by yard artists—old washing machines and rusting cars up on blocks. I've seen old trailers framed in Christmas lights, bordered by rebel flags and keep out signs. But the best art in these backwoods hangs from one hot wire that drapes across the highway, houseladder high: eight pairs of shoes dangle from the wire, each pair's shoestrings were tied together and flung toward the wire like a bolo, wrapping around the wire to hang until the shoestrings rot. The lowest-hanging bolo was a pair of cowboy boots. You'd expect a pair of cowboy boots to hang over this road to Duke, Missouri.

Duke is the kind of commercial town that depends on the kindness of strangers. They come here to paddle down a remote Ozark stream. Duke supports a barbecue joint called Duke Barbecue, and a convenience store called Duke One Stop, and a fire department called Duke Volunteer Fire Department. That's about it. Canoes outnumber residents five to one, since the town is only a country mile from the Big Piney River.

At the end of a dirt road, along the bank right before the river bends against a towering limestone bluff, Rich's Last Resort waits for floaters to arrive. It was nearly seven o'clock when Erifnus stopped sucking dust into her air filter and found a sandy berm to park for the night and chill her oil pan. On this evening, I was on a mission, joined by three other musicians who had traveled as far as I, and we played music for the floaters as they beached their canoes, dragged their drunken asses up the bank, ate and drank and partied like Bacchus, and watched a full moon rise over the bluff. The last campers crawled into their sleeping bags at five-thirty a.m. With sunrise only minutes away, I tried to get some sleep before I began the next busy day.

Mid-morning we drove out of the wilderness, a trip that took the better part of an hour, past Duke and its canoe trailers, past the shrine of the hanging shoe rack, through the pine veneer. Erifnus veered north, and for miles I saw only one building, a business called Ace

Grease Service. I don't think they serve breakfast. And Erifnus was well-oiled.

We reached Route 66 at a spot where even this famous Mother Road had difficulty taming the wilderness. From Jerome through Sugar Tree to Doolittle, Route 66 cuts through the most rugged terrain along the entire length of that fabled highway. It was the last section of Route 66 to change from two lanes to four. The surrounding countryside is a great place for survivalists to hide.

That's what happened nearly three decades ago when a Rolla police officer confronted suspected burglar John David Brown. Brown shot and wounded the officer, then fled to Doolittle where he killed a church volunteer and stole the man's car. He later broke into the home of an elderly lady and bound her, then ate the raw eggs in her refrigerator.

Law enforcement officers mounted an intensive dragnet, but Brown eluded them. Eventually, 250 officers from all over southern Missouri joined in what became the state's longest manhunt, searching for Brown with bloodhounds and helicopters. Brown, a self-styled survivalist, evaded capture for two months, while searchers locked arms and combed the rugged countryside.

Brown's elusiveness became legend. Ozarks residents became accustomed to roadblocks and searches, and the manhunt inspired ballads and T-shirts. One local told me a popular story. Authorities were closing in on Brown, and when he was close to being cornered, he reportedly joined arm-in-arm with searchers to walk through the woods, and then sneaked off quietly.

The FBI finally captured Brown in an Oklahoma motel. He was sentenced to life in prison.

* * *

Even though I-44 is the newer, smoother, straighter daughter of Route 66, as the two roads intertwine the old Mother's icons are visible: ghostly gas stations overgrown with trees, and native stone walls that used to be road houses. They show their age, but remain unbowed.

Just outside Rolla is a unique apparition seen only in the Ozarks. Beside the Mule Trading Post, a giant hillbilly flails at the air like a windmill. He's a distant cousin to the tie hackers and a caricature of Ozark culture. This statue was first seen at Devil's Elbow, standing twenty feet tall, painted on both sides with a hillbilly beard and a hillbilly hat that looks like a cone head with a brim, and hillbilly overalls and a corn cob pipe, and arms that rotate backward like an airplane propeller. This giant Bunyan-sized Ichabod looks as aerodynamic as any windmill. His arms pinwheel in perpetuity, making him seem like he's logrolling, or roller skating, always about to fall down.

He never falls. And he helps perpetuate the hillbilly aura. The hillbilly stereotype. The hillbilly stigma.

Bad News at Painted Rock

Even before I arrived at the twisting trail, I knew I wouldn't get to see the area's prized possession, an obscure natural history museum tucked out of sight under a bluff. It's a series of ancient paintings on a rock face that overlooks the Osage River. As such, it's Missouri's first billboard.

Zebulon Pike saw it. And so did thousands of friends and relatives and descendants of the original artist, who painted that rock face about the same time as the Spanish Inquisition, although there's no strong evidence that the two were related.

It's hard to tell what the paintings were trying to sell, since the messages have weathered 800 years or so. Some people think one red image looks like a buffalo. But then, some people think the constellation Capricorn looks like a sea goat.

There's plenty of bad news at Painted Rock Conservation Area. The painted rock itself is not accessible by land. And authorities discourage visits by water, due to "the extreme risks of drowning, falling rocks and poisonous snakes."

Well, then. That sounds like a challenge. Remember, chickenshits also discouraged a *New York Times* reporter from taking a raft down the Mississippi.

So I lifted Gneid off Erifnus' back, put the canoe in the water and paddled past the bluff. As advertised, the red buffalo is faded and fuzzy, barely visible a couple of tree lengths above the water. But in its day, I'll bet it was a neon buffalo.

With Gneid once again safely conjoined atop Erifnus, we motored to the land above the artwork.

The spot nestles in the Osage River bluffs, just past tiny Folk, Missouri, with its cluster of houses gathered around a picturesque Catholic church. A tiny brown sign pointed to Painted Rock.

* * *

Years ago the land atop the bluff was a private retreat for wealthy businessmen from Jefferson City. It was called Painted Rock Country Club. But like so many private resorts, when the old country clubbers died off, and their descendants tired of the upkeep, they sold the property to the state.

Through the wilderness, a mile-and-a-half trail delivered me to a blufftop platform that juts off the ledge like New Hampshire's Old Man in the Mountain. Unlike the old man, this platform hasn't fallen off yet. Instead it yields a dramatic panorama of the Osage Valley, the major superhighway for our ancestors.

From this perch I could see Bloody Island. Nobody knows for sure how Bloody Island got its name. There are several stories, all sharing two common themes:

1. A search for treasure
2. Ending in slaughter

In other words, Bloody Island is a metaphor for the history of the world.

Looking downstream, just before the spot where the Osage River's mouth bites into the Missouri, my mind replayed a grisly scene. It's been two decades since searchers recovered Norma Helmig's body from the swollen Osage River. Norma was murdered. There's little doubt about that, since she was found with a cinder block tied around her neck. But her killer was never found. Oh, zealous prosecutors charged Norma's son with the murder. They convicted him, too, and he served seventeen years for a crime he didn't commit. Dale Helmig would've rotted in prison, if not for his brother Richard's dedication to proving his innocence. I played a small part, helping brother Richard organize a media campaign, and connect with *America's Most Wanted*, which aired the story twice, the second time devoting a whole hour to this tragic injustice.

Dale's conviction was overturned.

When I visited with Dale a few days after he walked out of prison, he was reflective. "On the first day I was free, it was kinda overwhelming. I kept thinking 'This is a dream.'"

But it was no dream. And no picnic either.

This beautiful river bluff is a sacred spot, or at least it was sacred to the Native Americans who flourished here before Zebulon explored it, and the country clubbers claimed it, and the clubbers' children sold it.

On my hike back from the overlook to Erifnus, I paused to pay my respects to a Native-American burial cairn, mostly obliterated by vandals. Whether they know it or not, those vandals will carry that burden into their miserable afterlife, bobbing in the boiling blood of Dante's seventh circle of Hell.

Or maybe the desecrators will be chased in perpetuity by a fuzzy red buffalo.

Dog Meat, Cement Ponds, Swinging Bridges & Noxious Aircraft

We followed the Osage River, and dipped into Meta, pronounced MEAT-uh, a quiet little town way off the beaten path, too small for a Walmart. But this is no ordinary little town. It's centered around two things:

1. The Catholic church, which feeds souls, and
2. Dog food, which feeds dogs.

Meta is the world headquarters of corporate giant Diamond Pet Foods. The company has built production plants in California and Carolina. But the owners maintain their headquarters and their lifestyle near the banks of the Osage River.

Down the road in St. Elizabeth, the Baptists outnumber the Catholics two to one, but both towns generally agree on their politics, voting three to one Republican.

That didn't stop the area from receiving America's very first stimulus project. The old Osage River bridge at Tuscumbia has needed replacing for decades. But its sparse constituency didn't have the clout to put the project anywhere near the top of the replacement list. Their best chance at replacing the bridge any time soon would probably be the result of an unthinkable catastrophe, like a school bus crashing to the river below.

So when the feds announced the economic stimulus package of 2009, Missouri's governor acted fast and did something laudable. Even amid squalls from the St. Louis mayor, who wanted all the stimulus money, and Republicans, who wanted none of it, the governor turned the first spade on the new bridge, and it became America's first project under the American Recovery and Reinvestment Act of 2009. So far, the new bridge has saved the lives of 1,308,222 greater St. Louisans, if any of them ever come this way.

Nearly within sight of that bridge, on a hilltop overlooking the Osage River, a part of your history sleeps. And I'll wager a fancy leather lunchbox full of Texas tea that most Americans probably have spent more hours absorbing this history than they did learning about Osage Chief James Bigheart or the slaughter of the bison in Missouri.

Most locals can tell you about this unique history, spawned by Tuscumbia's most famous permanent residents. You might not know them, but you know their stories. On the edge of town, Paul and Ruth Henning sleep the eternal sleep. They're in Tuscumbia Cemetery now, their unassuming gravestones in the shade of a giant cedar tree. There's no pronouncement carved in granite that "Here lie the maw and paw of the *Beverly Hillbillies*."

But their stories live on in celluloid. Although they made their mark in Hollywood, they made their final resting place in the land that produced the rich fabric of their stories, some of them only a stone's throw from this plot.

Ruth grew up here, and when she got a job at a Kansas City radio station and met her city-boy beau Paul, she enriched his life with her rural stories. Long before there was a restaurant chain focused on mammaries, Hooterville sprouted from Paul's mind, inspired by Ruth's childhood memories.

The Hooterville sisters knew about rich fabric. If their names ring a bell—Billie Jo, Bobbie Jo and Betty Jo—you're already familiar with the small town of Eldon, just down the road from Tuscumbia. The long-running TV tandem *Petticoat Junction* and *Green Acres* got much of their inspiration from a hotel in Eldon, where the old Rock Island railroad would deliver Ruth for summer visits. There, Ruth and her summer girlfriends engaged in the time-honored art of attracting boys.

As I stood beside their graves, it struck me that more people have formed their impressions of Ozarks hill people from Ruth and Paul and their *Beverly Hillbillies*, than from any history of the region. That's not surprising. Most people get their knowledge of classical music from *Looney Tunes*.

Leaving Tuscumbia is still an adventure on the back roads. No less than five swinging bridges aid in connecting Miller County. Four can support your car, if you're brave.

The fifth supports your drinking habit. I knew about the good people around Brumley, who love to party and sometimes end up in fights. So when I went to the Swinging Bridges Bar, I was glad I was part of the band. Usually people don't pick fights with the band. Beyond bad manners, fighting interferes with dancing, as dancers stop to watch grown men grope each other. But the place is charming, if you're looking for honest-to-God hillbilly culture, rustic as a ball peen hammer, and the people are friendly and appreciative that a band would venture into the backwoods wilderness to strut their stuff. Yeah, I always heard that Brumley was a rough and tumble place. Maybe it is. But the folks there treated us with respect. A few years ago, there was a murder nearby. But heck, I've lived places where there's a murder every week.

Obviously the Swinging Bridges Bar was named for the area's primary attractions. Without a movie starring Clint Eastwood or Brad Pitt, the people of the world are unlikely to unite to preserve this network of swinging bridges that hide like tax evaders in the folds of Miller County. Like drawbridges over a moat. these swinging bridges cause squeamish travelers to turn back. Not my car. Erifnus approaches danger like Harry Houdini. And those bridges fit her perfectly.

Joe Dice built them back in the late '20s and early '30s, a tremendous feat for the day, especially considering that Joe left his Warsaw, Missouri, grade school at the age of ten because he couldn't see very well. He was never formally trained as an engineer and never drew a blueprint. He built these bridges by feel, using twine to measure distance and curves, and horses to pull the wire cables across the streams. And he built them to last. He designed forty bridges, and he built at least seven of them in Miller County. Erifnus quickly found three of the four that still feel rubber tires on their backs, and we crossed all three.

The swinging bridges of Miller County are scary, since this network of spans hide in the most remote part of the world, and they're among the oldest of their kind in service. The bridges are not particularly pretty. Nor are they romantic in the sense of covered bridges like the ones Robert Waller made famous in Madison County, Iowa.

But they sure are unique. And remote. Did I mention that? It's a bad place to have a flat tire or engine failure. Sprouting from banks overgrown with jungle-sized vegetation, the supports to the old bridges look rusty. Hell, they *are* rusty, suggesting that maybe the suspension cables have been compromised by weather and time. Each bridge is a twenty-ton reminder that a chain is only as strong as its weakest link. The bridge floor is a chain of ten dozen wooden planks. Could a car fall through the old deck? As unlikely as it is that all the wooden planks would give way, don't look down through the gaps to the swirling current below.

Laying those fears aside, we searched for the fourth swinging bridge. Our biggest problem was an autumn sun that would set within the hour. Undaunted, I wanted to give Erifnus a present. She was approaching a milestone, and I timed our approach to give us both a thrill. We rolled across the Auberge Swinging Bridge as Erifnus' odometer rolled over 250,000 miles, square in the middle of that span. I got out to take a picture, but my camera had reached the end of its film roll. As bizarre as seeing a shooting star split in half, a car came up behind us. They were tourists, a young couple from Illinois, friendly as hillbillies, adventurous as Amelia Earhart. I convinced the woman to take Erifnus' picture on her cell phone camera and email it to me. She took the picture. I'm still waiting.

It might not sound like much, but it was a leap of faith for me to entrust my car's quarter-millionth birth mile to the back of an ancient bridge built ninety years ago by an unlicensed guesser.

* * *

The area is crawling with unlicensed guessers.

Case in point: Much of the business development at the Lake of the Ozarks can be traced back to one event. Flash back to the late 1960s. In a move that forever changed the face and fortune of the lake, then-Governor Warren Hearnes entered a bid to host the 1970 National Governors Conference at luxurious Tan-Tar-A Resort, one of America's newest—and most remote—four-star playgrounds. The event promised significant economic benefit, and Hearnes would get to show off the lake to other governors. Back then, the lake featured miles of undisturbed beauty along its forested shores. It was a relatively unspoiled paradise in the Midwest, and real estate developers salivated at the thought of fifty chief executives—all savvy marketers—visiting this potential land boom.

All the boom needed was a fuse.

But to win the bid, there was a logistical problem to overcome: Missouri had to figure out how to get all those chief executives and their sycophants to this remote area. At the time, the closest airports that could handle jet aircraft were more than an hour away. The resort itself was accessible only by taking chances on old, twisting, two-lane highways, the kind with dangerous angled curbs called lips.

One of the governor's resourceful gurus had an idea. Build an airport at the lake that would be capable of handling big jets. It would serve the governors, then become an economic juggernaut for the lake for decades to come. To expedite the process, the state would use state-owned land to build the runway, and the governor could use his influence with the feds to expedite the federal approvals and subsidies. Done. Missouri won the bid for the conference.

The state carved a jet-ready airstrip before you could say, "Stop building an airport in the middle of Lake of the Ozarks State Park!" Park lovers were livid, since park lovers prefer to gravitate toward the peaceful quiet of nature.

But now, when planes land at this airport with a park wrapped around it, they buzz low over campers' tents. Through a thousand ups and downs, fights and lawsuits, commercial service and the lack thereof, Lee C. Fine Memorial Airport still serves the lake today.

Park lovers did achieve one small victory: they successfully prevailed upon state officials to decommission the commercial charter for the airport, and for years only smaller private planes landed there.

But economic developers at the lake had a plan.

A few years ago, I was enlisted—ordered, really—to help dust off the sleepy airport and find a way to increase air traffic. The chair of the tourism commission assigned me to research and encourage the necessary steps to re-certify the airport for big jets and eventually enable commercial service.

The lake's tourism officials salivated at the prospect that the airport would soon feel big charter jet tires on its runway again. But the airport could not legally allow big jets for several reasons, primarily because the facility had no emergency services: no fire trucks or crews. So I worked with a local team to achieve the steps necessary to re-certify the airport's commercial status.

Lake promoters were ecstatic. But in a reckless move similar to the story of the original Oklahoma Sooner, the promoters jumped the gun. Before the ink was dry on the airport contracts, before all systems were in place, before all final approvals gave the green light to commercial air traffic, somebody invited a charter jet from Chicago to use the airport. Ironically, that chartered 737 was full of retired commercial airline pilots.

Promoters thought nobody would notice. Jet flies in, occupants drop money into the economy, jet flies out. It would have worked, too, except that the pilot piloting the retired pilots ran off the runway and got the big jet's wheels mired in the mud. A photo landed on the front page of the local newspaper showing an unlicensed jet stuck on the side of the runway.

Some locals do carry licenses. In this case, it's a fishing license. . . .

Wheaties & Parties, Cool Bull & Two Alarms

Far as I can recall, I never sat in a boat with somebody whose picture is on a Wheaties box. But if you're talking about the son of somebody on a Wheaties box. . . .

I was in Los Angeles to promote Missouri, when I faced a decision. Should I stay another day and have lunch with Arnold Schwarzenegger? Or should I return home to the Lake of the Ozarks and join some Missouri fishing greats to welcome a group of outdoor writers? The answer was easy, since Governor Schwarzenegger would be hosting 6,000 other lunch guests. So I returned home to help put Missouri's best fins forward.

Angling aficionados know that Chad Brauer joins his dad, legendary pro bass angler Denny Brauer, at the top of the fish food chain. On a crisp, cool morning, Chad joined several other fishing guides to help these outdoor writers seek the feisty bass.

Fishing is an individual sport, like swimming, diving, and pole vaulting. Nobody can do it for you. So the pinnacle of success achieved by both father and son is virtually unparalleled in the competitive sport of tournament bass fishing.

Chad Brauer must've drawn the short straw, because he got stuck in a bass boat with me. Patiently, Chad responded to my questions about the best fishing lakes in North America. For him, the Lake of the Ozarks is among the very best. Sure, it's home, and he knows the best fishing holes. There's another reason. With thousands of docks extending into the water, the Lake of the Ozarks provides some of the best habitat anywhere for fish to thrive and seek shelter.

I rediscovered the truth about habitat the hard way. While Chad showed the skill and grace of a true professional, I snagged a dock, and a cedar tree, and dredged up an old abandoned line and lure. Then I caught my first largemouth of the day. Releasing the fish back to the deep, I reaffirmed why fishermen and golfers always come back for more. They get hooked.

Later in the day, a violent hailstorm sent all boats for shelter. Even under the roof of the nearest dock, the wind pelted us with hailstones the size of shooter marbles.

Yeah, the Lake of the Ozarks provides great habitat for fish and fishermen. Unfortunately, the population growth among animals at the top of the food chain is causing stress. And the stress isn't coming from what we eat; it's caused by what's coming out.

* * *

The Lake of the Ozarks has more shoreline than the coast of California. But the lake was privately built, by the same utility company that owns the dam that failed and unleashed the torrential flood on Johnson's Shut-Ins State Park.

There's no indication that the company has had any problems with the lake's Bagnell Dam, a hydroelectric powerhouse the company owns and operates. The only horror story I ever heard about the dam involved a legend about a scuba diver. Descending to the bottom of the lake to inspect the base of the dam, the diver was swallowed by a giant catfish. I think it was an exaggeration. But nobody ever saw Jonah the diver again.

Since the lake is privately operated and not restricted by the Corps of Engineers, people can build houses and cabins and resorts on the waterfront. Early investors bought lakefront property for a song. Back in the 1940s and '50s, there were few regulations restricting the disposal of sewage. Some toilets emptied directly into the lake, or into septic tanks, which could overflow if neglected. Back then, sewage from a relatively few cabins wasn't noticeable in such a big lake. Because of the remoteness of these Ozark hills and valleys, it took decades for developers to make a noticeable splash. I can remember weekends as a kid, traveling with friends to the lake and spending whole days in a cove by ourselves. No other boats, save the occasional fisherman.

Not any more. That's a bygone era, when you could operate a sailboat without fear of being T-boned by an ocean-going triple screw speedboat.

The lake has grown up, and grown crowded, with the afflictions that come with crowds: Accidents. Incidents. Pollution.

And racing boats. Reaching speeds of ninety mph, these speedboats are faster than torpedoes, and just as deadly. These power racers can scarab from the dam to dang near anywhere in minutes. And they're everywhere, churning the water into swells that make it uncomfortable to swim and impossible to ski. The qualifications to drive one of these monsters? Gas money. Lots of gas money.

This lake has become so crowded that a 2006 U.S. Coast Guard study revealed the three most dangerous bodies of water in America:

1. the Atlantic Ocean,
2. the Colorado River, and
3. the Lake of the Ozarks.

* * *

I swung around to the northern edge of this lake to see an old friend. She's a first-generation lake resort, and she's showing her age. Route O leads to Millstone Lodge, what's left of it.

Millstone Lodge, as I remember it, is gone. Too bad. In her day, the lodge provided one of the hotspots that kept the Lake of the Ozarks steaming.

I miss Millstone. For a while, the resort boasted the world's greatest bartender. Dick was efficient, quick witted, fast with a comeback, and raked in obscene stacks of tip money. It helps that he looked like Dom DeLuise.

His method for emptying a bar at closing time still resonates. "OK, all you ugly people get outta here! You know who you are. Don't make me turn up the lights and point you out."

My view of the Millstone party was from the inside out, as a musician in bands whose members, many of 'em, either turned out to be Republicans or died. Either way, I lost contact.

Millstone Lodge exuded charm, if not class. Through billboard-sized picture windows, diners feasted on a panorama of sailboats skimming across the broad channel to the Barge, a floating restaurant, another long-time favorite watering hole that got old. The Barge sank a few years ago, a grim reminder that we all have a date with Davy Jones, in one fashion or another.

Speaking of fashion, most folks around Millstone kept their clothes on, at least outdoors. But across the channel, swimsuit shucking was *en vogue* at a new phenomenon called Party Cove. Decades later, the party is still cranking every Sunday. Over the years, Party Cove has worn out its welcome in several spots, continually relocating to new coves in successive moves up the main channel, its hordes taking over the new spot like a plague of locusts. But thirty years ago, Millstone hedonists had only a short blast through two no-wake zones to America's Party Cove. And revelers could party with impunity, since the lake's water patrol was a squirt gun compared to today's force.

The year was 1984. Many of the free-love generation had sold out and taken jobs in some obscure corner of Big Brother. But most of 'em will now admit they sneaked a peek at Party Cove. I remember my first time. One glorious Sunday afternoon, after a Saturday-night gig at Millstone, our band loaded onto a pontoon boat and plowed across the channel to become the first band ever to play at Party Cove.

Sandwiched in the cleavage formed between two giant cabin cruisers, our band plugged into those two floating bookends of power, and provided the electric Viagra for a whole new breed of water nymphs. Through twenty-five years of stretch marks and sea changes, Party Cove has evolved into the world's largest floating trailer court, with jams and jiggles, pimps and hookers, and a water patrol circling like sharks.

Yeah, we saw nakedness and debauchery. But the setting was intimate, only about eighty-dozen boats.

Nowadays there are twice that number: 2,000 boats, 6,000 people, and a serious lack of toiletry.

Like a girl who writes bad checks, Party Cove keeps drifting to new locations. For a while it found a home in Anderson Hollow Cove, nestled near a former Boy Scout camp and a former Girl Scout camp.

Meantime, the Lake of the Ozarks gets more crowded. There are so many houses and cabins, you can just about jump from dock to dock. And the first surprise for many lakefront property owners is that they don't own the water in front of their cabins. The electric company built the dam, so they control the water level. Oh, the electric company works to maintain the water level, to avoid dock damage. But shore residents are helpless to shoo unwanted water striders from their views, since their property lines stop at the water line.

Around water, property lines and property rights get people fighting mad.

* * *

Nowadays, there are two speeds through the congested lake traffic: fast or fun. If you want fast, take the bypass that cuts through the hills like a laser. If you want fun, hop on the old treadmill and travel at the speed of the slowest car.

Fun happens when you get off the superhighway and find all the cracks and crannies. Harold Koplar filled in a lot of cracks with resorts and golf courses along a spot where the lake makes a hairpin turn. It's called Horseshoe Bend, and it's much tighter than a horseshoe, really, unless your horse wears a 22AAA shoe. But the name really doesn't matter, because people name river bends the way they name constellations. If something looks the least bit like a shoe or a face, they'll name it after a horse or Judy Garland. It's the phenomenon known as "This potato chip looks a lot like Mary Magdalene."

Harold Koplar didn't name Horseshoe Bend, best I can tell, but he may have had a hand in naming just about everything else on both sides of the bend. Harold was an entrepreneur, a promoter, and a developer who had a public persona because he owned a TV station in St. Louis with call letters that followed the consonants in his last name. In the early days KPLR-TV broadcast old nostalgic movies and St. Louis Blues hockey games, and it aired game shows during the traditional news hour.

At the Lake of the Ozarks, Harold built the Lodge of Four Seasons, a world-class resort for its time, with a symphony of vacation delights including golf and tennis and swimming and shopping.

In the years since Harold left the land to his heirs, the lodge has changed: a facelift here, a divestiture there, a town's worth of condos, and at least three more days worth of golf on courses that challenge your handicap, hills that challenge your equilibrium. So the lodge survives, and Harold's family still does a pretty good job running the place.

But I miss seeing Monte Davidson, who sang country songs at a bar in the underbelly of Harold's resort, a little cantina called the Wild Times Saloon. It isn't Monte's music that I miss. I miss his barroom persona, his bull-in-a-china-shop style. Every night he rode into the saloon on Gomer, a real live Brahman bull. The bull would sway through the crowd, between tables with drinks and hors d'oeuvres and patrons, some amused, some petrified. Monte wore an electric cowboy suit that lit up like a movie marquee, and he'd sing and strum his guitar while Gomer moved through the crowded bar. I never saw Gomer get excited or kick a table over or spill anybody's drink. I think they must've kept Gomer pretty happy. I know everybody else seemed sedated when Gomer plowed through. And when he left the building, I can't recall that I ever saw any Gomer piles. But that was years ago, and I assume Gomer is glue, or stuffed, and the wild times are mostly outdoors now.

* * *

On this day, Erifnus weaved along the strip that leads to Bagnell Dam, a commercial boulevard where motorists stop to browse through souvenir shops and arcades. It's a stretch of old highway that became a permanent carnival midway, as indelible as a tattoo. During my entire youth, I marveled at the culture along this strip. Throngs of pedestrians moved faster than the cars backed up for miles in both directions, a scene one buddy described as white trash turned loose at the carny. There's nothing wrong with that, really. It's what happens when you build go-kart tracks and rickety roller coasters and carny stands with big stuffed pandas as prizes if you can master the hoops and balls and rings and bottles that tempt your skill, and shops that sell T-shirts that say, "I'm with stupid." For years these funhouses and outlet malls have cranked out fun and outlets. Most of 'em, anyway.

One fun outlet may never be heard from again. Lee Mace's Ozark Opry struck its first note in 1953, back when Branson was still a quiet little town on the banks of the White River. By the time the first '57 Chevy drove down the strip, Ozark Opry had opened a theater just up the road from the dam. For more than half a century, the Ozark Opry vibrated with pickin' and grinnin' and hillbilly humor. The opry survived the death of its founder, when Lee Mace crashed his experimental airplane into a boat dock. But recently a fire damaged the old opry, and now, at least for awhile, the place is silent.

We crossed a new bridge, the replacement for the infamous Grand Glaize Bridge. The old bridge was the site of a rite of passage for high school graduating seniors who mixed too much booze with too much testosterone. They'd walk out to the middle of the bridge and jump off, a fall of thirty feet or so, into the main channel of the lake. Back then, pretty much everybody survived the jump. Today, jumpers would risk being shredded by an ocean-going speed boat.

Much of the lakeside has been paved and populated, layered in concentric rings around the water, often extending high into heretofore forested hillsides. Pavement replaces porous soil, and after a cloudburst, the resulting runoff can really change the complexion and chemistry of the water. Meantime, in many spots surrounding the lake, the hillsides begin to look more and more crowded.

Down the road and around the corner, Tan-Tar-A Resort was the site of our honeymoon. Tan-Tar-A is a Blackfoot Indian word meaning "one who moves swiftly."

During our honeymoon eons ago, I tried to move swiftly down a slick novelty for these Ozark hills: Tan-Tar-A's ski slope, complete with its own artificial snow machine. I managed to wrench both knees at the bottom of this short slope, because I didn't know how to stop.

Cheryl didn't hurt herself, but in her only downhill ski attempt, she fell thirty-two times. If she were advancing a football, she would've punted eleven times. I finally dragged her over to the lift, which was nothing more than the world's largest fan belt, a low slung rope that looped around a low rpm spindle the size of an automobile wheel. The rope had knots in it, an Ozark equivalent to a ski-lift chair. The knotted rope dragged her up the hill to the lodge, with its warm fire and comfy couches, where she became a dedicated snow bunny. Our marriage survived the honeymoon.

* * *

Tan-Tar-A Resort survived, too. And around it, over the years in every direction, cabins and houses and businesses and tourist attractions sprung up like children and grandchildren and great-grandchildren of the first old resorts. In the early days of development, there was little planning from one building project to the next, not much coordination, few regulations. The road builders followed the developers, who followed the contours of this lake that looks like a dragon, along shorelines and roadsides.

Around the corner I found a roadside attraction that has snagged generations of kids and their caretakers off the road with its most alluring Lorelei: Its splashy blue water slides are visible from the highway.

Big Surf Waterpark is fun, as far as water parks go. Swirly tubes and wave pools. One slide mimics dropping off a cliff, which probably causes some folks to involuntarily add to the water level. Big Surf rules a hilltop, and like many such attractions, the land is covered by almost as much parking lot as park. So the runoff from their hill could be significant. I don't know if they capture the rain from that runoff to recycle through the water park.

Not long ago, Big Surf's advertising touted the park's clean water.

Well, sure, folks are concerned with the potential for pee and poo and bodily spoo to end up in pools. But I think something bigger is going on. There's been a bit of controversy lately over the cleanliness of water in Missouri, and Big Surf is trying to reassure mothers of young kids that at the water park, where the water is treated, they won't get sick.

* * *

Just a short drive southwest, there used to be a rodeo. The J Bar H Rodeo was one of the summer's best wild west extravaganzas when I was a kid, with big-time bronco busters and big stars like Rex Allen and Michael Landon. But for all the fun I had when the rodeo came to town, I remember J Bar H for another reason, another time.

It was on the Fourth of July in 1972, during an all-day rock 'n' roll fest with the James Gang and Jo Jo Gunne, Brownsville Station and Black Oak Arkansas. Tens of thousands of rock fans showed up, despite the 100-degree weather. Soon, folks were passing out from what a buddy termed "heat frustration." Promoters hired local helicopters to hover over fans and send them cool breezes. The copter noise drowned out the performers, but nobody cared by then. Sun-baked and boozy and then some, the crowd made the best of it. If Woodstock was a washing machine, this was the dryer. More like a kiln. Best I can remember, nobody died.

* * *

On the outskirts of Camdenton in tiny Greenview, we stopped at Tres Hombres Mexican restaurant, a local fixture for thirty years. I'd heard that the chips and salsa were worth the stop. Good thing. In the tradition of great Mexican restaurants, the surroundings were remarkably unspectacular. But to misquote the Bard, the food's the thing.

I sat in a dark corner, and a server immediately brought me warm chips with a wonderful homemade salsa, flecked with cilantro. In a matter of seconds, I smelled the smoke. It wasn't the familiar sizzle of fajitas I smelled; more like burning wires. Servers waded through the dining room and whisked us outside the building. Kitchen fire. I consumed only half the salsa, but in that short introduction, that was the hottest Mexican meal I'd ever had. Two alarms, I think it turned out to be.

Spuds & Space Rocks & a Nipple Tooth

It's not very crowded. That's really not surprising for a lake named after a potato. Pomme de Terre may be the world's most overlooked lake. That just means there's more walleye for me. You know you've caught a walleye when you yank something out of the water that looks like Marty Feldman.

I headed to the State Park Marina at Pomme de Terre, where Teresa Barr served up one of the world's greatest walleye sandwiches. Teresa and the rest of the marina crew are proud of this lake, and they have a right to be. It's a relaxing alternative to the crowds at Lake of the Ozarks.

But there's a fundamental difference between the two lakes. At the Ozarks, you can build a house on the shore and a dock in the water. Pomme de Terre is a Corps of Engineers impoundment, and no building is allowed near the shore unless it's a regulated concessionaire. Even though the Lake of the Ozarks is getting more and more congested, and houses are crowded together ever tighter, there's a real demand for lakefront footage.

So folks put up with the traffic, and the unfortunate boat crashes that result from over-served boaters driving in overcrowded waters whipped into sea-sized waves in the main channel. And most visitors shrug off the occasional warnings about pollution. Hundreds of thousands of people have fun there every warm weekend, in the water, in the cabins, in the restaurants and bars, the golf courses and entertainment venues lined up along the coves and highways.

Meanwhile, Pomme de Terre, the "apple of the earth" in French, remains placid and playful and ready for people. Most local fishermen don't mind that the lake gets overlooked. The walleye don't mind either. Most of 'em, anyway. I finished my sandwich, thanked Teresa, and headed out the door.

* * *

Using my detailed county maps to match blacktop to gravel to blacktop again, I helped Erifnus find Highway 83, which led to Highway 82, which led past beautiful, undeveloped rolling hills amid what's left of the vanishing prairie. The land is surprisingly rugged and remote, with long stretches of highway straightaways that dip

into valleys, presenting penetrating views of the Sac River. We rolled
into Roscoe and detoured to get a look at the beautiful Osage River,
swollen into a lake.

We passed Cedar Springs and stopped in Eldorado Springs, where
the Osage Tribe used to bring their sick to heal in the mineral springs.
When Europeans settled the area, the Osage left for their own safety,
and the springs were ignored for generations—until the 1880s when
the Hightower family rediscovered their benefit. Eventually, the
springs became commercialized, with fences to keep out the hogs
and cattle and two iron pipes delivering the healing waters—one pipe
for Democrats, the other for Republicans. You think I'm kidding.
Democrats and Republicans around here hate each other, which
is not unusual. But their hate doesn't come from budget matters or
immigration policy or same-sex marriage. It comes from the Civil
War.

Anyway, this area's biggest upheaval happened long before
Democrats and Republicans and the Civil War. . . .

* * *

Too often, travelers don't realize what their wheels are touching.
Erifnus is no different, so I accompany her to interpret the scene. Such
was the case as we moved across the Weaubleau Plateau. Weaubleau
rhymes with "low blow." Geologists suspect that at one point, the
operative phrase was, "Look out below!" suggesting that this place got
punched pretty hard by a space rock. Beneath the plateau's surface,
geologists say this spot contains "deformed strata."

If it had been left undisturbed by the meteor, the layers of sediment
beneath this area would be like sheets and blankets on a mattress after
you slept in the bed, wrinkled and folded, but layered. By contrast,
a cross-section of the Weaubleau area looks like a Jackson Pollack
painting. Some geologists point to a twelve-mile-diameter circular
feature punched deep into sediment, which leads them to think the
meteor struck in the Mississippian Period, which was before they
made cars or people or Mississippi.

At Collins, I turned toward ground zero of the meteor impact,
between the towns of Vista and Gerster, whose residents generally
are glad they weren't around to welcome the meteor. This may be the

safest place on earth, if you believe that lightning won't strike twice. Well, this suspected meteor crashed into the area about 340 million years ago, so it has long since stopped smoking. When does the statute of limitations expire on lightning striking twice?

Nearly two centuries ago, an archaeologist struck something else. Albert Koch was searching a spring along the Pomme de Terre River when he discovered the bones of a nipple tooth. That's what mastadon means in Greek. He assembled the bones and sold them to the British Natural History Museum, where that mastadon skeleton still stands on display. The bones came from what is known today as Koch Spring, which is next to the aptly named Boney Spring, and Phillips Spring and Trolinger, Jones and Kirby Springs too. So it was a handy gathering place for mastadons and other heavy drinkers.

Today the big drinkers are gone, and some of the springs are beneath Truman Lake, but up the hill Anvil Rock still acts as a sentry, same as it did 30,000 years ago when mastadons frequented these bars.

Erifnus didn't care. Impressed only by the smooth surface of Highway 54, she stopped briefly in Wheatland to let me imbibe at the Common Ground Cafe. The name is inspired, according to the menu, by Mark Twain's *Prince and the Pauper*, where the two main characters find common ground. I found natural foods and wonderful folks committed to living the life of Rodney King's plea.

I made it back to Pomme de Terre State Park, where I skidded into a campsite and pitched my tent in the dark, using Erifnus' headlights as lamps to build my shelter.

I didn't build a fire because the darkness hid any measurable amounts of firewood. What meager wood supply I might find would be smaller than kindling, strewn about a manicured campground, scoured for wood a hundred times over by previous campers. By flashlight, I planned my next day, and crawled in my sleeping bag. *Je tombe dans les pommes.*

Next morning I visited Hermitage. It's not hard to figure out which president influenced the naming of this Hickory County seat, named the year Andrew Jackson died. This area is far enough north of the Trail of Tears that homesteaders wouldn't have heard the footsteps of the surviving Cherokees along that death march. So folks around here don't mind all the references to Jackson. He'd be pleased to know that around here, a twenty-dollar bill still goes pretty far.

Heading south out of the lake area, I saw the mileage sign: "Bona 5." I grabbed my map from the passenger seat to survey my route, but it was so worn that one of the middle folds finally tore the length of the map. I now had two maps, east and west, each held together with brittle tape along their threadbare folds so that both were in grave danger of further breaking down into smaller maps. I made a mental note to retire this map and start a new one.

Within minutes I passed the longest continuous school building in the world. The school, in tiny Morrisville, unfolds along the road like a geologic timeline, one addition cabbaged onto the next. It must be a quarter mile of schoolhouse, and a perfect record of the advance of civilization, as successive generations used their best techniques to plan and build the next addition to the school. As I passed the long low building, it struck me: This is an assembly line, with the first graders entering at one end, the graduating seniors coming out the other end.

Just past Flying Feathers Game Bird Hunting Resort, a year-old calf had found a hole in his pasture fence, and was running along the road, free.

"You better go home," I yelled.

It scared him. But he was free, and he felt free. As I drove away from him I watched him in my rearview mirror. I hope he doesn't wander too far, because at some point, he'll want to return home, where there's food and Mom and familiar surroundings like the windmill with a tree growing inside it.

The structural oddities kept coming. In Dadeville, I saw the world's smallest funeral home. It might be twelve feet square, barely room enough for a casket and a preacher. I looked for the drive-up window, but saw no windows at all. Just one door to the great beyond.

Sail Missouri

Hard to believe, but it's true. Missouri is a great place to sail. Some sailors say Stockton Lake is one of the top ten sailing lakes in the nation, but I couldn't track down that rumor's origin. No matter. Even if the Book of Revelations promised great sailing in Missouri, people would be skeptical. Can't blame them. In Missouri, travelers might rank sailing somewhere south of downhill skiing.

I chartered a sailboat on Stockton Lake and scheduled a photo shoot. As I drove south toward the lake to meet the photographer, whom I'd hired sight unseen, my cell phone buzzed. It was my photographer, saying he was being detained by a state trooper in Fair Play, Missouri, for running a stop sign, and for some issue with his driver's license. He said the patrolman would release him to my custody. So I drove toward Fair Play. But before I reached that town, my cell phone buzzed again.

"Mr. Robinson, this is the Polk County Sheriff's Department. We have your photographer here in jail, and he needs somebody to bond him out."

Well then. I veered east to bail out my never-before-seen photographer. At the same time, a virulent squall line of storms ushered in a cold front from the north, dropping the temperature by thirty degrees in a matter of seconds. A stiff thirty-knot wind howled across my windshield. As we entered the town, a thunderstorm pounded us, offering strobe glimpses of the road between my wipers' swipes.

When I reached the jail, a bondswoman said my photographer was in the process of posting his own bail and would be freed shortly. She introduced herself as Shanda and handed me a card: *"Ass in a sling? Call Shanda's Downtown Pawn & Bond."* I signed over my car as assurance my photographer would show up for trial. That wasn't easy for me, risking Erifnus like that. Truth is, the car had barely enough monetary value to cover the bond. Erifnus Caitnop's hail damage complexion has earned a salvage title, making her virtually worthless to anybody but me. But I needed a photographer, and with any luck and a little less wind, we'd be filming a sailboat in a couple of hours.

When he walked through the cell door, I stuck out my hand in the most unusual meeting I'd ever had with a photographer. Oh, it wasn't the first time I bailed a photographer out of jail, just the first photographer I had to rescue before I'd had a chance to meet him.

Leaving the jail in Bolivar, I looked up at the cupola on the county courthouse, which appears to have a statue of Joan Collins on top. No, it's not Simon Bolivar, for which the town is named. His statue stands, sword drawn, across from the Bolivar McDonald's. Some things even Simon Bolivar could not conquer.

"Hungry?" I asked the photographer.

"Sure!"

I pointed to a sign advertising Cookin' from Scratch restaurant. "Can't go wrong there," I said. We ate the local favorite: homemade Kelsey's bologna, fried and slapped between two slices of bread. Then we headed for the lake. I saw a billboard with the question: *"Ass in a sling?"*

No longer, thanks to Shanda. And Erifnus.

* * *

We crested the hill overlooking the harbor at Stockton State Park Marina. My pulse quickened as I saw scores of masts, waiting patiently for mates to hoist a mainsail. Then I saw the waves. Outside the protection of the harbor, a mile of whitecaps waited like an army of Philistines.

Over the years on the seas, our sailing crew has battened down in a hurricane, and felt the sting of tropical storms. We've survived episodes with shredded sails and busted prop shafts and running aground, and fuel leaks inside hot diesel engines, and empty rum bottles with no refills in sight on the horizon. But we've never actually set sail in a thirty knot wind.

On our sailing adventures, Mike Dallmeyer is a trusted ally. More than that, he's a good friend, and we've been through the kinds of scrapes that form a strong bond between high school buddies. Mike has been the captain on my vessel more often than not, but on this late afternoon, as we approached Stockton Lake to test the wind and waves, I was the captain. The decision to sail would be mine. The storm had blown over, but the trees still danced in a steady stiff wind, a constant near-gale that wailed and whistled between cars and buildings and boats bobbing at their marina moorings.

We walked down to the marina and greeted Chris Lefferts, half the tandem that manages the marina, lodge, cabins, and campgrounds. Her husband, Harry, scurried about the docks, supervising work crews preparing for the summer season. He stopped to huddle with us about weather conditions. Even though the storm had just passed, the wind continued to gust to thirty knots. That's about the upper limit of sane sailing. We looked beyond the seawall that protects the harbor, and into a sea of whitecaps. I should've known better. I should've exercised caution. But hell, this is an inland lake, for God sakes. How bad could it get?

"You may want to wait until tomorrow," Harry advised.

"I'd really like to get some shots today," I persisted, thinking like a writer instead of like a sailor.

Undaunted, or maybe just too eager, we boarded our chartered twenty-two-foot Catalina and prepared the boat for sailing in strong winds. We reefed our mainsail, which shortens it, thus reducing the amount of wind it will catch and making it less likely that the boat will capsize. Ready for adventure, we cast off all lines. Harry wished us luck, and within a few minutes we hoisted the mainsail and glided past the seawall out into the open lake.

From way back in my memory, the phrase jumped into my conscious: "An inexperienced sailor will challenge a gale. A good sailor will handle it. A great sailor will wait on shore for better weather."

There's a reason they say that.

When we cleared the protection of the harbor's seawall, the unabated wind hit us with a blast that laid the boat over, almost sideways. Mike struggled to hold the tiller. It took all his strength to guide the boat into the wind.

Meantime, we had a major problem flapping and flopping above our bow. I crawled out on the front deck as the boat pitched violently, and tried to gather a loose jib—that's the triangular sail on the front of a sloop—and pin it down into the front hatch. Trying to gather a loose sail in a gale force wind is asking to get flogged. I'd much prefer to piss into the wind. It actually was a benefit that the jib was loose, flapping like a flag rather than catching wind. It's probably the only thing that kept the boat from capsizing. Harry circled us in a pontoon boat, yelling instructions we couldn't hear in the howling wind, while the photographer, ballcap backward on his head, shot a hundred photos of Mike and me in various stages of wide-eyed panic.

After an hour of the most white-knuckle sailing I'd ever experienced, we retreated to safe harbor. The boat was unharmed, the sailors were wet and tired but whole, and the only thing damaged was the faith in my judgment. But I knew we got dramatic photos.

Sailing energizes the senses, especially that seventh sense: hunger. We drove nine miles into Stockton to break bread at Bongo's, a delightful little restaurant specializing in Italian dishes and steaks. There, we sat down with Larry Strait, who operates the sailing school at Stockton Lake. With an easygoing manner and a gray beard, Larry exudes the wisdom you'd expect from an experienced sailing instructor. Wannabe sailors from throughout the Midwest seek Larry's instruction. They get a conscientious teacher, who's more interested in making sure students get plenty of time at the helm, rather than packing people on the boat like sardines. In a weekend, he can teach you basic sailing.

But he can't fix an overzealous sailor.

He chuckled when I told him that today, we were outmatched by the wind. We swapped scary stories about the sea. And we ate. Then our photographer gave us the bad news: His film card was corrupted. No photos of white-knuckle sailing.

"I should have left you in jail," I almost chided him. But I held my tongue, because, truth is, those photos should never have been attempted in the first place, not if I had been a great sailor. I was lucky the water spray off the lake didn't ruin his whole camera. Our crew retreated to the state park's cabins to recharge for the next day's sail.

Next morning, we found the local gathering place, a breakfast grill in the back of a nearby convenience store. We inhaled a hot breakfast off of Styrofoam plates and listened to the morning coffee council debate a range of issues, mostly related to fins and flippers.

Under sail by ten a.m., we maneuvered alongside a local salt, Harry Rowe, who could sail circles around us in his smaller, faster sailboat. But it wasn't the boat that was better than us; it was the sailor. We asked him if he competed in the Governor's Cup Regatta held on this lake every October.

"Yes," he replied, "I came in second a time or two. But it's expensive." He meant that racers take the Governor's Cup seriously. They buy new sails and gear and prep their boats to get the best advantage.

Out of my league, I realized.

On this day, our photographer captured dramatic shots of the wind in our sails. One of his photos landed on a magazine cover.

* * *

The Stockton winds can be dangerous in other ways. On May 4, 2003, an unwelcome wall of wind swirled into a nearly mile-wide tornado that destroyed much of downtown Stockton, Missouri. Another tornado from the same system decimated Pierce City, south of Stockton.

Television footage of the devastation couldn't convey the power of that wind. It knocked over tombstones, splintered almost every tree in its path. Tin roofs were ripped from their rafters and sent flying in the wind, wrapping tight as wet T-shirts around surviving tree trunks.

I remember vividly the storms that night, although I was camping with my grandsons about forty-five miles northeast of there, near Warsaw, next to Truman Lake. As I crawled into our pup tent, the thunder over the hill was getting louder, the lightning giving me more and more strobe glimpses of the dark surroundings. I lay on top of my sleeping bag and sweated in the damp warm night. The tent was breathing, billowing big, then shrinking as the pressure of the swirling air changed in fits. The boys were fast asleep, even in the impending storm. Within minutes, the storm would hit. I had a decision to make: Stay in the tent beneath two giant oak trees or move inside a trailer, with all the tornado protection offered by a mobile home.

I chose the trailer, figuring that if a tree fell on our tent, there was no chance of survival. At least a trailer offered some protection from small stuff like limbs and hail. The storm struck with a punch, thrashing and gnashing and rocking the trailer. It tore the tent stakes out of the ground. But the tornadoes missed our little spot, and we survived.

Stockton was not so lucky. Three people died in the storm, and the city was an open wound. Shock gave way to grief, and eventually resolve, as residents rallied to rebuild the town. They had lost friends, and much of their proud history, including the old jail, rocked off its foundation by the wind.

But they rebuilt the town, and city leaders realized the opportunity to design with an eye toward serving the town's biggest draw: boaters, fishermen, sailors. They built a functional town square, catering to tourists. And taking a lesson from the "Three Little Pigs," this time they built with bricks.

Blue Cats & Backroad Camps

I found my way to Warsaw, a town that runs hot and cold. It got down to a state record -40° Fahrenheit on February 13, 1905. And forty-nine years later Warsaw set the state record for highest temperature, 118° on Bastille Day, 1954.

On the edge of town, I felt comfortable as I crossed another bridge built by the unlicensed guesser. But for this crossing I had to leave Erifnus Caitnop on the side of the road. This swinging bridge still stands over the Osage River, as it has since Joe Dice rebuilt it in 1928. His original span, built in 1904, was ripped apart by a tornado, the only apparent nemesis to a Joe Dice bridge, except for time. Although they closed the bridge to vehicles in 1979, and they don't let visitors like Erifnus cross it anymore, I walked the entire length of the span.

Below the bridge flows the river sacred to the Osage Tribe, and named for them. It's also the stomping grounds of the blue catfish and the fish's savior, though Jeff Williams doesn't call himself that. He's a fishing guide, and a one-man juggernaut bent on saving the big blue catfish. The big cats, which can grow to almost a hundred pounds in a few areas of the country, used to rule the Osage River. But commercial fishermen and trophy fishermen have depleted the big cats. That's dangerous, because the big ones are the successful breeders, the moms and dads and grandparents of the smaller catfish.

Jeff told me that a recent shock test by the state conservation department showed a severely declining number of the big blue cats. "People come from all over the world for the chance to wrestle a big blue," Jeff said. He encourages fishing, cleaning and eating the smaller fish, ten-pounders or less. But when it comes to catching a giant, he gently suggests the fisherman free the hook from its mouth, pat it on the head and push it back into the water. That's a sustainable way to fish for these leviathans and generate some tourist dollars, too.

So far, the commercial fishermen aren't biting.

Neither are the wild turkeys. I stopped by Turkey Camp, a favorite event hosted by a good friend who invites a bunch of folks to a remote lakeshore spot to hunt turkey. Don't worry: The turkeys are safe. The closest most camper-hunters get to birds happens when folks take a pull on the fifth of Wild Turkey that passes from hand to hand around the campfire, bathed in the warm glow of bluegrass ballads. And every morning in the wee hours, when the fire burns low and the last refrain of "Let's Talk Dirty in Hawaiian" fades into the woods, and the Big Dipper sets over the horizon, two or three hunters wake to hunt, greeting a dozen pickers and grinners as they stumble toward bed. It's a changing of the guard.

Turkey Camp forces attendees to choose their passion: Get up early, or stay up late. Hunt or hoot. It's a metaphor for lifestyle. For the record, I generally hang around the hooters.

Just up the road, folks around Deepwater know how to hunt and hoot. At one time the area offered jobs in the strip mines, which dredged the two most important ingredients for building brick shithouses: coal and clay. Actually, much of this high-quality clay was fired into tiles. Nowadays, the children of the old miners find work wherever they can, and it's not a sure thing.

So they're good hunters. For food, and for bargains.

The town has shrunk. Main street has too many empty storefronts, no different than 200 towns I'd already seen. But Deepwater still has a spine, and its roots run, well, deep.

Erifnus waited one evening while I walked into Carol's Place, the local watering hole. I ran into an old buddy who warned me, "There may be fights." He should know. As an area attorney, he'd counseled a fair share of the fighters for one misstep or another.

It wasn't long before I ran into Carol, who was flamboyant in her generosity, saying, "Order anything you want from the bar. I got it." A couple of beers later, I got the bill. Carol was nowhere in sight. Wrong Carol. The owner, Carol, was wearing a red T-shirt like all the other help scurrying around the bar, through a crowd so tightly packed it would make a sardine uncomfortable.

The Deepwater Festival was raging outside with carnival rides and musical entertainment. Still, the tavern was packed asshole-to-elbow with folks who simply wanted to drink, and maybe fight. And sing. Carol knows the power of alcohol: It makes the brain feel the need to express itself, and on this evening, folks were lined up to prove they were American Idols. The generally accepted translation for the word "karaoke" is "sing a few bars and prove you're a fool." But the singers and listeners were having fun, and nobody was throwing punches yet.

I paid my tab and left. Outside, a county sheriff's car, lights off, sat at an intersection a block away, trolling for drunks driving away from the bar, dumbasses who think they're invisible and can piss—or drive—anywhere. It's the same kind of opportunity a shark must feel at the edge of a reef.

Full, I knew I needed to seek shelter, so I grabbed my sleeping bag out of the trunk, and picked a spot to sleep, across the street in the carnival grounds, in the cool under the portable trailer of a sno-cone vendor. The deputy, intent on traffic, never bothered me. Next morning I left a tip in the door of the sno-cone trailer and headed for the birds.

The birds hang out just north of Montrose, in a wetlands conservation area made for ducks. And geese. Not much else. Hunters want to keep it that way.

I circled around through Bullard down to Appleton City, home of the world's best community organizers. These activists call themselves the West Central Community Action Agency, and when I first noticed them back in the '70s, they were doing a pretty good job of weatherizing five or six old homes per month. Over the years, that number increased to about forty homes per month.

Weatherizing homes makes sense. It offers a more stable return on investment than the stock market. Most often the recipients are elderly people on fixed incomes. Simple inexpensive weatherizing makes their homes less expensive to heat and cool, and they use less energy.

The weatherization program fixes two problems. Instead of subsidizing inefficient homes through cash payments to utility companies, the weatherization program gets to the root of the problem. Fix the damn holes that let the heat out.

* * *

Lowry City hides on old Highway 13, bypassed by a sleeker, faster, less superstitious superhighway 13. So the town doesn't have much of a presence on the main road. It hides just out of sight, like a hundred other towns whose hearts got bypassed. If you're cruising at breakneck speed past Lowry City on a Wednesday or a Sunday, hit the brakes.

Dip into town and delve into the best fried chicken this side of the pulley bone. Landmark Restaurant is on Main Street, and for more than two decades, the place has attracted diners from everywhere to ingest succulent yard birds.

Only a minute south of there, I found a giant rock outcropping so big they gave it a name: Dave. No shit. *Dave.* Well, its technical name is Dave Rock Natural Area, and I'm not sure which Dave it's named after. But the rock forms a glade, nearly a quarter mile long and an eighth mile across, big enough to land a fleet of helicopters. I waited around for an hour. No helicopters, but a whole battalion of stripe-assed lizards.

So I drove on down the road and discovered another outcropping, this one made of cheese, with a name made with cheese and a cheesy story to go with it. It all began down by the Osage River back before I was born, when dozens of milk trucks rolled into the Riverview Cheese factory at all hours of the night to deliver their milk and turn it into cheese. This process continued undisturbed for most of my youth, until Truman Dam came along and guaranteed that the factory would be inundated by Truman Lake, which was good for geese and fishermen, but not good for cheese. So they moved up the hill and changed their name and like all great cheese factories, they opened a car wash. But as the cheese got more popular, the car wash didn't, and it shut down.

These days, a bus wash might work, since Osceola Cheese gets thousands of visitors from buses headed to Branson. The bus drivers know that Osceola Cheese has eight bathrooms. Even with the short wait for a bathroom, it makes sense that a gift shop would evolve.

Somebody named the gift shop Ewe's in the Country. But that's OK, because usually the next bus stop on the way to Branson is Precious Moments, featuring a replica of the Sistine Chapel, including a ceiling reproduction of Michelangelo's famous masterpiece, except that the Precious Moments painting features doe-eyed cartoon characters. So Ewe's in the Country kinda gets folks in the mood.

Erifnus waited wistfully beside the car wash that no longer washed cars. I bought a bag of honey mustard pretzel chunks, and we disappeared into the wilderness.

The road from Warsaw to Clinton has a fun string of tasty town names: Tacker is so small it doesn't even show up on Google. Racket serves homemade ice cream at Grand River Resort. Coal got its name bituminously. But the crown jewel in this archipelago shines, even through tough times. . . .

Tighten Up

It's tough when everybody wants a piece of you. It might be because you're pretty, or rich. It might be because you've left a trail of bad deeds. But it's especially tough when people want you just because of your name.

Tightwad struggles. Oh, the town is doing OK, even after it lost its two major industries: the post office and the bank. That duo was their biggest draw. Taxpayers from hundreds of miles around used to drive into town on April 15 to postmark their tax returns from Tightwad. No longer. The post office closed.

But after a hiatus, the Tightwad Bank is back in the bucks, and seems to do a good business.

The town's most visible struggle is holding on to its city-limit signs, popular among thieves who incorporate the signs into their trailer house décor. It's easier than stealing a Picasso, and the Tightwad sign probably looks better on a trailer wall than a van Gogh.

Everybody wants a piece of the town's name. So to keep people from stealing the signs for their bedrooms, the state—or somebody— encased the city limit signs in steel frames, welded to each signpost. Every time I cross the city limit of Tightwad, I reaffirm that this is the most secure city signpost in the state.

Near one of those signposts sits a dance hall. Rural dance halls stand out from the crowd, using flashy neon beer signs and roadside marquees on wheels, backlit and beckoning with sin specials. The dance hall's neighbors, the rural churches, respond with their own signs and roadside marquees with messages about fighting sin. It's serious business, this battle for the souls of sinners. I feel strongly both ways.

The Tightwad Tavern is one of my favorite roadhouses, a wild wooden monument to the world of juke joints and dance halls that hide out in the sticks. It's a lakeland hideaway for folks from Kansas City, and they come down to cast for fish and fun. The bar is as rough hewn as its patrons, in this tiny town of sixty-three souls. On Friday nights, the place fills up with fishermen from nearby Truman Lake and locals from Clinton and Warsaw. Everybody uses liquor as bait or lubricant, depending on the gender and the inclination. Bands from Kansas City make it a weekend vacation, trolling for fish during the day, trolling for adoration at night.

A jack-of-all-trades entrepreneurial graybeard by the conspicuous name of Wino built the bar. He knew what he wanted, being a lifelong roadie for some big name rock 'n' rollers. At least he drops big names. I believe him. After all, he created the world's greatest authentic road house in the middle of nowhere.

Wino sold out and moved to Texas. The bar changed names. But it still rocks when the bass masters shuck their boats and the ass masters shake their booties.

* * *

Sometimes you walk into the past quite by accident. We finished a music gig in Tightwad late one Friday night. It's a thirteen-mile drive through Coal to the house where I was staying, outside Clinton. Our harmonica player and sober chauffeur reminded me, "We're making kraut tomorrow." Yeah, right. I crawled into bed and forgot all about it.

Next morning at seven a.m., here came the kraut makers, clanking their big crocks and cabbage shredders. It was raining that morning. So I did what anybody would do in that situation. I rolled over and went back to sleep. But krautmaking is a noisy business, and soon I joined the group to make thirty pounds of kraut.

It's an ancient art. And really simple, using the two cheapest items in your grocery store: cabbage and salt. The harmonica player had culled forty-nine good heads of cabbage from a farmers market. We cleaned the heads, and shredded them on a board with rails, a fancy plane grater, mixed the shredded cabbage with pickling salt in an eight-gallon crock, and mashed the mixture with what looked like a wooden fencepost until the mash sat comfortably in its own juices. I took my turn pounding the shred to the beat of Ingrid Lucia & the Flying Neutrinos.

Making kraut is easy as, well, making kraut. Grab a shredder, and keep a pinch of salt handy. Shredding is a little messier than playing the washboard, and a whole lot less fun. But if cabbage isn't exciting, it *is* health. Just pushing a vegetable the size of a Chicago softball through a shredder is an upper body workout. The whole process took less than a morning. We filled the crock full of bruised cabbage and covered the top with yesterday's newspaper to keep the flies out of the ferment, and forgot about it for six weeks. That's how you make kraut. Bratwurst is a little more involved.

I thanked my compatriots for the kraut lesson and caught the scent of a carnival that unfolded on the courthouse square in downtown Clinton. Clinton is the baby chick capital of the world, but it wasn't chicks I sensed as Erifnus nosed into a parking spot a safe distance from the bulbous buckets attached to whirling mechanical octopus arms.

Mixed in with the familiar carny smells of hot grease and tobacco were the turdular calling cards from two bactrian camels. The pair were docile, even while wild children rode their humps, proving why this breed is the world's longest-serving beast of burden. Camels are cute animals, with long eyelashes and longer legs. They're famous for their ability to go long distances between drinks of water, and even longer distances without taking a shower.

Folks were excited because a bike race was coming through town. This wasn't any ordinary bike race. It was called the Tour de Missouri, featuring an international field of the best racers on the planet, including Lance Armstrong, except Lance Armstrong didn't show up. Hurt or something. It didn't really matter, because the race came and went in the span of about ninety seconds. I had a better view of the dozen or so highway patrol cars that led the bikers through town. And all I could think was that I missed a great chance to speed out of town in the other direction, since all the law enforcement seemed to be escorting the race.

Erifnus took a shower at the local car wash, and we jumped onto Highway 52, headed for Sedalia. In a matter of minutes, I saw the skyline of Jugtown, USA. The Calhoun grain elevator is a wooden relic, standing four stories above this little town with its legendary jugs. Calhounians are proud of their jugs and their rural heritage. Upon closer inspection, I learned that there used to be a jug manufacturing plant there. I suspect their jugs held just about everything . . . kraut, corn liquor, silicone.

Gustav Spills His Guts

Just outside Windsor, Gustav's guts started spilling. Gustav had slammed into Louisiana as a Category 4 hurricane, and plowed north through Arkansas into southern Missouri. By the time it reached Sedalia, the storm had devolved into an extratropical depression, which meant that the system was going out of business, and the heavy clouds were liquidating all over the place.

Up ahead, through waves of rain, I saw my oasis from the storm, the warm glow of yellow light shining out of the windows of an old railroad dining car. Shifting wind gusts pushed me into the parking lot next to this old relic of the Katy Railroad, converted to a smokehouse restaurant called Kehde's Barbeque. Ducking under the restaurant's awning, I shook off the rain like a wet dog and took a window seat inside the dining car.

The great thing about a railroad dining car is that every table is beside a window, and the server has only one runway to check on guests. Linear. Efficient. Outside, the wind pushed sheets of rainwater against the big picture windows, and strong gusts gently rocked the dining car. The storm did what storms often do: electrify the senses, causing otherwise sane individuals to leave the dry comfort of their homes to seek food. On this day, everybody in Sedalia had the same idea: Brave the storm for comfort food at Kehde's.

John Kehde fixes a lot of fried sides, which his menu calls baggage: fried pickles, fried green tomatoes, fried portabellos, and five types of fried potatoes, including fried sweet potatoes. But this is a barbecue joint, and barbecue is about smoke, the sweet scent of which permeates the old rail car right down to its steel wheels. I looked at the menu, which was only a few pages short of a Tolstoy novel. The prosperity sandwich leaped at me, its burnt ends sprinkled with bits of barbecued ham. The meal gave me strength to tilt against the storm, and the weight to drown if I drove into a ditch.

Erifnus shot north, in an effort to move out of the storm, but made it only a few miles out of town when torrents of rain suggested we seek higher ground. Detouring to the top of a high cliff, I stopped to see an old friend. On a clear day, she's hard to miss, built on the edge of this bluff and sticking out of a forest canopy like a Bavarian castle. But on this day she was shrouded in rain clouds.

Her gestation period took thirty years to complete her thirty-one rooms, sprawling along the cliff in the arts and crafts style of the 1890s. Her builder was an attorney, a deft politician who helped establish the Missouri State Fair in Sedalia. Nowadays his blufftop fortress, the Bothwell Mansion, is a state historic site, and it suffers from an affliction common to most of us as we mature. At a distance, it's regal. Up close, you see its age spots.

The house has every ingredient to be haunted. It's isolated, a perfect playground for poltergeists and paranormals lurking behind its stone walls, under its gabled roof, at the edge of a towering cliff from which tormented souls can leap off and die. I greeted the guide, who met me at the door with an incredulous look, as if to say, "Why are you out in weather like this?"

I wanted to say that I came here to ride this castle when it loses its grip and falls off the cliff. But I held my tongue. The guide showed me around. We walked up the spiral staircase through the turret that guards the castle and peeked into the howling storm from third-story windows capped by gables worthy of Vincent Price's visage. Lightning struck nearby, illuminating the empty driveway, a waiting stage for a big silver hearse. Lightning struck closer. This might be the castle's last gasp if it takes a direct hit, and dies in a conflagration of fire and rain and steam. It's a wonder the old place has survived its hundred years. To be sure, angry taxpayers today would holler like a rodeo clown about the purchase and preservation of such a monstrosity, because angry taxpayers know that the end is near.

I thanked my guide and joined Erifnus, who was enduring a heavy thundershower in the parking lot.

We rejoined the unfolding pavement, pushing into the storm. An hour north, I traced the entire length of Highway 11, and as Erifnus shimmied through turns as tight as an Ozark mountain road, her headlights began reflecting off the heavy rain, signaling the advent of nightfall and the continued good health of Gustav, the ragged remnant hurricane.

In the middle of the storm in the middle of the night, in the middle of rural America, I reached New Boston, where a right angle in the road slowed traffic to ten miles an hour. Hell, if you slow down that much, you might as well stop. Appropriately, local folks erected two taverns and a hotel at this hairpin in the highway. The town's population struggles to reach a dozen, but nightlife seemed to be hopping, with cars parked solid along the main drag.

Erifnus kept going, goaded by my right foot. Despite her advancing age and wiper blades that played like finger painters on the windshield, she handled water pretty well. Until we got in a little too deep . . .

Stuck

Next day I found myself walking. I'd left Erifnus mired in mud, mostly because of my own dumb persistence to take shortcuts.

It was Sunday afternoon, only a few hours after Gustav had dumped a foot of rain on the fields and forests of Knox County. We had tried a shortcut between two blacktops. My detailed county map promised that County Road 246 was a gravel road, about three miles long, winding past two cemeteries. So I knew it was traveled, at least by pall bearers.

But as we drove deeper, the road deteriorated from well-kept gravel to muddy ruts. I persisted, forcing Erifnus to slip and slide past the two cemeteries. I was careful to keep her starboard wheels on the shoulder, her port tires along the center crown of this slickened path, straddling ruts that were a foot deep. As the road condition grew steadily worse, Erifnus eventually slid into the ruts and stopped dead in her tracks.

Stuck. It was almost six p.m. In the distance, I could hear another heavy thunderstorm approaching. I climbed out of the car to survey the damage. Her oil pan sat snug against the muddy crown of the road; Erifnus was high centered. The passenger-side wheels dangled in a deep rut, and vegetation pushed against that side of the car, making it hard to see how hopelessly stuck she was.

Worse, I wasn't dressed for a fixit. My dockers were no match for the mud, which ranged in consistency from cake mix to quicksand.

My city slicker shoes slipped and slid as I began to walk to the top of the hill, to look for any farmhouse nearby, though I knew it might be miles to the nearest living neighbor.

Near this very spot ninety years ago, my grandfather almost froze to death when his car broke down in a blizzard, and he tried to walk to the nearest farmhouse. He was saved by a passing farm truck. On this late Sunday afternoon, in the muddy middle of nowhere, I knew I wouldn't see a farm truck. Oh, maybe that silver hearse would come along, and the Grim Reaper would give me a lift.

Almost at the crest of the hill, I spied my saving grace. On the side of the road sat a bundle of sticks, a dozen branches, about as big around as your wrist and three to four feet long. I grabbed an armload of sticks and headed back downhill to Erifnus. I positioned the sticks in the ruts behind all four tires, shoving the small ends as far as I could push them beneath each tire. In reverse gear I slowly let out the clutch and rocked backward onto the sticks. Erifnus gained traction and backed up four feet, her oil pan sliding along the road's crown. Then she mired in the mud again. We repeated this maneuver three times. The last time, I couldn't get the car to rock backward onto the sticks, so I gunned her engine up to 4,000 rpms, and her tires finally caught the sticks, firing them forward like rut-seeking missiles. Erifnus lurched backward toward the water crossing at the bottom of the hill, and I used her momentum to roll out of the ruts and back onto the high ground. Erifnus was free. I looked like a 170-pound jockey atop a real mudder.

In first gear, we crept up the hill, careful to stay out of ruts, using every inch of road width to zigzag up the hill. The road condition at the crest of the hill was better, and we crept carefully for another mile to blacktop.

We made it to Edina, which, by the way, is a lovely name, evolved from my two favorite English words: eat and diner. Or so I believe. Anyway, the Blue Room was a great little place that served beer and pool and Pepsi, and tempted diners with an Elvis-like specialty: sour cream fries. Better still, they didn't shun a mudder.

I cleaned Erifnus at a BP station, which, given the company's history, should be well-equipped to clean up shit. But in all this billion inches of rain, the gas station's windshield squeegee bins were dry. A helpful lady attendant brought me a bucket of water. I thanked the station attendant for the bucket of water, and launched into another thunderstorm, and more uncharted territory. Erifnus had a floppy wiper blade on the driver's side, but we forged ahead toward the storm anyway. The sky was an eerie gonna-getcha green, and a fleeting calm flowed ahead of the black horizon that seemed to hesitate before unleashing a line of rolling sky breakers.

A short detour east of Edina brought me face-to-face with Troublesome Creek, bank full from the previous day's cloudburst. Troublesome Creek got its name decades ago because somebody found it troublesome, I suspect. Today, the trouble comes from sediment and pollution. According to conservation officials, erosion pushes tons of topsoil into this stream, a terrible loss of great farmland, which takes decades for Mother Nature to replace. To make matters worse, in a perfect storm, creatures who drink that water might get a toxic cocktail of fertilizers, pesticides, herbicides, and animal waste.

"CAFOs [confined animal feeding operations] are expanding in the basin," say officials, "especially in the Troublesome Creek watershed, where they may have significant negative impacts on water quality." CAFOs produce a lot of shit. One medium-sized CAFO can produce a city's worth of hog poop, which must be stored somewhere. Accidental releases of concentrated animal poop into the stream can cause trouble. Somebody drinks that water. Troublesome, indeed. The end is near.

There's another kind of runoff, too. I continued to see dozens of abandoned farm houses. Families have vacated them, no longer able to make the family farm work.

I stopped to reset the windshield wiper. A car passed, and the passenger shouted, "Don't get wet!" Seconds later the storm hit, and just down the road the shouters pulled into a gravel driveway and ran from their car to a house. They got wet. As I passed, I honked and waved at them through sheets of rain. They paused to see who honked, and just got wetter.

Several more times I stopped to rethread Erifnus' wiper blade onto the metal wiper arm. During one stop, a friendly local shouted from his front yard to see if I needed assistance. Right neighborly. And valuable, during the storm. I declined, thanked him, fixed the blade, and drove on.

It was getting dark when I drove thru LaBelle, the Queen of the Prairie. Stacked next to what looked like an old hotel were at least a hundred bicycles, massed together in one steel pretzel. A watchman walked along the bikes from one end to the other as the rain lessened. I never saw any cyclists. Maybe they were huddled in a shelter somewhere nearby. Or maybe those bicycles were for sale.

We slithered south through Knox City and Steffenville and Emden into Philadelphia, the village of brotherly love. Philadelphia is one of those shrinking farm towns that doesn't have a downtown or a main street any more. But it still has a heart. Some of my best meals have come from the collective effort of the cooks of Philadelphia, at family reunions, after funerals.

Philadelphia is a suburb of Greater Palmyra, which calls itself a Character Plus community, stressing the importance of self-control, integrity, responsibility, trust, honesty, motivation, kindness, self-esteem, respect and sportsmanship, all of which were lacking back in 1862 during the Palmyra Massacre, an event that shocked the nation, even during the Civil War. A Union sympathizer was missing, so the Union took ten hostages and promised to execute them if the sympathizer wasn't found in a few days. Sure enough, no *habeas corpus*. And the execution took place.

But things seem better now.

Eagles & Englishmen & Bent Tree Furniture

In a dark night made darker by a raging thunderstorm, Erifnus and I limped across the Mississippi River. We headed to a Quincy, Illinois, Holiday Inn. The storm had damaged Quincy's electric grid. Trees and power lines draped in surrender along streets. Stoplights had been knocked out, and drivers had to rely on hand gestures to take turns through intersections.

A song came on the radio: "Longneck Bottle, Let Go of My Hand." I pulled into the Holiday Inn and fulfilled the intent of that song, thrice.

Next morning, from Quincy we headed north, where Erifnus performed one of her favorite tricks. She reentered Missouri without rolling. We rode the oldest continually operating ferry across the Mississippi. At least it's the oldest right now. But the ferry is plowing into the headwinds of change. Since 1844, the *Canton Ferry* has forded this giant river with grain and goods on its back, animals, too, and pioneers on their way west.

Over that time, the cost for vehicles to ride the ferry has increased 1,000 percent, from fifty cents to five dollars. Captain John and Captain Teddy take shifts operating the modern incarnation of this 170-year-old ferry. The whole thing is driven by the *Paul B*, a powerful tug lashed to the side of a flat barge and its cargo. The ride is a dozen times faster than the old 1844 ferry, which relied on two horses on a circular treadmill that powered two wooden paddle wheels. That would've been a wild ride.

With big diesel engines packed into the tug, I felt safe. Erifnus was silent. The trip takes only a few minutes, and even on the mile-wide Mississippi, you're never far from land. Still, this is a ship, so it's ruled by the two immutable forces on this river: the water and the U.S. Coast Guard.

The orange life ring on the barge railing bore the name *Olen Fretwell*. It's a ninety-ton vessel built in Monroe, Louisiana. On water, almost every craft small or large, powered or not, has a name. In the vast roster of human appellations, covering the billions of people who trod this earth, there have been millions of John Smiths, I suppose, and thousands of John Robinsons. But there's only one Olen Fretwell, so far as I can tell.

Well, now, thanks to whoever named this barge, there are two.

Beside the ferry dock on each riverbank, there's a mailbox, and little else. I don't know how often mail crosses the river, but the mailboxes are a reminder that on the river, mail is king, and river etiquette awards the highest priority right-of-way not to the biggest barge, or the one with deadly cargo, or even the boat with human passengers. Nope, the one that carries U.S. mail goes first. I didn't ask, but I'd wager that these river pilots keep a box in the pilot house with one letter, addressed and stamped, always ready to stick in one of the riverbank mailboxes, so they can claim right-of-way as they cross the river. If Americans ever make the mistake of killing the U.S. Postal Service, I wonder if they'll give FedEx the right-of-way?

From the ferry, I gazed to the top of the towering hill behind Canton. There, a dome stands above the treeline, its shape and style reminiscent of Jefferson's Monticello, and it crowns Culver-Stockton College, the alma mater of every one of my family members but me. The ferry eased up to the riverbank to discharge its rolling stock, like it has at least a quarter million times, by my estimation. The ferry released us, and Erifnus rolled onto *terra firma*, between a conservation boat ramp and a campground scattered with a dozen camper trailers. In the rearview mirror I could see the ramp to the ferry and a sign next to the ramp: "Flash lights for service." Nowadays it's not a busy ferry, except for grain trucks in the fall.

On this day, I exchanged waves with a couple in a sedan that had driven up to the queue to watch the ferry. But I saw no activity around the campers, no campfires, no children playing. I guess most of the campers were fishing on the river. I heard the unique cry of one fisherman, and looked skyward to find the source of the cry. Circling high above my head were three sleek birds, big birds, black as night. I knew by their size, their movement and their coloring that they were young bald eagles, not yet wearing the white plumage that will someday frame them.

We left the ferry and the fishers to their business, drove into town, and hugged the Mississippi River down old Highway 61, now renamed Route B, less busy these days since the travelers with serious deadlines take the superhighway on top of the hill. Nowadays, Route B feels the wheels of locals, mostly, and visitors to the college.

And tourists looking for a river view or a ferry or an eagle.

I motored south, keeping the Mississippi at my elbow for miles, and left it only briefly to take a field trip to the banks of the Salt River, where a sesquicentury ago the Marion Rangers prosecuted their part of the Civil War, sort of. Their conquests were not noteworthy, and they only engaged in one midnight skirmish, when they shot and killed a poor innocent fellow who happened to ride his horse within their nervous sights. They disbanded when they learned that a Union regiment was bearing down on them, led by a colonel named Ulysses Grant, as later learned by the scribe of the Marion Rangers. His name was Clemens, and he would later call himself Mark Twain, and the murder of that innocent horseman greatly affected him, as did the other miserable aspects of war. In *The Private History of a Campaign That Failed*, Twain admits "that war was intended for men and I for a child's nurse." As the ragtag rangers wandered across "land that offered good advantages for stumbling," he learned something else: "I knew more about retreating than the man that invented retreating."

I retreated back to Hannibal.

With little effort, Highway 79 from Hannibal to St. Louis kept me entertained. It's a designated national scenic roller coaster, and at each apex, vistas become unavoidable.

My cell phone rang.

A television producer from Great Britain was calling, looking for stories as her crew prepared to retrace the journey of a world-renowned nineteenth-century novelist who traveled along the Mississippi River. But the novelist is not who you think.

I told her about the treasures along Missouri's east coast, even as I traveled it in real time.

I told the producer what I saw, and she delighted in the prospect of discovering the American art of the Provenance Project, stretching from Hannibal past the Victorian masterpieces in Louisiana to the towering river cliffs at Clarksville. It was fun to point out that her visit likely would coincide with the arrival of wintering bald eagles.

She was intrigued by the trip, even before she would arrive at the home town of this river's preeminent novelist. But she also was interested in the river south of St. Louis, because that was the route traveled by Charles Dickens, the star of her documentary. We talked about the vistas along the Mississippi below St. Louis, the mile-high apple pies in Kimmswick, and the settlement of Ste. Genevieve, lovingly preserved so that Dickens would recognize it even today. And we talked about Cape Girardeau and New Madrid, and their significance as two historic river ports near the confluence of the two great rivers where the waters of eastern America flow into the Mississippi.

Yes, she'd see Missouri's coastline the way Dickens saw it, from the Texas deck of a great American steamboat. Nowadays it's a rarely-employed perspective.

I was awed by a new perspective: As we chatted across 4,000

miles, each of us learned something. She learned about Mark Twain's hometown. I learned about Charles Dickens' journey.

Dickens was twenty-three years older than Twain, and Twain was such a Dickens fan that on Twain's first date with his future wife, Livy Langdon, they went to a Dickens lecture in New York.

We rolled into Clarksville, the last Missouri town whose business district faces the Mississippi River. Even today, hundreds of visitors still come by river. Never mind that they don't buy anything. They are attractions themselves. And I remember the first time I met them. . . .

* * *

"Don't be disappointed if we don't see any eagles," I warned my two young daughters as we drove round the last curve before we reached the river. A frigid January had tamed the top of the Mighty Mississippi. Only the churning water below the Clarksville lock and dam kept the ice from forming over a pond-sized pool.

That's where we headed.

As it turned out, we weren't the only visitors. The river came into view and, surrounding it, more white-headed sea eagles than any of us expected. You know them as American bald eagles. They were everywhere, in the sky, in the trees, on both riverbanks. Must've been a thousand, by my estimate.

Hitchcock never saw so many birds.

They were flying and fishing and tumbling through the air, and doing all the things that large birds of prey like to do. We did what we like to do: We watched. We walked. We ate. Then we left for Hannibal, driving up Highway 79, along Missouri's Great River Road. We vowed that we would return, when we had more time. That was a generation ago.

The intervening years have witnessed even more eagles. But queens are scarce.

The queens used to pass Clarksville a dozen times a year. But the steamboat *Delta Queen* has been docked permanently, and the *Mississippi Queen* has been scrapped, leaving the *American Queen* as the sole sister to ply the Mississippi. A few years ago a new paddlewheeler joined the fleet, but she's diesel-powered. And Clarksville's modern new port for the queens—a new port that allows steamboats to sidle up and drop shoppers on shore— is lonely for big paydays.

Still, the artisans persist along more than a dozen storefronts. Jewelry makers. Furniture makers and potters. A boat builder.

I entered the store of a soap maker.

"Open that one." I pointed to a vial of frankincense. From earliest childhood, I could recount the story of the three kings and their Christmas presents. Gold. Myrrh. Frankincense. But until my fifty-fourth year, two of those three gifts had remained a mystery. Tell you the truth, I haven't smelled much gold, either.

Geri, the attendant at Bee Naturals, plucked a slender vial from a rack holding scores of essential oils. I took my first whiff of frankincense. Then myrrh. Well, then. Been there, done that.

Up the street, Bent Tree Furniture's official greeter is Buddy, an adopted Jack Russell terrier mix. I patted Buddy as he accompanied me around the store. This is not your stodgy old run-of-the-mill furniture outlet. The tables, the chairs, the bed frames are made of bent hickory and willow branches, twisted and splayed and fanned out in patterns that excite the eye. No prefab laminated chip-mill products here.

In a neighboring store, I found a comfy theater seat behind a huge picture window overlooking the glassblowers' studio at Clarksville Glassworks. It's really more of a performance arena. I was lucky during my visit. Owner Gary Rice corralled his assistant and two artisan buddies, and they created the only ever attempted four-way, blown-glass creation. The effort became a circus of intensity. The four-fluted bulb looked kinda like a glass tire iron, and as four blowers put a final puff on the piece, it fell from their collective grasp and crashed in pieces on the floor. I gave them a standing ovation anyway, feeling very much like a Roman spectator in a tiny coliseum.

I gave up my theater seat and headed for a Windsor chair. At the Windsor Chair Shop, Ralph and Caron Quick welcomed me into their studio. As they worked, bending hot oak into classic Windsor chair forms, they explained that their business, like many other artists in town, almost didn't survive here. But now, to buy their award-winning Windsor chairs, get on the waiting list.

So things are looking up in Clarksville. Or looking down, depending on your perspective. After dormant decades of rust and rot, the old Clarksville Skylift is poised to jump back into action. A colorful, effusive character with the wild west name of Bill McMurtrey bought the lift, and with it, controversy. Before he could repair and reopen the lift, he negotiated an agreement to honor and preserve the remains of Native Americans interred at the top of the bluff. When reopened, the lift will deposit folks to the crest of Lookout Hill—highest point along the Mississippi—for a panoramic 800-square-mile view up and down the river.

If he needs a forge for the iron parts on his skylift, McMurtrey needs only to look down. Rinedollar Blacksmith Shop sits at the foot of this towering river bluff. Nowadays, you'd have trouble finding a blacksmith in most major metropolitan areas, much less in small towns. Clarksville has two. Down the highway, Iron Mike of Calumet Creek Ironworks offers a triple treat: blacksmith, sign painter, and boat builder. His handmade wooden canoes are sleek gems, built for deep water, not for the scouring and scraping that Gneid gets on the shallow gravel chutes of Ozark streams.

* * *

If your vision of retirement includes a post-card farm with a white fence running for miles along beautiful rolling hills, the backroads of Lincoln County lead to your Camelot. A drive down Route V revealed some beautiful homes blended into pastoral, forested scenery. But like a Caribbean island, the area's great wealth rubs up against great poverty. Continuing to the end of the road, I skidded into a candidate for a main street makeover. Briscoe needs help, wallowing in dilapidated buildings and trailers, no paving, no stores. On the plus side, I heard no banjo music.

I retreated to what I thought would be a safe escape. It turned out to be a dead end. In our travels, Erifnus and I have verified 142 exit routes from Missouri. Three of our favorites clump together along one twenty-mile stretch of border. Erifnus especially appreciates these escapes, since they don't add to the mileage on her odometer. I like them, too, since it allows me to park on something besides a street or a parking garage. So we crossed Highway 79 and rode down Route N to board the *Winfield Ferry*. Sadly, the route was a dead N. Approaching the banks of the Mississippi, we were crushed to see signs that the *Winfield Ferry* had closed.

Neighbors along the river confirmed my fears. The ferry seemed closed for good. "The last big flood shut 'er down, and she just never opened back up," a neighbor told me. "Oh, she might open if the river freezes downstream, and the *Golden Eagle Ferry* can't run."

The *Winfield Ferry* had operated for as long as I can remember, picking its spot, I suppose, for the same reason eagles pick the spot to fish: The crossing is just yards downstream from Lock and Dam No. 25. Water turbulence from the dam's spillway keeps the river from freezing over. So an eagle can fish. And a boat can cross. But no longer, at least not with rubber-rimmed land lubbing vehicles on its back. We could see the dormant ferry towboat across the river, pointed into the bank, ready to carry passenger cars and grain trucks and motorcycles and tourists. But alas, it had no barge. Another omen that the end is near.

So we retraced our route, away from the dead ferry, and followed a forty-mile rectangular land route to the *Golden Eagle Ferry* a few miles downstream. We weren't disappointed. As we took our place in line behind a half dozen vehicles, the ferry already was chugging toward us. With the skill of a dancer, the towboat maneuvered across the tricky current to drop its ramp onto the bank and deposit nine cars into Missouri. Then the deckhand waved our parade aboard, and in less than two minutes, we were sailing to Calhoun County, Illinois.

And back.

Erifnus Caitnop didn't question this seemingly needless maneuver, since she has spent a relatively high percentage of her effort doubling back from dead ends. We drove the cat roads to take one more river ride, this one on the *Grafton Ferry*, a few miles downriver from the *Golden Eagle*. The trip across the mile-wide Mississippi takes ten minutes. Grafton is a delightful town, worthy of an extended scouring. But my focus is Missouri. Illinois must remain an onlooker.

We returned to native soil aboard the *Grafton Ferry*. Twelve cars fit on three rows on the back of the barge propelled by the talented towboat *John W. Cannon*. Sometimes they can squeeze an extra car in each row, if they're compacts.

One thing I learned: On this boat, there's no free lunch. Everybody pays the ferryman. Oh, I didn't try to get a free ride. But owners

Derrill and Karla Machens posted a sign on the deck railing near the life preserver: "If we gave free rides to everyone who says they know Derrill or Karla, we'd go broke. They're very popular."

The boat's namesake, John W. Cannon was a seaman who lost his life aboard the USS Franklin, an aircraft carrier in the Pacific struck by Japanese bombers on March 19, 1945. He may or may not have been named for the famous John W. Cannon who piloted the *Robert E. Lee* to victory over the *Natchez* in 1870 during America's most famous steamboat race. But the ferry is named for the war hero. And somehow I felt good about that, riding a boat named for a hero, and not named *Minnow* or *Chug-a-Lug*.

I recently learned that Derrill and Karla sold the ferry to the city of Grafton. I hope it survives the dangers of progress.

Safely ashore, we drove down Highway 94, pausing for a moment to admire a venerable old Douglas DC3 airplane, sitting on the tarmac of Smartt Field. Today, folks call the airfield St. Charles County Smartt Airport, a catchy name from the creative mind of an economic developer, I'm guessing. I prefer Smartt Field, named for an airman who gave his life on December 7, 1941.

Smartt Field's sand brown buildings betray its original purpose, as a military airfield. An air museum sits on the property now. With a honk and a wave, we saluted the old DC3 and headed on down the road, humbled by flying machines and ferry boats, and hoping our wheels never touch deep water or become airborne.

We skirted the top of St. Charles past an area called Les Mamelles. Twin hills, they are—or were—so named by early French settlers because they looked like human breasts. Alas, Les Mamelles have been removed, victims of urban sprawl.

Boat Wrecks & Babbitt & Bullshit Bags

"Hands!" the sergeant barked at me. "Let me see your hands!"

I stuck out my palms, and the sergeant inspected them for calluses. Seeing none, he dismissed me with a grunt. "Yer too green to make the crew. You'd never survive."

I chafed for an instant. But I knew what he was doing. I had stepped aboard the replica keelboat that was preparing to retrace the journey of Lewis and Clark. The crew members, in uniform and in character, were demonstrating their recruiting techniques. They were screening for hardy souls who could withstand two years of pushing boats, hauling gear, hacking brush, plucking ticks and slapping mosquitoes, enduring rain and cold and ice and wet boots, eating bear meat without dipping sauce, and no air conditioning or Big Gulps or laundromats or Cheerios or candy bars or Sirius. The sergeant knew that the trip would be tough, and even intrepid explorers like Meriwether Lewis might crack under the strain. So the sergeant looked for tough.

Calluses.

That episode happened on the St. Charles riverfront. When the original Corps of Discovery Expedition launched from here in 1804, this spot on the St. Charles river bank was a door, a threshold. Sail downstream, and you'd retreat to the warm comfort of St. Louis. Head upstream, and you forged into wilderness.

Over time, St. Charles moved its front door away from the river.

Toward the end of the massive European migration called westward expansion, the Missouri River ceased being a superhighway. St. Charles used to load thousands of passengers onto steamboats to go upriver to catch wagon trains and head west. But now the steamboats are extinct, with a rare exception or two. And the town's main entry points are up the hill, along the highways.

The river looks different today, trained to stay in its channel until, of course, it decides to flood and change everything.

That's what happened to the *Goldenrod*. The *Goldenrod* is an old showboat, a fixture for years on the St. Charles riverfront. It was built on a barge, pushed by a towboat. It's one of the last American showboats in existence. The others got old, and sank or burned.

I remember great times on the *Goldenrod*, the music and the wine flowed like the river. But floods came, and damaged the boat, and the U.S. Coast Guard said she wasn't safe without a major overhaul. St. Charles didn't want to sink more money into an old boat without a motor, and not much of a future. So the Goldenrod left the St. Charles riverfront, towed to some spot in Illinois where she sits, dark, decaying.

On this day, the *Goldenrod's* old spot on the St. Charles riverfront was visited by a newer, sleeker craft. The *River Explorer* is a modern passenger vessel built on two barges connected end to end, pushed by a towboat. The whole thing measures 730 feet long, which makes it a challenge for pilots to navigate the Missouri River. So more often than not, the *River Explorer* generally runs the Mississippi and the Ohio Rivers. While it's a European-style barge and not a steamboat, the view is the same. The meals are nirvana for browsers and grazers who like to pack a plate with a dozen different foods. The cabins are modern, and larger than our postage-stamp stateroom on the Delta Queen.

I stood on deck, and surveyed the spot where old French fur trappers shoved off from St. Charles into the unknown. Lewis and Clark did the same, from right here. Eventually the first steamboat followed suit, trying its luck on this wild river.

* * *

As I stood on the top deck of the *River Explorer*, my mind wandered back to the golden age of steamboating. That whole era lasted less than a century. Yet this river's identity is branded by the steamboat, smokestacks belching black smoke as paddlewheels pushed against the current.

Many of the old steamboats were floating palaces, carrying all the creature comforts, with feasting, dancing and games of chance. Folks with money could splurge on a nicer cabin, up on the Texas deck near the smokestacks. Those stacks were called flutes. If you were living large on the top deck, you were high falutin'.

This modern vessel, the *River Explorer*, has only two decks, and no flutes since it gets pushed by a towboat. From my perch I could see the Wabash train trestle crossing the Missouri River. Was this the trestle that sank the *Montana*?

It was a strange story. The *Montana* was a giant sternwheeler, the biggest ship on the river, and at the helm was the greatest pilot ever to ply these waters. In sixty years of steamboating, William Rodney Massie sank only one boat, when he ran the *Montana* into the Wabash Bridge at St. Charles in 1884.

Massie was proud of his prowess on the river, but he had to endure humiliation when the *Montana* hit that bridge.

In a 1939 issue of *Waterways Journal*, "Steamboat Bill" Heckman tells a story about Massie's bravado, and a fellow captain who put

Massie in his place. When *Montana's* sister ship, the *Dacotah*, hit a stump and sank in Providence Bend, Massie sneered about *Dacotah's* Captain John Gonsallas: "Did Gonsollas not know an obstruction as prominent as that stump in Providence Bend?"

Gonsollas shot back: That stump, he said, wasn't near as prominent as the bridge where Massie wrecked the *Montana*, just three months earlier.

Massie usually beat the odds as a pilot on the river. Often, his gambler's swagger led him to the card table. His luck took a strange twist on August 2, 1876, when he sat at a poker table in Deadwood, South Dakota, with Wild Bill Hickok and two other players. Massie was winning and Hickok was losing. On this day Hickok's back wasn't to the wall, as was his custom, and Massie apparently refused to change seats with Hickok not once, but twice.

In Hickok's last game, as Massie laid down his winning hand, Wild Bill took an assassin's bullet in the back of his head. The bullet exited through Hickok's cheek and lodged in Massie's wrist. Wild Bill's fist still clutched his last poker hand with two pair—aces and eights—known to modern poker players as the dead man's hand. Massie carried that bullet in his wrist for thirty-four years and took it to his grave in St. Louis' Bellfontaine Cemetery.

Massie's good fortune at the poker table was surpassed only by his skill on the river. He could read the signs on the water's surface—ripples, colors, stream lines—and tell whether they hid snags or obstacles, and he knew how they changed depending on weather. He memorized the river like no pilot before or since.

Other pilots paid Massie so they could follow his course, and sometimes he'd lead a string of six or eight boats through dangerous passages. That's why it was so strange when Massie's *Montana* hit the Wabash Bridge.

With such danger, even for experienced pilots, why would anybody get on one of these boats?

According to Captain James Kennedy, who piloted boats on the river during the same period as Massie, "Loss of life is rare on rivers save in the case of an explosion."

Well, *that's* comforting.

Meantime, passengers could ignore the dangers and live in high falutin' style.

"As a rule," Kennedy said in his 'Memorys [sic] of Steam Boat Days,' "the tables on these steamers had the best food cooked by experts in that profession that no hotel of today could excel, and it was always abundant. Cabins for both men and ladies were clean and tidy, and on some the furnishings throughout were fine, and amongst all a piano was generally on board. Music was never lacking."

Neither was gaming. "There were no restrictions on gambling," Kennedy said. "Games would be started in the cabin every evening, frequently continuing all night, and any one could take a hand in the game or bet at will. Ladies frequently played, and for high stakes, too. A few of the boats would forbid gambling, but as a rule the games ran openly."

Most captains encouraged passengers to enjoy themselves. It kept their minds off exploding.

All those old boat wrecks are buried deep in the mud. And the river is quiet now. Too quiet for some folks.

* * *

Not long ago, a veteran policymaker of national stature stood on the banks of the Missouri River, and he spoke what he thought. It's not the first time he spewed blunt. Decades ago, *Parade Magazine* posed a simple question to half a dozen Democratic candidates, falling all over each other to be the next president of the United States.

"What's your favorite drink?" the magazine asked.

Al Gore and Dick Gephardt and Walter Mondale, and others I don't recall, gave safe answers. "Milk," one responded. "Tea," said another. "Lemonade." "Water." "Coffee." Blah, blah, blah.

Bruce Babbitt said he liked Tecate. That's beer. It's brewed in Mexico.

Babbitt's answer was Trumanesque. You may not like Tecate, or alcohol, or Mexico, or Truman for that matter. But you gotta trust somebody who will tell you the truth. Babbitt bared his salivary predilections to the world, even if it meant losing the Women's Christian Temperance Union vote. But Babbitt learned what Truman knew: If you're not pissing off half the voters, you're probably not doing your job. Or maybe he was channeling Twain: "Tell the truth. It will gratify some, and astonish the rest."

So when Babbitt came to the banks of the Missouri River, I was all ears. He doesn't live near the Missouri River. He's from Arizona, a desert land, mostly. Many of Arizona's inhabitants covet the Missouri River's wet benefit. Maybe that's why his vision impacted me. He said the Missouri River ought to be a national river trail. It's a vision many Missourians share. Resurrect "Big Muddy" from the list of endangered American rivers. Engage it, immerse in it, draw life from it, as our ancestors did.

Oh, and protect it from thirsty desert dwellers.

Not long ago, Bruce Babbitt was Secretary of the Interior. That's a Teddy Roosevelt kind of thing. The job is important to people who like wide open spaces. Even today, his words carry weight. And momentum is building to create the river trail, before South Dakota siphons off all the water and sells it to Arizona.

* * *

For two-thirds of my life, the Missouri River ran right past my house. It still does. I was the one who meandered away. It got me to thinking about an old African proverb: "The man at the base of the mountain is the last to climb it." Hard to explain, our innate propensity to postpone things indefinitely. Especially hard to explain, when things postponed are pleasant experiences, awaiting. During a half-century of observation, I worshiped the Missouri River from afar and above and beyond. But not long after the pep talk by Bruce Babbitt, I was baptized into the world of the Missouri River, and I became a disciple.

We drove to Portland, Missouri. Erifnus found a pleasant parking spot under a shade tree by the river bank. I walked down the concrete boat ramp, where I joined a pair of friends, willing seafarers. We launched a johnboat from the conservation access point and motored into Big Muddy, upstream and upwind, toward a sprawling sand bar a mile away. Our most experienced hand assured us that the river, though deserving of respect and awe, is safe, if one uses his head. Then he told us to duck if a silver carp came flying out of the water at us. Use one's head, indeed.

The silver carp can grow to the size of a discus, with the impact of a sledgehammer. This presents a problem, because it's an excitable fish, imbued with the innate urge to high jump fast moving objects, boats and such. These river athletes are pretty accomplished, except, like cannonballs, they cannot change trajectory in mid-flight, not even to avoid human heads that stick up out of boats. Accepting this menace as a river fact of life, we cut a wake to the sand bar.

Sand bar. The words fail to describe this monstrous structure, more of an island. At its center, an earthen butte rose a dozen feet above the sand, held together by the roots of giant trees, bare-knuckled against floods past and future. For the next two hours, we examined the island and its contents. We waded through shallow floes and eddies. We studied the shore birds. They studied us.

Heraclitus was right: You never step in the same river twice. Our guide, conservation writer Jim Low, explained that after the river rages, then subsides, a walk on this same sand bar might reveal anything from an arrowhead to a mastodon tooth, or a bison's jaw. That drew a huzzah from Bill Ambrose, the other beachcomber who sidelined as my dentist until he retired to restore the environment, one prairie field at a time. He had interested me in this expedition as I sat in his dentist's chair and he tooled around on my teeth, talking the whole time.

"You might find a century-old jar dislodged from a shipwreck," he said. "Keep an eye out for old tools from cultures who landed here long before Lewis and Clark. Maybe even a misplaced tool from the Journey Discovery itself."

Yeah, I heard ol' Pegleg Shannon was always losing shit.

Immersed in our beachcombing, we ignored a welling thunderstorm, until its rumbling alarm announced it would chase us back to the access point a mile downstream. We launched from the island and boated downriver, dodging the silver carp, and I learned more about them.

Aside from their side gig as aerial schrapnel, carp seem to be harmless. After all, they're related to goldfish. They're bottom feeders. They don't prey on other fish. But they breed like guppies. With no natural predators, these silver carp are an invasive species, growing unchecked in an ever-widening circle, doing harm to the balance of nature. They were imported nearly five decades ago to clean catfish ponds in Arkansas. But they escaped from those ponds during great floods and found their way into the Mississippi River watershed, taking over more and more territory. Now they're thick in the Missouri River, and elsewhere, too. Along many stretches of the Illinois River, nearly nine of ten fish caught are flying carp.

It was on this trip on this river, with carp flying inches from my head, that I realized that Pogo was right. Pogo understood the *Art of War*, the manual found on the bookshelves of nearly every smart general in history. Napoleon studied the book, as did Mao and MacArthur. It didn't help MacArthur much because Truman read it, too.

The book's author, the great ancient military tactician Sun Tsu, explains ways to defeat an enemy without firing a shot. While Americans worry about immigration policies and fret over China buying American debt, they overlook invasions that can cause more harm, more lasting damage. Silent killers like kudzu. The emerald ash borer. Zebra mussels and Burmese pythons and a snail from Africa that grows to eight inches long and loves to munch on stucco houses. But it wasn't Asia or Africa that bundled these invasive species into our local ecosystem. As Pogo said from a forest on Earth Day, 1971: "We have met the enemy, and he is us."

We reached shore back in Portland as the first fat raindrops splattered the dust. We climbed out of the boat onto dry land. My nose led me directly to the threshold of one of my most cherished discoveries. Beside the highway, an old round orange Gulf petrol sign has been painted white and emblazoned with four simple words that hold the key to the contents of the old building next to it: "Riverfront Bar & Grill."

From the outside, the building's appeal is muted, in the manner of all truly great surprises. Under a steep tin roof, its white frame walls wear a coating of grime from the Jurassic period. Climbing steps that look like a Mayan ruin, I crossed through the screen door into gastronomic heaven, complete with pretty much every inch of wall space covered with necessities like life preservers and a bullshit bag, a cousin to the cuss jar, where tall-tale-telling patrons pay up when the bartender calls their bluff.

The barstools support big round red seats, the kind that swivel so you can watch the local pool sharks. I ate my fill of fried chicken and fresh catfish snagged from the river I'd just rediscovered. Good thing I'd noticed the lack of credit card logos on the door, a strong hint that they don't take plastic. I was right. The nearest ATM is probably a dozen miles away. No matter, I had cash, and gladly forked it over.

Miserable with sustenance and steeped in the perfume of an active deep fryer, I drove into the hills, scouring the backroads for another treasure.

Loose Creeks, Ferry Ghosts & Frankenhogs

People tell stories. Stories require names. Names are useful. Useful sits in eastern Osage County, just south of Freedom, which is also useful. Two Useful antique stores define this town of five or so people, with even more antiques in the Useful Cemetery. Enamored with this name and other curious monikers within honking distance, I turned Erifnus loose on Osage County.

Among towns with 1,354 people, Linn may be America's longest, skinniest. Its nickname as the Mile Long City is grossly undercalculated. The town towers on a ridge, parted neatly along its crown by Highway 50. For years I've marveled at the linear layout of the community, built like its ancestor towns, in a pattern called "string cities" by the Germans. Although in recent years, development seems to be spilling down the mountainside. I stopped in town to pick up a copy of the world's best-named newspaper, the *Unterrified Democrat*. For a lark, I spit-pasted the newspaper's banner to my bumper, and drove through this decidedly conservative land bordered by two great American rivers, skewered by a third.

Heading east, we turned north onto Highway AA into the little sister of Lenk, Germany, a town called Loose Creek. I wondered if the creek is still loose, all these years after European settlers hung that wayward name on it. The name strayed from the original French *L'Ourse*, which means "bear." L'Ourse Creek evolved into Loose Creek. The new word fits, since the valley sees more floods than bears.

Above the creek, the road traces a series of ridges with spectacular views cascading down deep valleys to port and starboard. As Route AA descends toward the Osage River near its confluence with the

Missouri River, the highway bends sharply right. Erifnus went straight, and descended the steep entrance into Bonnots Mill. We crept slowly downhill, to avoid losing a grip on the road and smacking into a church at the bottom of the hill. It's that steep.

Bonnots Mill unfolded before us, an old river town unspoiled by change. The name of the town suggests there's a grist mill. But the town was named for a sawmill that fashioned wooden ties for a voracious new railroad plowing along the riverbank. That was back in the 1850s.

I stopped for a meal at Johnny Mac's Bar & Grill, a new name for an old building that remembers serving rail passengers who would stop in for a drink, back when it was called the Old Voss Saloon & Cafe for its younger ninety-three years. Johnny Mac and Ruth Bowen serve up prime rib and prime cuts in a delightfully wooden bar and grill and museum with a bazillion relics hanging on its walls and rafters. Fish traps. Surf boards. Kayaks. I had lunch sitting next to a full suit of armor, which, thankfully, didn't try to steal any of my fries.

The ground shook as a train rumbled past, only a dart throw from the restaurant's picture window. It was a coal train, one of many that roll through the town every day, on their way to the power plant downriver. The Union Pacific Railroad does a tidy business in the untidy shipment of coal from Wyoming and points west. And the railroad barely tolerates passenger trains that share these tracks. Hey, these are Union Pacific's tracks, not Amtrak's. In the hours I've spent in Amtrak's club cars on rail sidings, waiting for long slow coal trains to pass on the main line, I hatched a plan in my mind to give Amtrak the right-of-way. Simple idea, really, borrowed from my earlier discovery about the reason passenger steamers had right-of-way over barges. Why not restore the old mail car on Amtrak? Or forget the mail car; just one packet of mail would give Amtrak the right of way. Legislators said that's too complicated. Complicated? Touchy, maybe, for Amtrak management and labor and the U.S. Postal Service.

Meantime, Union Pacific is trying to alleviate the traffic jams by building more bridges and sidings.

Unlike the railroad track and the river it follows, the unavoidable truth about Bonnots Mill is that if you walk anywhere, it's uphill. Felix Bonnot had that in mind when in 1852 he established the first plat in this protected hollow that opens into the Osage River Valley. The plats are French in nature, which is to say they're long, narrow lots, to allow for outbuildings behind the main house. Uphill from Johnny Mac's, toward St. Louis of France Catholic Church, original outbuildings peek from behind the Dauphine Hotel. Owners Scott and Sandra Holder gave me a tour of the old hotel, including three of the outbuildings, which are functional outhouses, for the adventurous. The Dauphine was built in 1840 before the sawmill came to town, so the timbers and planks and joists are hand hewn. It's a unique bed and breakfast, a walk back into time, where guests can choose from a handful of rooms, all retrofitted with indoor plumbing, for the less adventurous.

Atop the hill, I got on my tiptoes to see over the treeline to view the confluence of the Osage and Missouri Rivers, one of this continent's first commercial street corners, way before somebody named the continent after Amerigo Vespucci. In the other direction, the Missouri State Capitol sticks out of the horizon ten miles away. It's the third capitol building on that site, and likely the last of its kind, since replacement cost is prohibitive. Hell, the building is nearing 100 years old, and still it's not finished, at least not according to the original plans. No front porch connection to the railroad and river. No money to build one.

We continued along ridges and beautiful vistas to the town of Frankenstein, and a lovely stucco church with an equally unique name, Our Lady Help of Christians. We passed the Kremer farm, a small operation that's a vanishing breed. The hogs on this farm root freely in a pasture. Yeah, the pasture is a muddy mess, but the hogs delight in it. Most of their cousins who end up on your plate aren't so lucky. They spend their entire lives in crowded confinement that makes prison look preferable. Kremer sells his happy hogs direct to Chipotle Mexican Grill. The farmer and the restaurant chain share a commitment to raising animals in a humane environment. Yes, the hogs still become burrito filling, but while they breathe, they live a lot more like hogs. They root around in the pasture and head for the lean-to shelter when it rains, a trick they learned from the farmer.

Down the road, we passed through a driving thunderstorm. I stopped in Chamois and dried my car, then peeked around the Old

School on the Hill bed and breakfast. Like most buildings that survive in these old German river towns, the old school is made of brick and will last well past the end of civilization. But there's not much left of the old railroad roundhouse and repair shop, the center of commerce 100 years ago.

Along the Missouri River is a sign stating, "Future home of the *Chamois Ferry*." It's hard to say when the ferry will become operational, since most forms of public transportation must rely on federal subsidies to survive. Of course, that includes the very highways on which Erifnus Caitnop rolls. My car could only dream about riding on the back of the *Chamois Ferry*.

But around the bend from Morrison, on Route J, the *Fredericksburg Ferry* was doing a booming business. Erifnus and I rode the ferry's deck across the Gasconade River, a trip that takes every bit of a minute. The skipper deftly fielded a boatload of questions. "What happens during a flood? Why doesn't the highway department build a bridge? How many cars do you ferry on a Saturday?"

"I have no idea," the skipper ended our short, one-sided conversation. I think he knew the answer to some of my questions. He just didn't care to waste his time.

Later I found out why. He died a few months after our conversation, and the ferry closed down.

Even with 231,418 miles on her odometer, Erifnus sprinted like a thoroughbred up the short, steep incline from the ferry, leaving the barge pilot in her backwash. We didn't make it far, just forty feet or so, to the River's Edge Restaurant & Bar, a treat of an eatery that is the official address for "the middle of nowhere."

I ate a catfish that I suspect swam through this very restaurant during the last flood. Back on blacktop and gravel, we drove through the tiny settlement of Deer, where the four-legged namesakes easily outnumber bipedal residents, and Mint Hill, and a town with an Aud name. We drove past an elk farm and a deer farm and a coyote farm, so I'm told, though I didn't see any of the shy doggies. I passed through ghosts of towns once called Welcome and Triumph, neither able to hold onto the promise of their names. Crook and Judge are two settlements that take their positions on opposite sides of the main highway.

Highway 63 crosses a long bridge at the confluence of the Maries and Osage Rivers, a spot somebody named the Mari-Osa Delta, in the rich tradition of functional contractions. Crowning the towering river bluff, visible to traffic from three sides, an old mansion serves travelers in its newest incarnation, a bed and breakfast called Huber's Ferry.

As the name suggests, William Huber built the house when he operated the ferry that crossed the Osage River a hundred feet below the bluff. Just as impressive, the homestead's bluff-top barn has survived through 125 years of storms. Both buildings can almost remember when the neighborhood included the Osage Tribe. But under the threat of musket balls and cannon balls and bowling balls, the Osage moved out of the neighborhood.

Across the highway is America's most remote bowling alley. Rainbow Lanes is miles from the nearest town. It's been there forever. There's a rumor that Lewis and Clark stopped there to bowl on their way back from the wilderness. Lewis bowled a thirty-three and later committed suicide. Most of that rumor is false.

I stopped in to find out how much business the bowling alley picks up from people on the highway, just passing through on their way to Arkansas or Wisconsin. "Spare change," a bowler told me.

As I crossed the bridge, I thought about stopping at Soda Popp's worm ranch. Soda is a longtime friend, and the best school teacher in Missouri, according to both my daughters. Today Soda raises worms, a thriving business in the fertile bottomland of the Osage River. For those who doubt the economic power of worms, confer with the founder of the Bass Pro Shops chain, who started his empire selling worms for bait in his daddy's liquor stores.

It's not easy for a teacher to prosper. But Soda was successful with whatever the task: teaching students, running a radio station in the rural Ozarks. And now, while corn and soybeans struggle to survive weather and blight and commodity prices, Soda's soil feels the tender loving caress of the worms.

The Pits & the Pinnacles

Nowadays on the drive north of Columbia, fewer people get killed. Highway 63 never really looked like a killer. Lots of roads were curvier, hillier, more treacherous. Maybe that's what made the road a killer. It looked innocent.

But the highway has been tamed.

Tamed too are two geologic oddities that sit just off the road, a dozen miles north of Columbia. The formations sit nearly side by side. One oddity is a scar, the other a monstrosity. They're so bizarre and so different from one another that they might have inspired a dark tale from Edgar Allan Poe or a strange case from Robert Louis Stevenson. The scar was called the Pits. The monstrosity was the Pinnacles.

The Pits were a coal mine, created by man. The Pinnacles were carved by nature. In the evolution of these formations, the Pinnacles became a private park, and the Pits became a nude beach.

Until a recent visit, I hadn't been to the Pits and the Pinnacles since the days of that nude beach.

Back then, during the Watergate era, I was in college at Mizzou, and everybody knew about the nude beach. On warm sunny afternoons, the nude beach was pulsating. It was far enough from campus that only students with cars and gas money could get there, and if you were lucky enough to hitch a ride, an afternoon at that beach could help ease recurring nightmares about grades and parents and conformity and Vietnam.

Students called the nude beach the Strip Pits, a fitting nickname for a nudie bar, even if this bar was only a strip of sand. People really didn't start showing up there and shucking their duds until the late 1960s. For eons before that, the only *au naturel* inhabitants were deer and squirrels dressed provocatively in buckskin and fur.

But during the mid-'60s Peabody Coal Company began extracting bituminous combustibles from the ground. They gave these pits a formal name, a sweet sounding literary name—Mark Twain Mine— and dragged giant scoops across the surface to strip 1.3 million tons of coal. When the strip mines closed in 1967, the pits filled with water, forming long narrow lakes.

For the next half-dozen years, the abandoned pits became a wild playground with mud slides, tie-dyeds, and bare hides. There were no rules and no lifeguards, and only an occasional sheriff's deputy showed up to dampen the party.

When new federal land-reclamation laws went into effect in 1972, the U.S. Department of the Interior began looking for old strip mines to reclaim for recreation. Two years later, Missouri was awarded one of only two federal grants for such reclamation projects. Peabody Coal donated the strip mines to the state, and the land was transformed. They left the pits—now lakes—intact, and they became a state park.

The result is stunning. From the air, the small lakes look like skinny fingers, hence the new name: Finger Lakes State Park. The lakes are flanked by smaller ponds all sitting at different elevations along the terrain. Sprawling across more than 1,000 acres, the lakes and trails wait for swimmers and hikers and bikers and fishers. But since a park ranger patrols the area, there seem to be fewer skinnydippers around.

I drove a couple of miles north to the other, very different geologic marvel: a naturally sculpted breath-taker called Pinnacles Youth Park. The privately owned park is free and open to anybody, but it really focuses on introducing youth groups to nature, hiking, and camping, along with some of the most stark geologic formations this side of Pickle Springs. As the name suggests, the featured attractions are the Pinnacles themselves, eighty-foot limestone towers carved by water and wind and pointing like fingers into the sky. And on these fingers people with the right combination of courage and skill can pretend they're mountain climbers, or mountain goats. Closer to earth, back at the base of the Pinnacles, if you catch Silver Fork Creek just right, it can be a hair raising kayak ride.

Heading back toward civilization's mainline, just across Highway 63 from these two parks, I spied the crown of a building peeking above the long earthen berm that separates the modern highway from its mother road. At the peak of the building's roof, a "Busch Bavarian Beer" sign stood like a big plastic flag, backlit so that it was easily visible from the new highway, alerting the observant traveler that Heuer's Country Store & Cafe sits comfortably behind the berm, refreshingly behind the times. In the dusk, the old country store was dressed for dinner, framed in a string of white Christmas lights, permanent, I assume, since this was July. The outline of lights gave the effect of a rustic chalet.

Well, rustic, anyway. Inside, I realized that I was in an authentic old-time country store. I took a seat surrounded by shelves of canned goods and packaged goods and the eyes of at least one mounted buck and four trophy bass, sharing wall space with seven homemade pictures of Heuer's, among them a pencil sketch, a watercolor, a charcoal rendering.

My server was patient as I pondered the evening's menu choices: liver and onions, fried oysters, a prime rib sandwich, burgers and fries of course, catfish filets, or smoked pork chops. I picked a trio of house favorites: a Reuben sandwich with cucumber salad and carrot cake.

"Are you a Heuer?" I asked the lady at the counter as I paid my bill.

"I'm the mama."

"Well, thanks, Mama Heuer." She has a right to be proud. I hope this old chalet lasts a few more generations, and under the watchful eyes of the trophy bass, old folks can tell stories about the nude beach across the highway.

Bridge to Nowhere

I was running late. Hannibal was still an hour away. So I took a short cut. Making good time on the backroads of Monroe County, I succumbed to a suggestion from a small brown sign that pointed down a blacktop road to a relic from the past.

The detour led to a dead end. I knew it would. At the end of that road stood a covered bridge, all alone, isolated in space and time. Union Covered Bridge survives, off the beaten path. It shares the same oxymoronic fate of the three other covered bridges that survive in Missouri: They lead nowhere. Their roads changed course, and the march toward civilization took another route. Having served their time underfoot, they retired to the highest rank in the bridge family: destinations.

Union Covered Bridge stands as graceful and elegant as the oaks from which it was sliced. A dozen generations of young lovers have courted through its belly, making dreams, popping proposals.

And carving graffiti. Seriously, I think someone transcribed a phone book across the mighty span's oaken shoulders. Names and numbers. Hearts and arrows. And dates. Like a big wooden wedding register. No matter. The carvings are superficial wounds in the skin of the oaks, long since drained of their blood.

Amid the bridge, one horizontal clapboard is removed, forming a long slit in the structure's side, so that from a distance, the span looks like a wooden grandchild of the Bridge of Sighs, pulled like taffy to fit onto its banks. Now this old covered bridge is a bookmark in history, with only a pair of modern purposes: beauty and picnics. The state maintains the bridge as a historic site. Some folks want to drop the bridge from public support. They may prevail. Nobody goes there, they say.

From the middle of the bridge, I spied a family on a Sunday picnic within the bridge's shadow. I stuck my arm out of the slit and waved. They waved, smiling their approval that the bridge, in its evolutionary journey, had sprouted arms. I thought about joining the family picnic, and accept a fried chicken thigh and a cold beer from the red cooler, or a Coke from the blue one, and learn about their homes and their families and find out if one of their grandparents carved her name in the bridge. How else would a whole family know about this remote place that goes nowhere? Instead, I retracted my arm from this big wooden shell, and left them to their picnic peace, content in this connection to their past. After all, I was running late.

I got back into my car, back onto the blacktop short cut. Hannibal was still an hour away.

* * *

Weeks later and a hundred miles further west, we found another old bridge, this one crossing the Missouri River to Glasgow. It had just been closed, and a ferry transported cars and trucks across the water while a new bridge grew out of pylons in the river. The ferry crossing takes all of ten minutes. But like every good ride at an amusement park, the wait for the ferry is considerably longer.

It was an opportunity to study the travelers trapped in the queue: locals, farm vehicles, and a family in a van with kids crawling over it like ants, excited about crossing the river on a boat. Collecting the nine vehicles that gathered during a twenty-minute wait, the barge arranged its cargo and plowed across the river. As we crossed, I felt a connection with the millions of ancestors who forded this river before there was a bridge. My trip was quicker than my ancestors' crossing, and safer too; I patted the scar from my smallpox vaccine for good luck.

Erifnus rolled off the ferry and drove up the embankment into a city whose charms are regularly overlooked. Like the other river towns up and down the Missouri River, Glasgow's history extends to the beginnings of westward expansion. Its oldest homes saw the early settlers clutching the handrails of steamboats, and felt the heat from the Civil War. Those homes survive today to flavor the town's hilltops. Nearer the river, the business district maintains the feel of the nineteenth century, including the oldest continuously operated soda fountain west of the Mississippi at Henderson Drug Store.

The town inherited an old barge from upriver, its decaying superstructure betraying its sinful past: It once served as the old St. Jo Casino, where, they say, the great grandchildren of Pony Express riders used to gamble. Today the old casino barge is tied to wild trees along a muddy riverbank, hoping to rekindle its old spark, sans slots. Alas, recent floods loosed a barrage of trees and debris down the river, big wooden torpedoes that helped deep six the old barge. So it sits half submerged at the edge of the bank, choking a stump, bobbing in the rushing brown water, calling for help that can't come in time.

A similar thing happened before, not far from here, but long ago, on September 17, 1840.

The *Euphrasie* was one of this river's first steamboats, a side wheeler named for the wife of owner George Collier, and it did a brisk business transporting hemp and tobacco from eleven tobacco stemmeries and factories around Glasgow. The boat left town headed downstream, loaded with 150 bales of rope and bagging, and at least $14,000 worth of insurance on the seventy-one hogsheads of tobacco on board. Four miles downstream, the *Euphrasie* struck a snag and sank in what became known as Euphrasie Bend. Salvage efforts recovered the boat's furniture, and even the engine, which was later installed in the steamer *Oceana*. Nobody died, but the insurance settlement claimed a victim on shore. The Glasgow Marine Insurance Company went bankrupt covering the loss.

Euphrasie Bend became a liquid dead man's curve, the graveyard for at least six more steamboats.

Not far upriver, Malta Bend might be the most-repeated name of a shipwreck bend on the Missouri. Since that wreck the river has changed course, and the bend no longer exists, but the town of

Malta Bend is still there. Back in August of 1841, Captain Joseph W. Throckmorton was piloting the *Malta*, a steamer he originally designed as a comfortable excursion boat. Its cabins even had innerspring mattresses. But Throckmorton had adapted the boat to the fur trade, and on this day he was guiding the *Malta* around a sweeping bend two miles above Laynesville when the boat struck a snag.

The *Malta* sank in a little more than a minute, but resting in only twelve feet of water, its upper decks stood above the waterline, where passengers waited to be rescued. Nobody died in the *Malta* wreck, though the boat and cargo were a total loss.

That was a typical shipwreck when a boat hit a snag: The boat found a shallow bottom, and passengers found the upper deck.

But not always.

On a hill overlooking the Missouri River, Lexington bleeds history from the site of the oldest continually operated corporation in the entire state. Macpelah Cemetery did a brisk business during America's westward expansion, burying pioneers who succumbed to typhoid and cholera and boiler explosions and drowning. Within the cemetery's walls are thousands of tragic pioneer stories, mostly forgotten, buried by time. A whole section of the cemetery contains scores of Mormon pilgrims scalded to death when the steamer *Saluda's* exploding boiler blew them onto the river bank.

It was Good Friday, a cold day in 1852. The river was pushing chunks of ice through a narrow chute just upriver from Lexington. The *Saluda's* Captain Francis Belt had tried for two days to power his ship through the icy chute. On this morning, he was determined to make it around that bend, and steam upriver to his destination in Council Bluffs, Iowa. He ordered more steam, and within seconds the boiler exploded, throwing a hundred bodies onto the banks or into the river, which swept them away. The recovered bodies, many of them children, were laid to rest at Macpelah.

Blackwater Reborn

Further up the Missouri River, a few miles away from its banks, we found an old town tucked in obscurity. Near a tributary called the Blackwater River, the old dried up railroad town had struggled for years to avoid the wrecking ball.

Blackwater isn't the center of commerce for anybody, really. But it's the center of inspiration on several layers, brought back to life by a New Orleans hotelier and a colorful cast of characters right out of Central Casting, including Jay Turley.

Turley was "the Charles Dickens among American playwrights." Don't take my word for it. Tennessee Williams called him that. Turley lived in Blackwater off and on. And although our paths crossed many times, I met Jay Turley only in his last year, at his home in Blackwater. He was feeble, but gracious. He showed me his home, a converted garage on Blackwater's main drag. The exterior was forgettable. The interior was a castle.

Turley died in 2004. But his work remains, in a lasting legacy. You can still see his plays if you time it right, or you're lucky. *Orphan Trains West* is a true story about how folks back east got rid of homeless children by packing them onto trains and sending them out toward the frontier with a one-way ticket. Ah, those were the days, when social services were cold and imaginative.

Turley's beloved Blackwater didn't collect many of those orphans, but over time the town became a collection of inanimate orphans: old buildings, old furnishings and other antiques up for adoption.

When the passenger trains stopped coming, and freight trains no longer needed infusions of coal and water, the town started to wither, on the verge of collapse. Years passed, and bulldozers loomed, ready to raze the village as it sagged under the weight of time and neglect. The end was near.

That's when a character worthy of Dickens—or Turley—stepped up to save his hometown. A world traveler who can tell you his adventures in five languages, Bobby Danner had a vision. Just as important, he had a unique set of skills. He became mayor of Blackwater. He knew how to run a hotel, since his family still owns the Olivier House Hotel on Toulouse Street in New Orleans' French Quarter. And yes, he told some amazing stories about Hurricane Katrina.

But he also knew how to fix a town. Under Bobby's leadership, the sewers were revamped, and the homes began to dress up, thanks to some historic preservation grants. He even persuaded prodigal Blackwaterians to donate money for old-fashioned street lamps.

He bought and transformed the old 1887 Iron Horse Hotel into a place that you and your sweetheart won't want to leave. Don't be distracted by the appellations—shoot, with room names like *Marrakesh Express* and the *City of New Orleans*, you just might have the ride of your life. Anyway, each room has its own charming ambiance that runs anything this side of the Ritz out on a rail.

Inside the Iron Horse Restaurant, I ordered a salad with an original dressing that made me wanna lick the bowl. Or, as one guest said, she'd like to fill her bathtub with the stuff and eat her way out.

Not long ago a building burned on Main Street. The burned-out space was too small to build a Walmart. So Blackwater built a park. Sure, Walmart would bring big tax revenues to help the little town. But the park helps raise money, too, because of its centerpiece: a water fountain.

The theory is beautifully simple. Build fountains, and people will throw money. Selfish cynics who gripe about taxes will swiftly fish their pockets for loose change to make a wish and change their dumb luck. It works at theme parks, where long waiting lines snake past fountains. And you thought fountains were put there for beauty, or to keep you cool. Kansas City figured this out a long time ago. Now KC has more fountains than any city but Rome.

Blackwater remains insulated from the most-traveled path. But it's an easy jump off I-70, a three-mile detour to discover this hidden gem, one of the most delightful towns in the western hemisphere.

Think I'm kidding?

Name another town of 199 people that has a Museum of Independent Telephone Pioneers. A walk inside this bank-like brick structure at the main intersection of town rewarded me with a Disneyesque display of dialing history, and kept me cranking for just enough time to forget about cellular Hell.

I walked another block to the remarkable chainsaw carving of an Osage Indian chief. He holds a scroll, a deed of title to about 30,000 acres the Osage tribe gave to trading partner and friend Pierre Chouteau. The federal government didn't recognize the scroll as a true deed of title, saying the Louisiana Purchase made the contract moot. Chouteau sued, and won.

Down the street, the West End Community Theater just might

open your mind. It's an old Baptist church which changed hands several times until it took on a theatrical perspective. Before he died, Jay Turley bought the building and willed it to the Blackwater Preservation Society, so the show can go on.

* * *

Decades ago, according to local lore, a lady from Blackwater entered a Mars Candy Company contest to name a new candy bar. She suggested the name Snickers. Mars agrees there was a contest years ago. They just can't recall the winner.

No matter. Blackwater rolls on. Not far from Snickers Street, the old grain elevator snuggles against the rails. It has a new purpose now, as a farm museum, farmers market, bat habitat, and ornamental Grain Garden laid out with grain crops.

Jay Turley would be happy. So would Tennessee Williams, depending on how they ferment the grain.

Erifnus rolled toward the city of fountains.

Connie & the *Arabia*

Connie stays across the river from downtown Kansas City at the old municipal airport. She's known more formally as a Lockheed Constellation, the airline workhorse of the 1950s. If you saw her, you'd instantly recognize the plane, with her curvy porpoise fuselage, three tail fins and four propellers. She's the poster plane for the last great American airline company, Howard Hughes' TWA.

The Save A Connie Foundation is in Hangar 9 at the old Kansas City Municipal Airport—now called the Charles B. Wheeler Memorial Airport. The airport itself is a relic, replaced by the larger, safer Kansas City International Airport. Tucked into a tight river bend beneath the watchful eyes of the Kansas City skyline, this airport museum gets overlooked by just about everybody, one of Kansas City's best-kept secrets.

I was looking forward to climbing aboard Connie. Until dumb struck.

On the day we visited the old airport, foul weather had grounded flights. Forecasters were predicting a foot of snow behind an early spring cold front that was poised to push through. So Erifnus delivered me through the howling wind and rain, into the parking lot.

As I left Erifnus to see the alluring Connie, I realized I'd just locked her doors with the keys in her ignition.

I stood, numb, frozen—not from the wind and rain that pelted me, but from my own stupidity.

Erifnus Caitnop doesn't deserve such rude neglect. She's performed nearly flawlessly as my Trigger, my Lassie, and my Old Faithful all rolled into 140 horsepower. She is my one constant companion along this journey across every mile of every road on Missouri's highway map, my trusty steed for fifteen years and nearly 300,000 miles.

But on this day, she sat protecting my keys from the wind and the rain.

And me.

I must confess that this is not the first time I've locked the keys in this car.

In fact, I've probably tied a world record: performing this stupid feat twice in one day. That memory is painful:

She was new and sleek and shiny, and we were still getting used to the road together when it happened. The first time was like any time you've done it. And don't tell me you haven't done it.

The second time, hours later at a Casey's General Store in tiny Madison, Missouri, I jumped out of the car to fill her tank with the corn-laced liquor she loves. I hung the hose on the gas pump and returned to open the car door.

My heart sank.

It soothed my ego only a tiny bit when the locksmith arrived an hour later and told me, "Yeah, these cars have a protective locking system. So when you leave the keys in the ignition and shut the door, it automatically locks. Keeps thieves from hopping in your car."

And me.

I promised Erifnus I'd never again treat her with such neglect.

But over the years, as with most partnerships, there were stressful moments. Most were caused by driver error. Spinouts. Warning tickets. Getting stuck in mud. Sliding sideways under downed power lines. Stuff like that.

And now this.

In the windswept parking lot of Hangar 9, with a blizzard on its way,

I regained my composure and entered the museum hangar, confessing my stupidity to the friendly folks inside. They were extremely helpful, being pilots and mechanics and classic airplane lovers.

But try as we did, we couldn't make a coat hanger unlock my car.

So after a delightful tour of the museum, and a walk down the aisle of that classic old aircraft with its three tail fins and four engines and porpoise-shaped fuselage—and ninety dollars for a locksmith—I thanked my hosts, tucked my tail fin in the driver's seat, and drove home.

* * *

It's not the first time I'd had trouble around that old airport.

One dark night I tried to drive to the airport from downtown Kansas City. I had to cross the river, so I began looking for the ASB. That's a bridge, though for the life of me, I couldn't remember what ASB stood for. Worse, I couldn't find the ASB. I drove around riverfront streets for what seemed like a week, until finally I spied a police car parked two blocks ahead. I parked Erifnus and walked toward the officer, a block away. As I got closer, I realized he was talking to a man who had been beaten to a bloody pulp. The victim was propped against a building. I stopped, and began to turn back when the officer noticed me, and shouted, "What do you want?"

"I'm looking for the SOB," I stammered.

The cop looked puzzled. "You mean the ASB?"

"Yeah, that's it."

"This isn't my precinct," he said, "and I don't know how to get you there."

"I do," said the derelict wearing a quart of his own blood. "Go two blocks down here, hang a left, stay left and then make two more rights. You're there." I was dumbfounded. I didn't absorb any part of his directions. I thanked them, and returned to my car, and drove around lost for another hour.

That old district, called the River Quay, used to be quite entertaining. It featured an eclectic collection of nightclubs and whorehouses along the riverfront. Well, most of the bars and skin joints have been obliterated, thanks to a lethal mixture of mob ambition and dynamite. That all came down in the late '70s, and the area slowly recovered as the mob enforcers killed each other or ended up in prison.

The River Quay evolved into a peaceful collection of farmers markets and museums, under the constant smell of fresh roasted coffee from the Folgers Coffee plant up the hill. But Folgers moved away. Now, coffee connoisseurs gravitate to the Road Hard Coffee Company, featuring exotic javas from Kenya and Sumatra, Ethiopia and Arabia.

As Erifnus rolled into the River Quay, I was looking for another Arabia.

That *Arabia*, what's left of it, is a steamboat resurrected from beneath a cornfield where it sank on September 5, 1856. Technically, it didn't sink in a cornfield. The three year old boat was making its fourteenth trip up the treacherous Missouri River, long past its life expectancy, and as evidenced by hundreds of other shipwrecks in that river, the odds were mounting against the *Arabia's* survival. Rounding Quindaro Bend near Parkville, the *Arabia* hit a snag, a submerged walnut tree, which punctured the hull below the waterline. Within minutes, the steamer was swamped, and it settled to the bottom of the river, its upper deck sticking out of the rushing water. Only one passenger was killed, a mule that drowned because it was still tethered to the railing.

The boat was loaded to capacity: 130 passengers and 220 tons of freight. Mr. Able D. Kirk was aboard the *Arabia*, and gave this account: "We embarked on the boat in St. Louis and had been on the water about 10 days. The boat was heavily loaded with freight but did not have a large number of passengers. One evening when many of the passengers were at supper the boat struck a snag. We felt the shock and at once the boat started sinking. There was a wild scene on board. The boat went down till the water came over the deck and the boat keeled over on one side. The chairs and stools were tumbled about and many of the children nearly fell into the water. Several of the men on board seized the life boat and started for the shore, but they came back and the women and children were put in the boat. They called for a small man to go with the boat and I was small and got on board. The river bank at the point where we landed had been carving off and was very steep. I climbed out and pulled the women ashore. Horses and wagons came down from Parkville, and took us to the hotel for that night. Many of the trunks and valises were taken off the boat and stacked up in the woods near the river. That night they were broken open by thieves and all the valuables were taken out. We were taken on the steamboat, *James H. Lucus*, and when we went aboard all that could be seen of the *Arabia* was the top of the pilot house. That sank out of sight in a short time." Kirk's account appears in the definitive book on the shipwreck, *Treasures of the Steamboat Arabia* by David C. Hawley (1995).

In a less dramatic way, the shipwreck itself survived. Over the century and a half that followed, the river piled up a protective layer of mud around the boat and its contents. Then the river changed course. In the mid-1980s a search and excavation team found the wreck a half mile from the river's channel, buried beneath forty-five feet of mud. David and Greg Hawley and their father were joined by friends and family in the Herculean effort to unearth the giant boat.

The *Arabia* was a supply ship, a floating forerunner to Home Depot. Excavators brought up what's left of the wooden hull, its steam engine, and 20,000 artifacts that populate the Stramboat *Arabia* museum, a fascinating glimpse into the past, a preserved presentation of Pompeiian proportions. Many of the artifacts are in controlled-environment storage, but thousands more are on display. Leather shoes and rubber boots. Dishware and medicines. Guns and knives. Cognac and cheese. Tools for sewing and stitching, banging and building, cooking and kindling. Wedgwood china and beaver hats. The museum's shelves look like a grocery store: jars of beans and beets, tomatoes and cucumbers. Bottles of fine liquor have waited nearly two centuries to prove the art of their vintners and distillers. Meanwhile, skilled hands have lovingly restored the boat's steam engine, and its twelve-ton boiler.

On my visit, I talked with one of the excavators of the *Arabia*, who confirmed that after they uncovered the ship and its contents, he opened a jar and ate a 150-year-old pickle. "It was good," the Hawleys' friend Jerry Mackey reports. And Jerry's still alive, a tribute to your great-great-grandmother's canning prowess. Sadly, Greg Hawley was not so lucky. It wasn't a jar of pickles that killed Greg. Or a shipwreck. It was a car wreck, and Greg was a casualty.

* * *

How can you top a morning among jars of antipasto at the *Arabia*? More antipasto. Although Kansas City's cattle drive history conjures visions of steak houses, the town draws from St. Louis roots to offer several of the best Italian restaurants this side of Palermo.

From its outside appearance on a cluttered stretch of old Highway 40 in Independence, Salvatore's Ristorante doesn't look like the kind of place that would have tablecloths.

Ah, but it does.

Great Italian restaurants can put a table cloth on a table, light a candle, and still allow you to dig in to your food with abandon. And from Salvatore's friendly greeting, I knew I'd found more than a pretty table setting. Salvatore carries on the great Garozzo family tradition in Kansas City, with savvy that traces its roots back to the Hill in St. Louis.

I started my meal with an addictive mix of olive oil and garlic and Parmesan, sopped up with enough bread to bind my colon for a week. The antipasto prepared me for one of the best *insalatas* west of Madison's Cafe. I ate a veal marsala, said a prayer for the calf, and licked my plate.

Sal looked the other way.

Transition

One minute from Mound City is one of America's biggest rest areas. It sits along an interstate. Yet this rest area is not for people. It's for the birds.

Squaw Creek National Wildlife Refuge has been here since the Roosevelt administration designated it in 1934. While the area is protected and preserved by humans, it's not manmade. Migrating waterfowl have been using this area around the Missouri River for a few million years before we came along. I knew that if I stayed long enough, I'd see many of the 301 species reported to have checked in, ducks and geese, of course, but also rare sightings, including the Olive-sided Flycatcher, the Red Phalarope, the Black-legged Kittiwake and the Parasitic Jaeger, though I might have to wait an eternity to see them all.

In these wetlands near the Missouri River, as many as 300 bald eagles hang out during the fall migration, waiting to feed on sick and wounded Canada geese.

It was getting dark as I found refuge at a cabin on Big Lake. The lake formed when the Missouri River changed course, cutting a new channel, and leaving the abandoned riverbend as an oxbow lake. The cabin formed when Missouri made the lake a state park.

A few years back, I came to this area for another purpose. . . .

* * *

Arising before the birds, I drove in darkness to the banks of the Nishnabotna River to wave goodbye to a hardy group of explorers. The Lewis and Clark Bicentennial reenactors had camped in the natural shelter along this tiny tributary to the Missouri River. We stood in a farm field a dozen feet above the river, looking down mud banks upon the grizzly Corps of Discovery as they broke camp and prepared to leave Missouri. The reenactors loaded their pirogues and the big-ass keelboat, shot their guns in a salute to us shorebound onlookers, and paddled around the corner into the swift current of the Missouri.

I wished them well.

But major expeditions—even reenactments—can be tumultuous. Upriver, the reenactors met a band from the Lakota tribe displaying a banner: "Why celebrate genocide?" The Lakotas demanded that the party turn around. Only after intense discussions did the reenactors proceed.

Along the way, the curse of Captain Meriwether Lewis surfaced. The actor who was playing Lewis quit the party in a dispute. I heard the rumor that he believed that the reenactors should stay on mission, in character the whole time, without pausing to visit schools and city halls and folks who wanted to interact with them. Maybe he was a bit too rigid, too caught up in the experience, and too much like the character he played. For Meriwether Lewis, the end was always perilously near.

* * *

Within minutes, strong shoulders had moved the boats upriver, out of sight. We watched them disappear, then turned back to the state park.

The words "state park" lead you to believe that the contents within its borders are solid, fixed, permanent. But the river only loans this pinched-off oxbow to us, and it reserves the right to wash the park away without notice. The park already has been washed away once. It'll wash away again.

This Land Is Your Land

Lewis and Clark's Journey of Discovery opened the flood gates to westward expansion, and manifest destiny muscled across the land. And from Missouri, wagon trains laden with settlers and supplies fanned out along trails named for exotic destinations: Santa Fe, Oregon, California.

The history of Missouri is the history of the wild west. Missourians settled Texas. Missouri loaned its greatest writer to the Gold Rush. From Missouri, the Pony Express raced across the wilderness, and thrived for eighteen months, killed by the garrotte of the telegraph wire. Railroads cut through the landscape, and like a great army, dropped supply depots every few miles.

The wild west started right here. Cattle drives and Sooners. Riverboat gamblers. Frank and Jesse, Kit Carson and Calamity Jane.

Over time, outposts became settlements. Trails became highways. And in the Ozarks, one of the last American holdouts to change, water power was finally replaced by electricity.

Now the land is civilized. The roads are paved with fast food choices.

But I can still find wilderness. I retreated to my favorite spot on earth.

* * *

It was after midnight when a pickup truck splashed into the river and drove onto the gravel bar near our campfire, where a few diehard night owls still sat. Two men in their thirties got out of the truck and approached us.

"Wanna beer?" one man wobbled as he held out a six pack toward me.

"No thanks, I got one," I held my beer up in the firelight for them to see. Others in our group did the same.

The pickup driver popped the top on a can of Milwaukee's Best. "Y'all aren't from around here, are you?"

We told him we were from the Ozarks. Surrounding counties.

"Y'all aren't from around here. I grew up here. This river is in danger. . . ."

We nodded and grunted in agreement.

"This river—this whole area—is being destroyed by people like you. You come down here and trash it. And then you leave and go home. I live here."

I remained calm. "We don't trash it. We leave it cleaner than we found it."

"If the park service wasn't around to take care of this river, people like you would destroy it," the pickup driver spoke as if he didn't hear me.

"Wanna beer?" his drunk buddy offered up the dwindling six-pack again.

The driver continued his rant, speaking rapidly through meth-rotted teeth. "You all don't live here. I've lived here all my life. You don't realize you're destroying this whole area."

I tried one more time to reason with him. "You're right," I agreed with him. "There are people who come to this river and trash it. Not us. We bring our children and grandchildren to this river, and teach them to respect . . ."

"People like you are ruining this river. I grew up here . . ." His rant was endless, a broken record from a bruised mind. I slowly rose from my chair and walked to my tent. Others in our party did the same. The firelight cast the man's shadow on my tent wall as he raved. He was oblivious that his audience had deserted him. After a few minutes of silence, I heard the doors slam on the pickup. The engine started and the driver revved the motor, ready to drive off the gravel bar. The driver spun his wheels, spraying gravel like it was shot from a gatling gun. Finally, the driver eased the throttle, the tires bit the gravel and they drove up the bank onto the road. And stopped.

"Now what?" I muttered to myself.

The driver cranked up the pickup's stereo so our whole camp could hear Everlast cover the last two minutes of "Folsom Prison Blues." Then the truck sped up the hill, out of earshot.

The fear of such a hostile encounter is what keeps a lot of people away from these Ozarks rivers. Why take a chance that they may encounter a chemically impaired local with a chip on his shoulder?

For me, the lure of this Garden of Eden is worth the risk.

Flow

On the way home from my favorite spot, we took a backroad. And another. In my head I took inventory. Along our journey, nearly a dozen years had passed behind us. Erifnus showed 284,661 miles on her odometer. We'd covered all the roads on my highway map. I had dipped into every lake, crossed every river, and paddled most of 'em.

Our journey was not without loss. As Erifnus and I moved like a tiny red blood cell through the state's capillaries, life went on around us. Friends died. Grandchildren were born. I left jobs, found others.

That's the sad tradeoff to my travels. If you're gonna drive like this, you'll miss home. Back deck barbecues and birthday bashes down the street, morning golf outings with your buddies and yard saling even earlier than that, and throwing the Frisbee with grandchildren and neighborhood picnics. Your dogs and cats will assign their trust to another more reliable family member. Your lawn will jungleize, your houseplants will grow indifferent to your voice. Your grandchildren will have no choice but to turn to their parents for help with their homework. You'll miss the sound of your own doorbell, and the smell of your sycamore. You'll miss your own easy chair, your own shower, your own bed and its companion. And an authority no less than Napoleon warns that you'll miss home cooked meals, unless you get lucky and find a blue plate diner. Or something close to blue plate.

Gneid, my trusty canoe with the one-of-a-kind name, she left me, though not of her own accord.

It was late autumn a few years ago when I stacked her against my backyard fence, a seven-foot wooden privacy fence that bordered the back alley. I left her there too long, I guess. Her bow jutted another seven feet above the top of the fence, like the foot of a mussel waving for a smallmouth bass that might drift by. Sure enough, late one night, a methmouth bastard brought a pickup truck down the alley and teeter-tottered Gneid over the fence into the truckbed. My canoe disappeared into the night, leaving a solitary seat cushion at the foot of the fence.

I haven't seen her since. But sometimes on the river, I'll see a canoe that looks like her, and I look at the decal on her bow for her name. If I ever found her, I couldn't prove she was mine. I'd just be glad that she still got a chance to feel cool water on her keel.

I drove on, meandering through the backwoods toward home.

* * *

We were still on the road when I heard the news. A newscaster's voice crackled over an AM radio station. "A man was shot and killed today on the Meramec River. . . ."

Details were sketchy, but apparently a group of canoeists had stopped at a gravel bar. A landowner confronted them with a gun, and in the ensuing argument about territory and trespassing and boundaries and river rights, one canoeist ended up dead, shot in the face.

My heart sank.

Without knowing any more details, I knew this wilderness had just become more dangerous. This one tragic incident would spark more confrontations. Even as I drove home, social media spread the news like wildfire. Through thousands of tweets and blogs, talk shows and coffee shops, armchair warriors lunged into battle half-cocked, even before the hands of justice began to sift through clues.

I drove on through the wilderness toward home, knowing only that on a river that everybody loves, one man killed another. But instinctively, I knew something else: On that gravel bar, there were at least two more victims: civility and respect.

* * *

In a reflective mood, I stopped by the old Union Covered Bridge to take a break and think about my travels. Heavy rains had pushed the river to bank full, and its swift brown current rolled perilously close to the bottom of the bridge. In the parking lot beside the old bridge, I got out of the car and reflexively started picking up trash. With an armload of beer cans and Styrofoam cups, plastic lids and potato chip bags, I wandered around looking for a receptacle.

A lone driver pulled into the parking lot. His car wasn't official, but he had a formidable antenna on top, the kind used by deputies and people who want to help the authorities. Or maybe this guy was the Grim Reaper in disguise.

The car stopped beside me. The driver leaned over to look at me through the passenger window. "Whatter ya doin'?" he asked.

"Lookin' for a trash can."

"Gone. Vandals threw it in the river."

"Vandals." I spat the word, as I dropped my trash in a neat pile next to a sign about the covered bridge. He climbed out of his car. We met in the gravel between our cars' hood ornaments. I stuck out my hand. "John Robinson."

He shook my hand. "Darwin Marshall," he replied, from under his "U.S. Army Veteran" ball cap. He explained that he stops by to check on this old relic just about every time he passes. That's almost every day. He travels to Paris, Missouri, a dozen miles north, to get the St. Louis newspaper. "Can't get one in Centralia."

I think he just likes to get out and drive.

Darwin told me that he has lived all over the United States, working as a first-class engineer for radio and television stations. But a few years back he retired to Centralia, a dozen miles south. "County Mountie says I oughta come by when I'm passin' through, check things out."

"I'm glad you do," I told him. "This is close to where I started my journey to drive every mile of . . ."

"So *you're* the guy." His voice perked up. "I love travel. I used to travel a lot . . ." His voice tailed off into wist.

I pointed to the bridge, which had suffered damage. The lower boards along its horizontal cedar siding had been ripped away, exposing the deck of the bridge. "What happened? Vandals?"

"Nope," he shook his head. "Big flood a few months ago. The river got up higher than the bottom of the bridge, so they ripped away the lower siding to let the river go through. Probably saved the bridge."

We talked for a few more minutes about the bridge and travel and television stations and life. Then I shook hands with Darwin Marshall. "Keep an eye on this ol' bridge," I said.

"Don't worry."

I turned and left. I was running late. And there still was a lot of territory to cover before the silver hearse rolls back by.

CPSIA information can be obtained at www.ICGtesting.com
Printed in the USA
LVOW06s0921121113

360984LV00003B/3/P